L I M I T L E S S

New Thinking for an
Explosive Christian Life

Art Thomas

SUPERNATURAL TRUTH PRODUCTIONS, LLC
Practical Training for Spirit-Filled Living
www.SupernaturalTruth.com

Copyright © 2015, 2017 Art Thomas

Limitless Hope: New Thinking for an Explosive Christian Life
Formerly titled *Limitless Hope: Renewing Your Mind for Supernatural Living*

Please note that Supernatural Truth Productions, LLC, chooses to capitalize various pronouns and metaphors used for the Father, the Son, and the Holy Spirit, even when such capitalization does not exist in an original source, including Bible translations. This is a style decision made for the sake of honoring God in our text.

ISBN: 0692616381
ISBN-13: 978-0692616383

Dedication

To my hope-filled wife, Robin Thomas, who regularly
challenges me with the great things she expects God to do.

Thanks for helping raise our children to anticipate
God's best in every situation. And thanks for
representing God's best to me.

LIMITLESS *Hope* — Art Thomas

My Prayer for You:

"I pray that the eyes of your heart may be enlightened in order that you may know the hope to which He has called you, the riches of His glorious inheritance in His holy people, and His incomparably great power **for us** who believe.

That power is the same as the mighty strength He exerted when He raised Christ from the dead and seated Him at His right hand in the heavenly realms, far above all rule and authority, power and dominion, and every name that is invoked, not only in the present age but also in the one to come. And God placed all things under His feet and appointed Him to be head over everything for **the church, which is His body, the fullness of Him** who fills everything in every way."

Ephesians 1:18-23, NIV, emphasis added

LIMITLESS *Hope* — Art Thomas

Table of Contents:

Preface

One day I grew tired of living in disappointment. I realized that I had limited God to a series of anti-biblical, unfounded concepts, which had locked me into a system of wrong thinking (the Bible calls it "unbelief"). Miracles rarely happened, and my prayers were rarely answered.

My erroneous views had produced what I would call "expected disappointment." I thought I was being polite to God by expecting so little, but the truth was that I didn't actually expect Him to love me the way His Word promises. When I shared the Gospel I didn't anticipate any immediate results. I thought I was being courteous to others, but the truth was that I didn't expect the power of the Gospel to impact the person in that moment. And if I attended a funeral I certainly didn't expect that the dead person could come back to life! I performed no great exploits for the Lord, and I was very comfortable with my mediocre Christianity.

But this lifestyle looked nothing like the ministry of Jesus in the Gospels, nor did it resemble the ministry of the Christians in the book of Acts. To make matters worse for me, I then started learning about ministries around the world who are having daily encounters with a very real God—miracles, healings, prophecies, salvations, and even raising the dead! I realized something had gone terribly wrong with my Christianity.

Limitless Hope **is a book born out of my own transformation from a life of expected disappointment to a relationship with an eternal, limitless God. It is an invitation to a new way of thinking, believing, and living that moves Christians like you and me from powerless busyness to explosive demonstrations of God's love, glory, and power.**

This "limitless hope" to which I invite you is not blind optimism. I'm not suggesting that we just "think happy thoughts" or "try to be positive." Jesus didn't pretend He was "okay" as He wept at the grave of Lazarus, but He was still convinced of His identity and the resurrection power of the Holy Spirit that was resident within Him. Limitless hope is not simply mind-over-matter. Rather it is what one of the senior pastors from my past, Otis Buchan, called "supernatural realism."

Supernatural realism, he said, is a mindset of genuine faith. It sets us free from the cloud of pessimism because we have faith and hope in a God who has overcome our circumstances and loves us enough to provide for our deliverance. Likewise it sets us free from the false mask of optimism because we don't have to pretend to "look on the bright side" while bad things are truly happening. You cannot "mourn with those who mourn" when you're constantly trying to put on a happy face. It is also not what the world would ordinarily call "realism" because it is not based merely on an honest assessment of the natural situation. Supernatural realism transcends all three earthly perspectives as we set our minds on things above and place our hope in a limitless God.

Today I live my Christianity from a completely different perspective. I often see Jesus heal the sick. I often see signs, wonders, and miracles that confirm the message of the Gospel. I regularly dialogue with the Lord instead of simply rattling off my "to-do list" of things I want Him to accomplish in my life. And when I go to a funeral, I expect that the deceased loved one might just wake up. I'm happy to risk myself and my reputation for the sake of the Gospel. If that makes you too nervous then feel free to put this book down now, but if it stirs something inside of you that is looking for the same results then you're in for the ride of your life!

What was it that brought me to my present way of life from the way I used to live?

Limitless hope.

Since making this change of mindset, I no longer place self-imposed boundaries on what God can do. When I minister healing I expect the finished work—not wise doctors or gradual improvement. When I minister to the spiritually oppressed I expect the demons to flee at the name of Jesus; I no longer simply pray for the person to have peace or better circumstances. When I give I do so beyond my means as the Spirit leads; I no longer hold back enough to make me comfortable with the budget that works in my head.

Limitless hope comes from a very real relationship with a limitless God. It is an expectation that He not only "can" do anything but that His love for us compels Him to act beyond our expectations. It is total reliance upon His infinite power and a knowing of the loving heart behind that power. It is unshakable trust that He will follow through on His Word without compromise.

Limitless hope is all about believing God for immediate results yet not crumbling when prayers go unanswered. Limitless hope is all about expecting God to reveal the secrets of His heart yet still being comfortable with unsearchable mystery. Limitless hope is all about allowing Jesus the freedom to be who He is.

In the opening three chapters of this book I have laid the foundation for what this hope really means. And in the remaining chapters I have tried as much as possible to tear apart the most common "intellectual strongholds" that exalt themselves above the knowledge of Christ. (See 2 Corinthians 10:3-5.) In other words, I have attempted to dismantle the wrong-thinking that has permeated Christian thought, robbed us of Biblical faith, and thereby placed unmerited limits on our awesome, all-powerful God.

As much as I'm excited to start sharing these thoughts with you, I do foresee one problem that could easily arise. As you read the statements contrasting between what I call "expected disappointment" versus "limitless hope," it would be easy to run wild with the thoughts presented and leave the Bible in the dust. The statements made about limitless hope are often extreme, challenging the mindset of even some Spirit-filled

Christians. And the statements made about "expected disappointment" are often what we might deem to be sound wisdom or even good, Christian theology (not because of what the Bible says but because of what has become comfortable and "normal" in our culture).

Naturally, one could start thinking things that are unbiblical while assuming that he or she has continued in the same flow of thought. For example, just because God desires everyone to be saved and that none should perish doesn't mean that there is no hell. There is indeed a hell, and people who have not come to Christ will indeed end up there. That's not limitless hope. Rather, limitless hope recognizes the reality of hell and believes it is possible for that horrible region to be plundered of its future residents. Consider the stated goal of Evangelists Reinhard Bonnke and Daniel Kolenda's ministry: "Hell empty; heaven full." It is right to hope such a thing as a means of fueling evangelism. Biblically, it is a plausible goal—at least for those generations that still have the opportunity to repent. Jesus paid the price for all. (See 1 John 2:2.)

Even the most outrageous declarations in this book have firm Biblical grounds for being stated the way they are stated. This is not a book about "undermining the establishment" or creating new theology. Rather, it is all about destroying man-made excuses for powerless Christianity and offering a biblically sensible and hope-filled perspective to embrace. As such, Scriptural foundation is key. If we can't root our faith in the Bible, then what basis do we have for anything we believe? Limitless hope does not contradict the Word of God; our "expected disappointment" does.

As you read this text, let the chapters challenge

your way of thinking, but do not let the enemy drag you away from the plum line of the Bible.

Perhaps like me you will come to grant God the liberty to act in your life without limits. Perhaps your changed perspective on God's heart and desires will cause you to live with greater faith and see greater results. Perhaps you will see an increase (or even a beginning) of signs, wonders, miracles, and healings in your life and ministry. I pray these are all true.

It's time to stop expecting to be disappointed with God and choose to place our unbiased, unfettered, unshakable hope in Him. It is time to have limitless hope.

Be blessed,

Art Thomas
Missionary-Evangelist
www.ArtThomas.org
www.SupernaturalTruth.com

Introduction

" A friend at work suddenly died of a blood clot and left behind a wife and two small children," stated a gentleman at the men's group I was attending. "Please pray that God would comfort his family."

I had just returned from my first trip to Africa where I had witnessed hundreds of miracles—blind eyes opening, deaf ears opening, cripples walking, tumors disappearing, and more. With as much tact as I could muster, I suggested that maybe we should pray that God would raise the man back to life.

That's when I encountered one of the most awkward "blank-stares" I have ever received from a group of Christians—the silence only briefly interrupted by the uncomfortable creak of a chair as someone shifted their weight.

To be honest, I suddenly felt like I was the only person in the world who believed that God could do anything at all. This was a room full of seasoned Christians—men I looked up to—in a church that teaches and expects the active presence of the Holy Spirit. Yet the civilized debate that ensued revealed all manner of reasons—which might be better called "excuses"—for why God rarely intervenes in human affairs. Rather than expecting God to actually change circumstances, my friends had more faith in His ability to change our emotional perspectives on those unchanged circumstances.

This bothered me deeply. Jesus didn't come to earth to make people comfortable with their life-situations; He came to set us free! He didn't teach people how to honor God with their sicknesses; He just healed them! He didn't wrap His arm around the widow who lost her son; He put His hand on the casket and brought the young man back to life. To excuse away sickness, disease, turmoil, death, sin, and so forth is to rob Jesus of the reward for His suffering. Jesus paid the price for all of it, and we must be actively involved in seeing that He receives everything for which He paid.

In your hands is a guide to a new way of thinking. In short, this way of thinking is what the Bible has been teaching all along. In the coming chapters we will dismantle the systems of unbiblical unbelief that have crept into much of Christendom and take a fresh look at what the Bible says at face value.

If you're anything like me during my own discovery process, you may find yourself shocked or stirred with every new page of this book. And if you're anything like me, you'll also welcome such jolts to your thinking-patterns.

I realized some time ago that Jesus frequently rebuked and corrected His disciples for their lack of faith. And this made me think: *If I'm never being corrected for my own lack of faith, am I really following the same Jesus?* With that realization came a simple prayer: "Lord, please rebuke my unbelief, and teach me to truly trust You!" I encourage you to adopt this same prayer as you read.

Most of my wrong thinking about God came from people who also had wrong thinking about God. Well-intentioned as they may have been, their authoritative statements of unbelief had me convinced that their way of thinking was the right way of thinking.

Theology, experience, and sermons are all great and necessary things. Nevertheless, if what we hear is incorrect, these things can also ignite and fuel unbelief in our hearts.

Faith comes by hearing, but so does unbelief. Are you listening to the words of God? Or are you listening to the unbelief of human beings who have no track-record with the miraculous? We are not disciples of books, experience, or church leaders; we are disciples of Jesus. If the books, experiences, and church leaders we follow don't look like Jesus (as revealed in the Word of God), then we need to reevaluate the spiritual food on which we're feasting. (For the record, I'm not suggesting hopping from church to church until you find one whose theology you like. God works best within the context of committed relationships. First try to be a respectful voice of hope rather than bailing on people God loves. I am, however, suggesting that you evaluate any television preachers, authors, radio shows, commentaries, and anything else that regularly feeds into your understanding of Scripture.)

The less a person has been wrongfully convinced of a limited God, the more likely he or she is to see Him do the things He did in the Bible. Rather than miracles being rare occurrences with possibly coincidental explanations, miracles become everyday experiences that are undeniably God. Rather than healings being gradual improvements through the power of medicine, science, and physical therapy, healings become instantaneous transformations of the physical condition performed in the name of Jesus. When a person has limitless hope in a limitless God, limitless things begin to happen!

Let's go back to my friend's prayer request in that men's group. I challenged my Spirit-filled friends to consider the ramifications of the Holy Spirit being within us. This stirred up all manner of replies until one man finally caught it.

"Maybe the reason we don't ask these things," he mused, "is that we're afraid of God not answering the prayer."

He was right. If I pray for the family to be comforted, then no one will know if God answered my prayer or not—and I can go on feeling like I look good in their eyes. But if I pray for the man to be raised from the dead and he stays dead, then people might think that my prayers have no power. I'll look weak.

Such is the tragic end of fearing man more than we fear God.

So I prayed for the man to be raised from the dead.

Unfortunately, he stayed dead.

Limitless hope isn't a magic wand that suddenly

produces supernatural results. But it is definitely the mindset that creates opportunities for such results. If I hadn't chosen to hope during that situation, no one (at least within our little group of men) would have sought God for a resurrection. Limitless hope is about creating opportunities for God to move that might not otherwise exist. And while in this particular case the man stayed dead, I have continued in this way of thinking for more than six years and have witnessed nearly 4,000 miracles within that short time.

If you're looking for a magical string of words that will make God do whatever you want, then you have the wrong book (not that such a book exists). But if you're looking for something to rip the roof off your faith and open your life to a brand new world of possibilities with God, then you're in for a mind-renewing, transformative journey in the coming pages.

When I prayed for my friend's coworker to rise from the dead, I wasn't concerned with what would happen if he stayed dead. I was okay with whatever people might think of me. What I couldn't handle was having resurrection power living inside of me and praying for comfort as though there were nothing else I could do. If the same Holy Spirit who raised Jesus from the dead dwells in me, then I must give Him opportunities to minister to people through me. Sure, we can pray for comfort too; but if the person raises to life, then the comfort is no longer necessary, is it?

My role is simply to believe that Jesus is the resurrection and the life and then to do something with it. My job is to take Him at His word and stick my neck out with the expectation that He will be consistent with His

Word. My job is to have limitless hope.

What tends to happen, though, is that we stick our necks out one too many times, and then we start to second-guess our convictions. We then start to form unbiblical and antichrist arguments that I call "expected disappointment." If you pray for enough dead people to be raised and never see results, eventually you might start to think that God doesn't want to raise the dead. You might start to expect that dead people stay dead—never mind the countless Biblical and modern-day examples (which we will address later in this book). And then you begin to only pray for the families to be comforted.

I prayed for hundreds of people to be healed before I ever saw someone actually receive healing. I wonder sometimes if this was God's way of humbling me and keeping me from thinking I had some special power of my own. Regardless of why, the fact remains that God wanted to heal people all along. Whether or not He used me to do it was irrelevant. My personal experience does not trump the reality of God's nature or desires. With limitless hope, I kept expecting that the Bible was infallible. I took Jesus at His word and expected that "those who believe" will "place their hands on sick people, and they will recover." (See Mark 16:17-18.)

In your hands is a book about living like the disciples in the Book of Acts (rather than living like the Pharisees—believing in the spiritual realm but being more focused on this world). (See Luke 12:54-56.) This is a book about knowing a limitless God and investigating the depths of His heart. It is a book about limitless Christianity that turns the world upside-down. And in case you haven't picked up on it by now, it is a book about limitless hope!

My hope for the Church is that a day will soon come in which there are no more Christian meetings like I experienced. My hope for the Church is that the principles of this book will invade our thinking and change the ways we respond to this fallen world. My hope for the Church is that we all rise up as radical followers of Jesus who are unashamed of the Full Gospel of Jesus Christ. My hope for the Church is limitless.

How about you? What do you hope for the Church? If you read my statements above and thought, "Oh, that will never happen," then you're illustrating my point. Limitless hope is not about expecting the most likely natural outcome. Limitless hope is about engaging a limitless God.

Are you expecting disappointment? Or are you expecting the best-case scenario that is available in Christ? It's a dangerous mindset to embrace—and an uncomfortable one at that—but I can tell you from experience, it's the only way to live.

Rise up, Church! Fix your eyes on Jesus, and begin to dream about what He purchased on the cross. Allow yourself to be stirred into thinking that He wants to do more than you've ever witnessed. Allow yourself to risk your reputation for the sake of what you know to be true about God. Allow yourself to have limitless hope.

Chapter 1:

The Anchor of Hope

The baby had been diagnosed with a heart murmur, and the parents were understandably concerned. Rather than the blood pumping forcefully through the heart, one of the valves was allowing some blood to slosh back into the previous chamber.

Heart murmurs are tricky issues—they might never cause a problem or they might result in congestive heart failure and untimely death. Risk was elevated because the child's grandfather had died of a heart issue. Worse yet, this particular type of heart murmur was significant, and the doctors considered it incurable. As you can imagine, this news was not happy news for the two parents who were already in their early forties at the time of the child's birth.

The parents brought the little boy to their small

Assemblies of God church and asked for prayer for their son's heart. They could have requested prayer for peace in their emotions, financial provision for possible surgeries, skillful doctors, wisdom for parenting a child with special needs, or any number of other things which would have left the baby's heart unaffected; but no. They knew that Jesus had paid the price for their son to be healed. They didn't waste time asking for any of those things. If God healed their little boy's heart, they wouldn't need those things anyhow.

Why hope for anything less?

People often use the word "hope" to say things like, "I hope no one notices my socks don't match." Maybe it will happen, or maybe it won't; but one option is usually more favorable than the other. Yet this middle-aged couple with a new baby boy didn't see it that way. If God didn't heal their son, they would manage; but they were coming to their limitless God with an expectation that He can and will work this miracle. They were banking on the sufficiency of Jesus Christ's sacrifice.

The parents returned to the doctor only to learn that the hole had closed and the heart murmur was completely gone. Sure, it might have gone away on its own—that was the doctor's best explanation—but these parents knew that there was a direct correlation between the hope they had in the Lord's power to heal and the transformation in their baby boy's heart.

What do I think?

I'm convinced that it was a supernatural healing.

What authority do I have to speak on the matter?

I was that baby boy.

Limitless Hope in a Limitless God

I've been healed of more things than anyone deserves (not that any of us actually deserve to be healed even once). Today I'm living free from a heart murmur, scars on my face, ADD, severe dental problems, tendonitis, degenerative disc disease, Crohn's disease, and many more sicknesses and problems that fled at the name of Jesus. Some of the healings happened the first time someone prayed, and others happened after years of persistent prayer. But healing always happened.

I regularly bank on it. I expect to be healed every time someone prays for me. My parents taught me that our God has no limits, and so it would be wrong of me to limit Him with a thought that "it probably won't happen."

Jesus has no limits! The only limits God has are found in our own unbelief. It's not that He is incapable of acting beyond our expectations (because He often does). The issue is that He has chosen to live in loving relationship with us. The nature of love is that you willingly sacrifice your own desires in order to respect another person's boundaries. God often limits the fulfillment of His desires out of respect for our boundaries.

Sometimes my wife wants my undivided attention, and sometimes she wants her space. I may want to spend every waking moment with her, but it wouldn't be love if I overstepped the boundaries she is presently requesting. In the same way, God rarely imposes His desires on us when we have our walls up. He loves us too much.

At the same time, though, occasionally my wife will see my desires and willingly lay aside her own boundaries in order to show love to me. This is the way we, the Church, should be with God. As we learn that Jesus paid the price to heal all our diseases, we have a choice.[1] We can limit God by saying, "I don't really think You want to heal me," or we can lay down our boundaries and say, "I know You want to heal me. Would You please do it today?" Then we humbly speak with the authority of Jesus—certain of the price He paid—and see what happens.

The nature of true hope is that we're not swayed if the healing doesn't happen or if the prayer isn't answered. Our personal experience does not change God's limitless power—nor does it disprove His desire to heal. Our limited experience should not put limits on our limitless God. Rather, we must continue to have limitless hope— letting down our boundaries of unbelief and allowing God room to do what He has wanted to do all along.

What is Hope?

The Greek word for hope (*elpis*) literally means "expectation," whether of good or of evil. What defines hope in a specific instance is the object of that hope. Either you are expecting good or you are expecting evil, and this determines whether hope is positive or negative.

For the Christian, the object of our hope is always God Himself. We don't have hope in a circumstance or hope in a possible outcome—we have hope in a Person. He is the One we expect. And if it is true that God is good, then our hope truly is a positive hope! The apostle Paul tells us to take joy in our hope. (See Romans 12:12.) Biblical hope, then, is a joyful expectation that our good God will triumph.

I've heard it said that "hope is the excited

expectation of good." I love that idea! Hope is not a wish that may or may not happen. It is the excited expectation of good based on the certainty of God's own goodness.

In the summer just before I turned fifteen, I was severely sunburned to the point of significant blistering and oozing sores on my face. I was told that these were second-degree burns. When the blisters healed, I was left with big, splotchy scars on my forehead, cheeks, and chin. My skin looked like military camouflage.

The doctor said he couldn't do anything and sent me to a dermatologist. The specialist then said that we could try to bleach the skin around the bright white scars to make them less noticeable. All that did was turn my skin yellow, but the scars were still obvious. (And now I looked like yellow camouflage.)

Clearly feeling for me, the dermatologist tried to offer me a shred of limited hope. "Scars like this don't generally go away," he stated, "but in the unlikely event that they do go away, it will take seven years because that's how long it takes a human skin cell to regenerate."

I came to terms with my condition and accepted the fact that these scars would likely be on my face for the rest of my life.

But a couple years later, I was volunteering at an elementary school when one of the children asked a question that had become all too familiar: "What's wrong with your face?"

No one likes that question. I had heard it a hundred times before from well-meaning children, but this one was the straw that broke the camel's back. I answered the little girl graciously, but by the time I reached my home, I was irate.

"What's the point, God? How are You receiving any glory in this? I'm sick and tired of having these scars. I don't want them anymore!"

At that moment, an image popped into my mind of a scene I had watched in church plays for years. I saw Jesus appearing to the disciples after His resurrection and saying to Thomas, "Here. Put your fingers where the nails were. Put your hand where the spear pierced My side."

In that instant I knew Jesus was saying to me, "I didn't just take the pain and suffering for your sin so that you wouldn't have to, but I also—even now—bear scars so that you don't have to."

I ran to the bathroom, stood in front of the mirror, placed my hands on my face, and prayed, "Jesus, take the scars!"

Can you guess what happened?

Nothing.

But I was convinced that I had received a word from God. The seemingly failed results did not have any authority over the word He spoke to me. So every day— even though it looked to me as though nothing was happening—I would put my hands on my face and pray, "Jesus, take the scars." My limitless hope in a limitless God transcended the reality I saw with my eyes.

Within a month, the scars were completely gone. Two-and-a-half years after receiving them from second-degree burns and four-and-a-half years before it was medically plausible, the scars had totally disappeared. I still can't tell you if they disappeared suddenly or gradually—I just remember one day realizing they weren't there anymore. Today I have the photographs and eyewitness testimonies to prove it. In fact, I met my wife while I still had the scars, and she saw the healing herself. Jesus truly is that powerful!

Because of limitless hope in the word of the Lord, I never lost an expectation that God would fulfill His promise. My hope transcended my experience. I had a joyful expectation of good despite the negative report from the doctor. Hope conquered disappointment.

Hope Beyond Natural Sensibility

In Genesis 22, we read a shocking story about an old man with a dearly loved son. Years earlier, God had promised Abraham that he and his wife Sarah would have a son, and that he would grow up to father countless descendants. (See Genesis 15:4-5.) To over-simplify a long story, Abraham believed God, and it ended up happening. Now, however, God had asked Abraham to take his son to the mountains and sacrifice him as a burnt offering.

Isaac went with his father, not knowing what would transpire. He carried the firewood for his own cremation while Abraham carried a knife and some fire (perhaps a torch or some smoldering coals). Isaac was smart enough to size up the situation and see that something was missing.

> **Genesis 22:7-8** — Isaac spoke up and said to his father Abraham, "Father?"
>
> "Yes, my son?" Abraham replied.
>
> "The fire and wood are here," Isaac said, "but where is the lamb for the burnt offering?"
>
> Abraham answered, "God Himself will provide the lamb for the burnt offering, my son." And the two of them went on together.

Isaac stood by as his father began stacking rocks to form an altar. Piece by piece, the wood was arranged on the rocks in preparation for the sacrifice. Even after all this, the old man was not too tired to seize his treasured son, tie his hands and feet, and toss him atop the altar. I often wonder if Isaac fought him—I know I would have! Today, a father would be arrested and locked away in a psychiatric hospital for claiming that God told him to sacrifice his son. Nevertheless, Abraham raised his knife in the air and prepared to thrust it down into his boy, who by now probably wished he had brought along a lamb.

What would possess an old man to do something so atrocious? The answer, I believe, is actually a good thing. The answer, I believe, is limitless hope.

> **Hebrews 11:17-19 –** By faith Abraham, when God tested him, offered Isaac as a sacrifice. He who had embraced the promises was about to sacrifice his one and only son, even though God had said to him, "It is through Isaac that your offspring will be reckoned." **Abraham reasoned that God could even raise the dead**, and so in a manner of speaking he did receive Isaac back from death. (emphasis added)

Abraham was convinced that he would return home with his living son whether he killed him or not. He had faith in a limitless God who could do absolutely anything. Abraham knew that even if he killed his son, God would still fulfill His promise to multiply his descendants through that son—and the only way to do that would be to raise him back to life. Abraham believed God's word over his experience or physical circumstances.

As you may know, Abraham did not need to kill his son that day. As the knife was about to thrust into the boy, a voice called to Abraham, stopped him in his tracks, and praised him for his faith.

> **Genesis 22:12-13** – "Do not lay a hand on the boy," he said. "Do not do anything to him. Now I know that you fear God, because you have not withheld from Me your son, your only son."
>
> Abraham looked up and there in a thicket he saw a ram caught by its horns. He went over and took the ram and sacrificed it as a burnt offering instead of his son.

Abraham never lost hope that God would fulfill His promise. He had a limitless hope fueled by his relationship with his limitless God. He didn't allow rationalism to interfere with obedience to the Lord.[2]

Rationalizing Versus Reasoning

There is a difference between rationalizing and reasoning. Reasoning has to do with weighing the factors and coming to a conclusion. Rationalizing, on the other hand, is a mathematical term that has to do with eliminating factors that don't make sense.

Hebrews 11:19 says that Abraham "reasoned" that God could raise the dead. It was indeed a reasonable conclusion when an all-powerful God is one of the factors. If God said Abraham would have a son and that the son would produce descendants, then it was reasonable to conclude that not even death could stop that promise from happening. God keeps His promises.

Faith-filled reasoning happens when we recognize the stability and reality of heavenly factors and the weakness and frailty of earthly factors. Rationalization, on the other hand, happens when we wrongfully believe that earthly factors are concrete while heavenly factors have no affect. The difference between rationalizing and reasoning is found in which realm we place the most confidence.

It would have been easy for Abraham to rationalize away the factors that didn't make sense to him in the natural realm. "Hmm…God said this son would give me descendants, so He couldn't possibly intend for me to actually kill him. Perhaps there's some metaphorical meaning. Maybe God is saying that I need to ignore my son for a while—pretending as though he were dead. Yes! That's it! Then again, God wants me to love my son, not ignore him. I guess that voice was the devil. Yes. Now I can reject that thought and go on comfortably with my life."

This is what happens so often today. Rather than taking reasoned steps of radical obedience to the voice of the Lord, we often tend to rationalize things away until we're comfortable enough with our conclusions. Other times we may move forward with faith-filled reasoning until something becomes uncomfortable, at which point we rationalize that we must have heard incorrectly.

For example when I first started listening to God's voice, I felt like the Holy Spirit asked me to go to a specific store and wait in a specific aisle for a woman with a specific hairstyle, wearing a red shirt. He said, "I want to set her free, and I want to use you to do it."

At first I was reasoning. *If the woman is there at that store in that aisle,* I thought, *then this really is God, and it will work.* As you may have guessed, there she was; but as it turned out, the woman was an employee who had significant cognitive impairments. Fear took over. I started rationalizing. *God doesn't actually need me to say anything out loud. Maybe I should just pray for her silently.* I walked away, praying for her under my breath. It wasn't until I finally reached home that I really started kicking myself for rationalizing away my obedience.

My hope-filled reasoning resulted in obedience and near-fulfillment of a prophetic word, but my rationalization resulted in disobedience and falling short of God's desires.

Reasoning is based on faith and hope, but rationalization is based on expected disappointment. Even though I knew I was supposed to verbally minister freedom to that woman, I started to rationalize that things like this don't happen in the natural world. If this woman was going to actually be set free, then it would take a miracle. Miracles aren't rational—and miracles happening right when we request them are even less rational.

However, if we believe in a good, loving, limitless God who made a promise (a belief I now hold), then miracles certainly are reasonable! I believe much of the Church needs to return to reasonable faith in a limitless God. We must nail our rationalizations to the cross.

Any theology that limits God needs to be called into question. If God placed those limits clearly in His Word, then that's one thing (for example, God does not lie); but if man placed those limits because God's Word seemed too uncomfortable or impossible, then we need to do something about it!

On another occasion I found myself alone in an

impoverished Ugandan city at night (alone, that is, except for my Kenyan guide, Wycliffe). The streets were swarming with people, and all of them—for obvious reasons—were staring at me! Unbeknownst to us, the taxi (called a *mutatu*) had dropped us off in the wrong town, and the man who was supposed to meet us was searching the wrong place. To make matters worse, we later learned that the city we were in—Naluwerere—was infamous for its crime and prostitution. On top of this, I didn't actually know if I could trust the man who was coming to meet us. Paul and I had only met through e-mail. I was only there because I felt that the Holy Spirit had told me to go.

To make a long story short, after we had waited for over an hour, word came to Paul that we were in the next city. Soon, three motorcycles roared up to us. "Praise the Lord!" declared the man whose face I couldn't see in the dark African night. I still didn't know if I could trust him, but he said, "Get on!"

My guide and I climbed on the backs of two of the motorcycles and were whisked away to the other city.

In hindsight, this was probably one of the stupidest things I've ever done (at least by earthly standards). I had traveled alone to a developing country on a continent I've never been to, met a guide who was a friend of an acquaintance, and traveled to an unknown city at night—all to meet a complete stranger who may or may not want to kill me…and all this without enough money to survive on my own and a return plane ticket that wouldn't be useful for another half a month.

You might think I'm out of my mind, but I simply believed that God had told me to go. What I did was irrational, but it was completely reasonable. God has spoken many promises over my life, so I knew that even death couldn't stop His plan. Like Abraham I reasoned that God could raise the dead.

The motorcycles turned down a dirt road, which became a dirt path, which became a dirt trail. Passing mud huts and banana trees, we traveled for over half an hour into the African bush. To be honest my human mind was wondering at what point the drivers would stop, shoot us, and take all our belongings. But in my spirit I had total peace. My heart beat normally, my muscles weren't tense, and my mind was clear. It was irrational, but my faith was well-reasoned. In Philippians 4:7 God promised us peace that surpasses all our understanding, and that's exactly what I had.

Reasonable Hope, Irrational Action

Hope is a powerful force, encouraging us to do irrational things in reasoned response to our limitless God. When we have hope it is as though we have one foot in the natural realm and another foot in eternity. Hope enables us to perceive what God wants to do even when we can only see natural circumstances.

> **Hebrews 6:19 –** We have this hope as an anchor for the soul, firm and secure. It enters the inner sanctuary behind the curtain…

Hope is an anchor for your "mind, will, and emotions" (soul), which is firmly fixed in the throne room of God. When we have this anchor of hope, it doesn't matter how hard the storms of this life beat against us— we are secure in the truth of eternity. Hope is a perspective fixed on the kingdom of heaven, which naturally changes the expectations we have about what God wants to do here on earth. Hope flows from a heavenly perspective because heaven is all about hope.

When I was a baby, my parents didn't look first for a rational solution to my heart murmur—even though they would have sought medical attention if prayer didn't work. Rather, they had hope firmly fixed in another kingdom—a kingdom where heart murmurs don't exist. And when it came to my scars, I had exhausted all rationalism when God finally gave me a word that made my healing reasonable—that Jesus bears my scars in heaven so I don't need to bear them on earth. And when it came to Abraham, rational actions were out of the question; but he reasoned that God could raise the dead— even though he had never seen it happen before. He believed this because he trusted unswervingly in the goodness and righteousness of our limitless God.

As you might have guessed (given the fact that I'm telling the story), the motorcycle drivers in Africa didn't kill me. As it turned out, the man in Uganda was completely trustworthy. Pastor Paul Basuule Habib hosted Wycliffe and me for half a month, taking us to several rural churches to preach the Gospel. By the end of my short time in Africa, we saw hundreds of people saved and hundreds of people healed. Deaf ears were opened. Blind people could see. Cripples were walking. This was not the fruit of rationalism. It's the fruit of a limitless God.

Having now traveled to multiple countries around the world—dodging bullets, sleeping in villages, and confronting Hindus, Muslims, witchdoctors, drunks, and armed gang members—I have learned a very important lesson: At any given moment, you are one irrational act away from a God-encounter; just make sure it's reasonable.

In the coming chapters you will discover the reasonable and mind-blowing potential of having limitless hope in a limitless God. I invite you into the exploration of a miracle-inviting mindset—one which was present in the Lord Jesus Himself as He walked this earth.

Admittedly, this won't be a comfortable journey. If you've been rationalizing away obedience, then this book is sure to be a challenge. My intention is not to simply make you uncomfortable. Rather it is to accomplish what the writer of Hebrews commanded:

> **Hebrews 10:23-24** – Let us hold unswervingly to the hope we profess, for He who promised is faithful. And let us consider how we may spur one another on toward love and good deeds...

Endnotes:

1. I understand that what I just said may be a new concept for many readers (and perhaps a bit of a stumbling block). The terminology that God "heals all our diseases" comes from Psalm 103:3. We will discuss some more of the scriptures that back this up later, so for now I simply request that those who disagree overlook any disagreement momentarily and trust that many of your questions will likely be addressed later.

2. I feel it would be prudent to offer a disclaimer here. I recognize that teaching the story of Abraham in this way opens the doors for dangerous things to happen—especially if a person thinks they are hearing from God but they are not. In Chapter Five, we will discuss hearing God's voice, and you'll see that the New Testament Church hears God within the context of community. For this reason, I offer the following advice: The greater the risk, the more important it is to consult with other mature, Spirit-filled, Bible-believing, Jesus-loving Christians for confirmation before taking action. I can guarantee that you are not the only person capable of hearing God's voice!

Chapter 2:

Unshakable Boldness

There were eight of us in the living room of the little apartment that night. The next day I would lead a seminar, training people in the ministries of Biblical deliverance and inner healing. But this night I was simply invited to the pastor's house for dinner with a handful of key church members and leadership. Little did I know that this would be the most dramatic encounter of the weekend.

The pastor asked me to share whatever the Lord put on my heart. So for the next half-hour I taught on the power and authority that we are given through the Holy Spirit.

The longer I talked, the more hope stirred in my heart and in the hearts of those listening. Colossians 3:2 was happening in our midst—our minds were focused on things above rather than on earthly things. As a result, our minds were being renewed, enabling us to reason with God rather than rationalize things away.

When the moment seemed right, I asked if anyone needed prayer for healing. As it turns out, five of the eight people did. Following what I felt the Holy Spirit wanted to do, I said, "You don't need some fancy 'man of God' from Michigan to lay hands on you. We're in a room full of Spirit-filled believers, and each of you has the same Holy Spirit that I do. So I'm going to have you minister to each other, and I'll mostly just stand back." I gave them some simple instructions for ministering healing and then had them lay hands on each other.

Within moments people were being healed. Even the kids were praying for people and seeing results! One woman had injured her ankle a few weeks earlier and had been in pain ever since. The rest of the weekend, though, she wore four-inch heels just to show off what Jesus did! The more healings we saw take place, the more hope we had for the next person; and the more hope we received, the greater boldness we had.

Now allow me to pause this story for a moment. As you may know, my first book was all about the spiritual gift of a Word of Knowledge.[1] In a very literal sense, you could say that I'm the guy who "wrote the book on it." But even I still tend to question the things I sense. Whereas in one setting, I could be incredibly bold with the level of revelation God is giving, I might in the next setting wonder if I'm really hearing from God. The most common determining factor, in my experience, is the current level (or intensity) of hope in my heart.

As I stood in that living room, the people present

prayed for a young man who had a circulation problem in his legs that was causing chronic pain, specifically in his right leg. During their prayer for him, the Lord told me through a word of knowledge that there was witchcraft in his family history and that it was somehow related to what he was experiencing.

If this were an average stranger on the street, and if I'd had that thought cross my mind while walking past them, it would probably take a lot more for me to speak up about it. But because of my presently renewed mind, heavenly focus, and the boldness springing from hope in God, I had total confidence in that moment. I had seen so many miracles in the last few minutes that I was operating in a level of boldness unlike everyday life (not that we shouldn't try to change this about everyday life!). I told him what I was sensing, and without even asking if it made sense, I proceeded to pray: "In Jesus' name, I break the influence of witchcraft in your family history. Jesus, I ask You to set him free by the power of Your blood. We command the enemy to leave now in the name of Jesus."

The man said he physically felt something leave his leg.

Later that night, he told me that during his childhood, his mother would have people over to the house who would practice witchcraft with her. The next day at the seminar, he testified that his legs were completely healed. Not only that but his mother attended with him!

Drop Anchor

Remember from Chapter One, hope is called an anchor for the soul. A good anchor should have more influence over the position of a boat than the wind or water around that boat. If I have an anchor firmly fixed in the throne room of God, then I will only be moved by what happens there. But putting my hope in the things of this world would be like a ship in a storm hooking its anchor to a piece of driftwood.

A firmly anchored ship looks rather bold as it withstands the waves around it. That's because it has taken on the nature of the rock to which it is tethered. In the same way, limitless hope in a limitless God causes us to take on His nature—unimpressed with earthly circumstances and motivated by the kingdom of heaven.

Second Corinthians 3:12 says that hope makes us "very bold." Take a look at how this same Greek word for "bold" is used in the following verses—all within the context of persecution:

> **Acts 4:13 –** When they [the persecutors] saw the **courage** [same Greek word] of Peter and John and realized that they were unschooled, ordinary men, they were astonished and **they took note that these men had been with Jesus.** (emphasis added)

> **Acts 4:29-31 –** Now, Lord, consider their threats and enable Your servants to speak Your word with great **boldness** [same Greek word]. Stretch out Your hand to heal and perform signs and wonders through the name of Your holy servant Jesus."
>
> After they prayed, the place where they were meeting was shaken. And **they were all filled with the Holy Spirit and spoke the word of God boldly.** (emphasis added)

Again, this "great boldness" comes from hope, and it is activated by interaction with God—having been with Jesus or being filled with the Holy Spirit. It is the result of being relationally anchored in another realm—a realm not affected by the decay and destruction of this fallen world. Unshakable boldness is directly related to being anchored in the Kingdom of Heaven via hope in our limitless God.

In the previous chapter, I told you about my first experience in Uganda. Five days later, I was preaching to a crowd of roughly 200 people in an all-Muslim village overrun with witchdoctors. (It's not uncommon in these rural African villages to find Islam and witchcraft coexisting. Both generally hate Christians, so they seem to get along at least in that regard.)

To my right was seated an intimidating line of men from the village. Some were likely witchdoctors or Muslim imams. They didn't participate in the singing, and I had a feeling that they weren't there for the entertainment factor. At any rate, they didn't seem friendly. In the back of my mind, I began to think, *If persecution is going to happen, then these are the guys who will soon be rushing the stage!*

But because of my limitless hope—because my soul was anchored in the throne room of God—I was not afraid. Boldness from the Holy Spirit came over me. I declared to the crowd something to the effect of, "If you are a witchdoctor or an imam, I want you to come up here on this stage and show me what your gods can do. Bring your biggest demons. Bring your Muslim god. I will prove to you that they have no power compared to Jesus. Muhammad has no power. The Koran has no power. Your idols and shrines have no power. Jesus is King; He has ALL power. If you disagree, come prove me wrong."

No one came. So I added, "Alright, then I'm just going to demonstrate how powerful and good Jesus is. If you're sick, injured, diseased, or have any other physical problem, I want you to put your hand wherever the problem is." Then I declared, "Be healed in Jesus' name... Now, test it out. If you're healed, raise your hand."

Scores of hands went up all across the field—a little over forty. That day, about fifty people converted to Christianity. In the coming days, the pastor of the new church in town was flooded with over a hundred people asking to know more about Jesus. His church, which consisted of some upright poles and three worn-out tarps, was overflowing that next Sunday.

The people of that village saw a man who wasn't afraid of persecution—a man who had limitless hope. I don't credit myself with this testimony. The truth is, my human mind kept thinking, *What are you doing? You're trying to start trouble! If this doesn't work, you're toast!* But Christ in me—the Hope of glory—produced supernatural boldness. The devil cannot stop Christians who have a secure hope. Why? Because he cannot stop Christ! True hope makes us more like Jesus.

The Eternal Reality of Hope

Do you know what eternity is going to be like? A lot of people think it's going to be the final culmination of all the things we ever hoped for in Christ—as though we receive the "fullness of life" that was promised and then just worship or sit around for the rest of eternity on a cloud. But that would imply that when we arrive in heaven, we no longer have anything left to hope for. What an empty, unfulfilling eternity that would be!

Romans 8:24 says something I find a little funny: "...But hope that is seen is no hope at all. Who hopes for what he already has?" In other words, the very concept of hope implies that you're looking forward to something you don't yet have (but that you eventually will have). Hope is the excited expectation of good.

Let me take you a little deeper. Colossians 1:5 tells us that faith and love "spring from hope." That's important because it means true faith and genuine love cannot really exist apart from hope. And can you think of another Scripture that mentions faith, hope, and love?

> **1 Corinthians 13:12-13** – For now we see only a reflection as in a mirror; then we shall see face to face. Now I know in part; then I shall know fully, even as I am fully known. And now these three remain: faith, hope and love. But the greatest of these is love.

Do you see it? Paul is talking about the end of time when we are all with Christ in eternity, beholding Him as He is, face to face. At that time, when it seems that we have reached the pinnacle of perfection, peace, and joy, we still enjoy the excitement and wonder of hope.

Think about that! What more do you have to hope for? Could it be that when we set foot on the new earth at the end of time that it's not really an end but rather a beginning? Could it be that even after "we've been there 10,000 years, bright shining as the sun," there is still more "good" to excitedly anticipate?

Absolutely! Faith, hope, and love will remain. We know it because it is promised, and we know it because faith and love spring from hope. Faith is the realization of things hoped for. (See Hebrews 11:1.) In eternity there will still be faith. There will still be love. There will still be hope!

Don't think of eternity with Christ as eons of sitting on a cloud playing a harp. On the contrary, see it as the adventure that God has designed it to be: A never-ending journey with the Lord in which we constantly experience the fun and beauty of faith, hope, and love.

It is also important to note that Paul said "these three *remain*." In other words, faith, hope, and love are already here now. How could they "remain" unless they already exist? This tells us that even though God's kingdom has not yet been fully realized, we are now in a very present kingdom, which is accessible to us already. We are presently capable of being anchored in that kingdom and living according to its principles.

This hope, rooted in eternity, gives us unshakable boldness. It prompts us to do things without fear of what may become of us on this earth.

> **Revelation 12:11 –** And they have defeated him [the devil] by the blood of the Lamb and by their testimony. And they did not love their lives so much that they were afraid to die. (NLT)

> **Philippians 1:20-21 –** For I fully expect and hope that I will never be ashamed, but that I will continue to be bold for Christ, as I have been in the past. And I trust that my life will bring honor to Christ, whether I live or die. For to me, living means living for Christ, and dying is even better. (NLT)

Real Christians don't fear death. Again, this hope in God makes us "very bold." Real hope causes us to be so secure in our heavenly position that no earthly condition can cause us to fear. That's why I wasn't afraid when I confronted the witchdoctors and imams in Africa.

Boldness that Endures

We don't simply have a responsibility to be bold in a given moment. Whenever we experience a new level of boldness, we are expected to live from that level of boldness in the future.

Hebrews 3:6 encourages us to "hold fast" to boldness and "rejoice in hope until the end." When a new and higher level of hope produces newfound conviction and boldness, it is our responsibility to "hold fast" to that boldness and keep that hope alive through rejoicing.

But new levels of hope don't mean new places to put our anchor. Our hope is always in Christ, and therefore our anchor is always in the same Rock. Entering a greater level of hope does not mean you've found a new Rock. It also doesn't mean that the Rock has changed. Rather, it means that your anchor has fixed itself more securely in that Rock, and your chain has become stronger.

The stronger your hope, the stronger the pressure you can endure in this fallen world. The nature of being anchored to something is that you find yourself locked to it. If a ship is tightly anchored to a rock fifty feet below, what happens when the water rises to fifty-five feet? Assuming the chains cannot break, the boat experiences a sort of pressure as though the rock were pulling it into the depths. The higher the water rises, the more intense that pressure on the boat. The same is true of us. The tighter we are anchored to the heavenly realm, the more uncomfortable this fallen world becomes.

What we tend to do, though, is loosen our chains so that we don't feel the pressure anymore. Even though we have the power and authority to command the waves to calm and the tide to subside, we let the waves toss us around. Rather than speaking into the circumstances of our fallen world, we adjust our level of tolerance to withstand more corruption. Rather than ministering healing in Jesus' name, we become more comfortable with medical science (not that it's bad—it just shouldn't become a replacement). Rather than raising the dead in Jesus' name, we become more comfortable with funerals. Rather than evangelizing the lost, we become more comfortable with worldly lifestyles. Before we know it, our chains are so loose and our anchors are so far away that we can't even feel the least pressure from the Rock below.

The solution to the storm is not to let out our anchor lines. The solution to the storm is to speak to the storm! This is how we live in hope.

The further we drift from the kingdom of heaven, the more we start to see that kingdom as something distant in the future for after we die. But the tighter we pull the anchor-line of hope, the clearer we can see its present reality. The corruption of this world begins to feel unnatural. Suddenly, we begin to say with Paul, "Living means living for Christ, and dying is even better."

Boldness in Relationship with God

The tight anchor-line of hope causes us to feel the pressure of this fallen world, and this pressure motivates us to do something about the water level. The first thing this pressure produces in us is boldness in prayer.

> **Hebrews 4:16** – Let us therefore come boldly
> to the throne of grace, that we may obtain
> mercy and find grace to help in time of need.
> (NKJV)

Limitless hope draws us into the presence of God. It stirs us to ask Him for help, knowing with confidence that He holds the solution to the problem we face.

Naturally, that solution is Jesus Christ and the price He has already paid at the cross.

Jesus came to earth to live like us so that we could go to heaven and live like Him. I'm not talking about going to heaven when we die; I'm talking about already living there now. As Paul put it, going to heaven when we die will be "even better," but living there while we're still on earth is the only way to bring that reality into this one. To live in this world is to live for Christ, sitting with Him on His throne. (See Ephesians 2:5-7 and Revelation 3:21.)

Those of us who have surrendered our earthly lives to the cross of Christ have already died. But since Jesus didn't stay dead, neither did we. The same Holy Spirit who raised Him from the dead now lives in us, making us new creations in Christ. (See Romans 8:11 and 2 Corinthians 5:17.)

Jesus is physically seated in the heavenly realms at the right hand of God, and He has invited us to sit in that same place—a place of unmatched authority and intimacy with our Heavenly Father. God becomes just as much our Father as He is Father to Christ. (See John 1:12 and Romans 8:14-17.) This gives us a whole new measure of boldness in the way we approach Him.

> **Hebrews 10:19 –** And so, dear brothers and sisters, we can boldly enter heaven's Most Holy Place because of the blood of Jesus. (NLT)

The work of Jesus is what grants us access to the Father. Without that access, we have no place to secure the anchor of hope. Why? Because without relationship with God, we have no hope! Limitless hope is based on the premise that we are in relationship with a limitless God who can do absolutely anything and loves us beyond measure.

Those who walk in loving relationship with God have access to a far superior reality than what we see in the physical realm. Hope keeps them secure in that reality even when this world stands in stark contrast.

Returning to that living room with the eight church leaders, recall that several people were miraculously healed. The more healings we witnessed, the more firmly our anchors in the throne room of God were secured. We started to see the reality of His will, which directly influenced our expectation in the next ministry situation. The more convinced we became of God's will, the greater the boldness we had for the next healing. The renewing of our minds produced clarity about the will of God.

> **Romans 12:2 –** Do not conform to the pattern of this world, but be transformed by the renewing of your mind. Then you will be able to test and approve what God's will is— His good, pleasing and perfect will.

As the group prayed for each other to be healed, two people—at different times—started to exhibit the signs of having demons influencing them. With boldness springing from the hope in my heart, I spoke confidently, calmly, and with authority.

"You may not make a show of this person. Be quiet in Jesus' name, and come out."

Sure enough, freedom came to both people.

It didn't matter how desperately the devil tried to intimidate us; I was free from fear. Limitless hope— through relationship with our limitless God—gave me the confidence to speak boldly to the "storm" rather than cowering in fear. The heavenly authority of Jesus Christ was expressed in the physical world.

The boldness God gives through hope is for a purpose. It stirs us to action and produces results. Hope is what keeps our focus on the Kingdom of God and the desires of our King.

Endnote:

1. *The Word of Knowledge in Action*, by Art Thomas. Destiny Image Publishers, 2011.

   In short, words of knowledge take place when the Holy Spirit makes you aware of something Jesus knows. It is a powerful tool in ministry and can be very helpful when looking for solutions to a person's problem.

   You can purchase this book at SupernaturalTruth.com or anywhere books are sold.

Chapter 3:

Overcoming Deferred Hope

I was in a rural African church, teaching the people to minister physical healing in Jesus' name. I decided the best thing to do would be to demonstrate, so I asked for everyone with eye problems to raise a hand. I picked one woman at random, brought her up in front of everyone, and said, "I want you to see that Jesus has power to overcome any problem."

You might think this was presumptuous on my part. What made me think this would work? Well, to be honest, I had already seen six eye conditions healed in the previous twelve days—including a man who was almost completely blind. It only seemed reasonable that it would work again.

The woman said she couldn't read because everything close to her was blurred. I placed my hands on her eyes and said, "Eyes, be healed in Jesus' name." Then I opened a Bible in front of her and asked if there was any change.

No. Nothing changed. So I did it again.

"Eyes, be healed in Jesus' name."

I opened the Bible again. Still there was no change.

I continued this process for about fifteen minutes. Ten pastors, thirty church members, and fifteen children watched in silence as nothing happened over and over again. One woman walked out of the church.

I eventually asked the people, "At what point should I stop asking God to heal this woman?"

They laughed.

But I continued, "Did Jesus pay for this woman to be healed?"

"Yes," they answered.

"Did He pay a very high price for her healing?"

"Yes."

"Then is Jesus happy that she can't see clearly?"

"No."

"Does Jesus deserve to receive what He paid for?"

"Yes."

"Then does it matter if I look like a fool as I keep trying the same thing over and over?"

The people smiled silently. I turned back to the woman, placed my hands on her eyes, and said, "Eyes, be healed in Jesus' name."

Nothing happened.

How many times should we pray for a person

before we give up hope? How many times should we ask God to bring our backslidden family member to repentance? How many times should we ask Him to give us wisdom, provide for our bills, or help us love others?

The right answer is simple: As many times as it takes until it happens. That's what Jesus taught us to do. When one of His disciples asked Him to teach the group to pray, Jesus responded first by demonstrating a model prayer that involved worship and requests for supernatural intervention, provision, forgiveness, and freedom from temptation and the enemy. He followed all that with this story:

> **Luke 11:5-10 –** Then Jesus said to them, "Suppose you have a friend, and you go to him at midnight and say, 'Friend, lend me three loaves of bread; a friend of mine on a journey has come to me, and I have no food to offer him.' And suppose the one inside answers, 'Don't bother me. The door is already locked, and my children and I are in bed. I can't get up and give you anything.' I tell you, even though he will not get up and give you the bread because of friendship, yet because of your shameless audacity he will surely get up and give you as much as you need.
>
> "So I say to you: Ask and it will be given to you; seek and you will find; knock and the door will be opened to you. For everyone who asks receives; the one who seeks finds; and to the one who knocks, the door will be opened.

Because of the man's "shameless audacity," the friend will give him as much as he needs! Some versions say "boldness" and others say "persistence." The point is clear: Keep asking God for the things He has made available, and He will respond simply because you came.

This story about the friend makes it sound like the midnight request was an inconvenience, but the analogy only goes so far. Our God is a loving Father—not an inconvenienced friend. How much more passionate about you is your Father in heaven? He delights in giving good gifts to His children! (See Matthew 7:11.)

The Father Grows Blessings

The Father is not a reluctant giver, but sometimes He waits while we are shaped in the fire of persistence, knowing that the result will be an even greater blessing.

When I turned ten, my dad said to me, "Son, you're in the double-digits now, so you're probably going to start noticing girls soon. I thought I'd give you a little advice about that. When I was your age, I asked the Lord to send me my wife early in life so I wouldn't waste all my money on girls I wasn't going to marry."

Funny as that statement was, I took it to heart and began asking God for the perfect person to marry. Now, I don't believe in the concept of "the one" except to say that "the one you marry" is "the one." Otherwise, the Bible would have listed that as being acceptable grounds for a divorce: "Don't divorce unless you accidentally didn't marry 'the one.'" What I do believe is that God knows me better than I know myself, and He therefore knows the perfect type of person for me.

Throughout my teenage years, while all my friends

were finding girlfriends and boyfriends, I kept waiting and praying. Every time a girl caught my eye as a possibility, I would pray, "Lord, if this isn't the right type of person, I ask that You would keep us from even having a conversation that would lead to a relationship." For seven whole years, this plan worked.

That's when I met Robin. I had asked the Lord for a list of things to look for in the ideal wife for me. Within the first couple hours of meeting Robin, every one of the items on that list was checked off in my mind. I was stunned. This was the right girl for me!

There's a long story about how Robin and I finally started our relationship, and there's an even longer story about our waiting seven more years to be married until she finished college (honoring her parents' request). Sparing you all the details, the important thing here is that Robin truly is the perfect wife for me. There are few women who could handle the emotional stress of sending their husband to dangerous places on the other side of the world while they stay home with the kids. Not only that, but Robin is the perfect ministry partner for me, often having insights into people's lives about which I was unaware. She's the perfect mom for our boys, and I love knowing that she's the one raising my boys when I'm traveling. Robin is smart, funny, and beautiful, and she loves Jesus and me.

Those seven years of waiting and praying before Robin came along were agonizing—especially with adolescent hormones running through my veins. But if God had sent Robin to me any sooner, I'm sure I would have lacked the maturity necessary to maintain a healthy relationship with this spectacular girl.

It's not that God derived some sort of pleasure

from making me wait. It's that He knew the only way to make this blessing work would be to bring Robin along at the perfect time. He didn't wait for my character to be perfect—I had a lot of emotional issues even at the age of seventeen—but He did wait until I was working on self-control and trying to live in spiritual freedom in Christ. Because God waited to answer my prayer, Robin and I met at the right time and bonded under the right set of circumstances. Today we have an awesome marriage that I wouldn't trade for the world.

Anytime God delays in answering a prayer, it's because He knows that there's a greater blessing coming later. It's like He has insider information about the stock market and knows that if you leave your money in a little longer, it will double in value. If God is saying "not yet," don't be discouraged. The blessing is growing.

Not Everything is God's Will

When it comes to things like finding a spouse or a job or something else along those lines, God's delays are expressions of His wisdom and divine foresight. But when it comes to things like forgiveness, deliverance from demons, physical healing, and anything else that the blood of Jesus directly purchased, His desire is always the same: "Now is the day of salvation." (See 2 Corinthians 6:2.)

If a person comes to the Lord for forgiveness and walks away without it, the problem isn't that God is waiting until a better time to forgive. He decided to forgive 2000 years ago. He doesn't need to make up His mind again. Rather, the problem is that the person didn't trust that Jesus' sacrifice was sufficient to remove all their sin. Salvation is a simple matter of a person's faith in God. Do they trust that His work is enough? Or will they continue striving to prove their value through their own efforts and trying to earn God's approval? If a sinner walks away from God without forgiveness, it's their own fault, not His. God freely forgives us and never says no.[1]

Spiritual salvation is the only result of Jesus' sacrifice that can only be acquired by your own faith. In other words, my faith can't bring you into a relationship with God. You have to trust Him yourself. However, the other results of Jesus' sacrifice—healing and deliverance—can happen through anyone's faith. In fact, while experience tells me that you can indeed minister healing to yourself, there is actually no scripture verse that expects or requires it. The only prescription for a sick Christian is to go to other mature believers and have them minister to you in faith. (See James 5:14-15.)

When it comes to matters of the atonement—things Jesus paid for with His blood—God responds to active faith. In the case of spiritual salvation, only the person's own faith matters. But in the case of physical salvation—wholeness of body and freedom from the demons who roam throughout the earth—the faith can be anyone's. The passage in James that I cited places the responsibility for faith on the ministers doing the praying, not on the sick person. In fact, I have seen people healed who didn't have any faith for themselves at all.

In the only biblical case where someone tried to minister healing in Jesus' name but without results, Jesus didn't blame the little epileptic boy for a lack of faith. He didn't blame the boy's father, even though the father confessed to having unbelief in his heart. And while He identified the surrounding crowd as an "unbelieving and perverse generation," He didn't blame the lack of results on the spiritual atmosphere among the onlookers. And He certainly didn't say God was delaying the answer for a higher purpose. Instead, Jesus healed the boy and later explained to the disciples why He could do it and they couldn't: "Because you have so little faith." (See Matthew 17:14-20.)

In the case of something like forgiveness, healing, or deliverance, a lack of results is not God's will. A lack of results is purely evidence of a lack of faith.[2] In these cases, God is waiting for a human being to trust Him fully and partner with Him to bring about His will in the earth.

When we don't fully entrust ourselves to Him, He doesn't act. Why? Because if He did, we would never learn to fully trust Him with our whole lives. We would go on thinking our faith was perfect because it produced results. In these cases, when God says, "No," He is growing us into a fuller expression of sonship—children who do their part (and only their part) and completely trust their Father to handle everything else. God is disciplining us and teaching us to trust Him. (See Hebrews 12:5-11.)

Now this is very important: I'm not saying that God is disciplining the sick person. The existence of sickness is the devil's work, which Jesus came to destroy. (See 1 John 3:8.) We are responsible to do everything Jesus did when He walked this earth, and more. (See John 14:12 and 20:21.) And Jesus healed every single person who came to Him, called out to Him, or sent someone else on their behalf. Everyone who touched Jesus' body was healed, and now we are His Body in the earth. If sickness remains, the weak link isn't that the blood of Jesus was inadequate. And the weak link isn't the sick person. (Jesus raised the dead. Dead people don't have to have faith or even figure out how to receive!) The weak link—as identified in James 5:14-15 and Matthew 17:20—is ministers who aren't representing Jesus as effectively as we could.

Whenever I minister healing without results, I look the person in the eye and say, "If Jesus were standing here, you'd be completely whole right now. Instead you got me, and I'm still learning to trust God like He did. But I am convinced that God wants you whole—Jesus paid the price for it. So I want you to keep making opportunities for Jesus to receive the reward of His suffering. Keep going to Christians for ministry. I believe we—the Church—will soon grow into the faith needed for your healing."

In the mean time, if you're sick and still waiting to be healed, be encouraged! First of all, your sickness is exposing a need for growth in the Church and challenging us to trust Jesus more fully. Even though God isn't happy that you're still sick, He will use this condition to strengthen the Body of Christ and grow our faith. And second of all, you can rest assured that your own blessing is building up steam—not because God is waiting for a better time but because He loves to overcompensate for injustice.

God Overcompensates for Injustice

When the devil destroyed everything in Job's life, God's response was to bless Job with double of everything he lost and then gave him 140 years of life to enjoy it all! (See Job 42:10-17.) When a swarm of locusts destroyed Israel's crop year after year, God promised to restore what was lost, meaning not only that the famine would end but that they would harvest more than they could consume until it was all repaid. (See Joel 2:25.) Solomon wrote that if a thief is caught stealing, he must repay seven times what was taken. (See Proverbs 6:30-31.) And God's overcompensation for injustice has its fullest expression when the singular death of Jesus Christ paid the price for all humanity's sin. (See Romans 5:19, 2 Corinthians 5:14, and 1 John 2:2.)

God loves to overcompensate for injustice. Whenever someone comes to a believer for healing and doesn't receive it, that's an injustice because Jesus shed His blood to make that work. Jesus deserves what He paid for.

Seeking healing is an act of worship because you are seeking for Jesus to receive the reward of His suffering. Don't let the enemy discourage you from seeking healing. You're not an inconvenience; you're a worshipper. And if, in your seeking for healing, the blood that Jesus shed didn't have the effect intended, that's an injustice against Him, and God will overcompensate for it. Every time you seek healing without experiencing results, the blessing grows.

I battled with degenerative disk disease and bulging discs for four years. I had bulging disks in my lower back that pinched nerves and caused chronic pain. Two to four times a year, my back would go out, and I would be on strict bed rest for at least a week until I could walk again—sometimes being out of commission for a couple weeks.

I couldn't tell you how many times people prayed for me over the course of my four years with that disease. Three times, I was partially healed for a short period, but the condition would come back.

Then, just days before stepping out into full-time traveling ministry, my wife and I were attending a conference when my back was completely healed. (I should note here that this was in April 2011, and I began healing ministry in August 2009. For more than a year and a half, I ministered healing to other people while I was still suffering. Limitless hope looks beyond our own condition. Limitless hope enables us to believe in what is possible even when our experience argues to the contrary.)

After I was healed, the speaker, Will Hart, asked for testimonies from those who had just experienced significant healing. I was third in line on the stage. The first person shared, everyone clapped, and he sat down. The second person shared, everyone clapped, and she sat down. Then I shared, and everyone clapped; but when I went to sit down, Will said, "Wait."

What followed was a very specific prophecy that confirmed everything the Lord had already been speaking to my wife and me. Will spoke about me traveling throughout the world, preaching the Gospel with the power of the Holy Spirit. He spoke about the accelerated season of favor that God was giving us over the next four years, during which time God would reveal the full extent of what He wants me to do for the rest of my life (and He did). It was a word of confirmation that I desperately needed from the Lord. My wife and I were both walking away from our careers with a newborn baby in our arms and an instruction from the Lord never to solicit for a speaking engagement. But that day, God strengthened us by prophetically commissioning us into ministry.

If I had been healed any time in the four previous

years, I probably wouldn't have wound up on stage to receive that word from God. The Lord redeemed my four years of suffering by granting four years of accelerated favor. Similarly, if I had stepped into ministry prematurely, I wouldn't have received that miraculous commission and may not have been healed in that way.

I'm not saying God was purposely holding off on my healing so that I could receive that prophetic word. I'm saying that since I sought healing for four years, the blessing continued to build up steam behind the scenes so that when someone finally partnered with God in faith, the blessing was even greater than if I had received it sooner.

If God regularly withholds healing for a higher purpose, then Jesus wouldn't have instantly healed all the people He healed. Instead He would have said things like, "It's not time yet. Check with me the next time I pass through your village." Jesus never contradicted His Father.

No. "Now is the day of salvation." When it comes to things Jesus paid for, His answer is always "yes" and "now." But His stipulation is always active faith, and He will withhold a blessing for the sake of the Body of Christ gaining a fuller connection to our Head, Jesus Christ.

In the mean time, God doesn't waste the time we spend seeking His will. Instead, like parents saving for their child's college, He sets aside the answer as we grow into the moment of receiving it—and just as the college money grows with compounded interest, so does the blessing we're seeking from God.

Never assume that waiting is necessary. Simply trust that if immediate results don't come when we expect them, God is growing the blessing behind the scenes.

When Hope is Deferred

People often ask me how I could keep seeking healing in my back for four full years. The answer is simple: It hurt for four years! But I know what they're really asking. They really want to know why I never settled down and accepted the fact that "this is just the way it's going to be." Why didn't I conclude that it must be God's will for me to have this condition?

Whenever we focus more on the delay than on the testimonies of the past, we run the risk of developing a sickness of discouragement. If you focus on disappointment, then you're a disciple of disappointment, and you will therefore reproduce disappointment. But if you focus on Jesus and the things He has done, then you're a disciple of Jesus, and you will reproduce the things He has done!

> **Proverbs 13:12** – Hope deferred makes the heart sick, but a longing fulfilled is a tree of life.

The longer it takes for hope to be fulfilled, the easier it is to become distracted from the truth. After about a hundred times of having people pray for my back, it would have been easy to stop expecting it. This expectation of disappointment is what that proverb calls a sick heart.

On the other hand, "longing fulfilled is a tree of life." Do you know what the Bible says about the tree of life? When John saw it, he wrote in Revelation 22:2 that it bears twelve crops of fruit—one for every month. In other words, it constantly nourishes—never running out of provision. When a longing is fulfilled, it becomes a tree of life meant to nourish you as you wait for the object of your hope. The testimonies of the past are a resource meant for us to draw upon as we wait for God's promises to be fulfilled. Not only that but John said that the leaves of the tree are for the healing of the nations. The testimonies of the past are not only for us but for the transformation of the society in which we live.

The healing of my scars became a tree of life for me. The enemy couldn't trick me into expecting disappointment. One of the easiest times to be tempted is when you're hungry—perhaps that's why the devil came to Jesus while our Lord was fasting. (See Luke 4:1-2.) Temptation comes when our desires become chains with which the enemy can drag us away. (See James 1:14.) But my spiritual appetite was satisfied—I was feasting on a tree of life. The enemy couldn't discourage me because I was continually reminding myself of the testimony from my past. Every time the enemy said, "Your back will never be healed," I would look in the mirror and try to find a scar.

Longings that have been fulfilled in the past are meant to encourage you and sustain you as you await the next fulfillment.

Limitless hope trusts God regardless of the present circumstances. My physical condition does not change who God is. God is Healer whether I am healed yet or not. God is Provider whether I can pay my bills or not. God is my Peace whether I feel it yet or not. We can't allow ourselves to live out of the disappointments of the past or present. We must lock into a clear conviction of who God is. This is our anchor for the soul.

We focus on God rather than circumstances. "Set your minds on things above, not on earthly things." When we look at the present mess in life, we often begin to wonder if we really can trust God. We wonder if we truly are secure in Him and whether or not He will actually come through for us. And this sickness of heart—this questioning of our security in the arms of our loving Father—causes us to waver in our boldness. We soon find it difficult to approach Him in prayer.

> **1 John 3:21 –** And, beloved, if our consciences (our hearts) do not accuse us [if they do not make us feel guilty and condemn us], we have confidence (complete assurance and boldness) before God. (AMP)

If we can't approach God boldly in prayer, then we won't pray. Circumstances will remain the same, and the sickness of our hearts will be reinforced. Remember, when the water level rises, the solution is not to lengthen the anchor chain; rather, it is to speak to the wind and waves.

When David was about to slay Goliath, he announced to King Saul, "This giant is going to be a piece of cake. After all, God helped me kill a lion and a bear who were after my father's sheep, and God will help me again." (See 1 Samuel 17:33-37.) David feasted his mind on the victories of the past. "Longing fulfilled is a tree of life." Again, the testimonies of God's action in the past are meant to nourish us continually throughout the future.

You can choose to feast your mind on testimonies, which will fuel your hope; or you can choose to focus on your present circumstances, which will make your heart sick.

You decide.

The Substance of Hope

The testimonies of the past only go so far. We also need to be convinced that those testimonies are evidence of a consistent God.

The substance of our hope—the thing that makes it tangible here and now—is our relationship with God. That relationship is one of total dependence on Him. The Bible calls this faith.

> **Hebrews 11:1** – Now faith is the substance of things hoped for, the evidence of things not seen. (NKJV)

Faith enables us to see the reality of that which has not yet taken place. Faith gives us access to the reality of our hope even when it has not yet been fulfilled. Faith spares us from the disappointment that makes the heart sick. And ultimately, faith brings that unseen hope into the natural realm. Faith produces tangible results. (See Matthew 17:20.)

I like to say that faith is a relational word. It's not a matter of belief. Suppose my wife, Robin, calls me on her way home from work and says, "Hey! I'm meeting some friends at Pizza Hut for dinner at six o'clock. You should come!" I know without doubt that if I go to Pizza Hut at six o'clock, she will be there. I have faith in my wife. Now suppose I drove to a McDonald's restaurant and believed with all my heart that she would come. Would she ever arrive? No. Faith and belief are different. It is possible to believe something (because you want it to be true) and yet have no relationship as a basis for that belief. But it is impossible to have real faith apart from a relationship.

God promised Moses that the Israelites would be

set free from slavery in Egypt and brought into a land flowing with milk and honey. (See Exodus 3:8.) However, this "Promised Land" eluded the Israelites for forty years as they wandered in the desert.

Why did they have to keep wandering in the desert? Because the people refused to have faith in God! (See Numbers 14:11-23.) When God appeared on the mountain to meet with Moses, the Israelites rejected Him. They were terrified of God and basically said, "We don't want a relationship with God. You speak to Him on our behalf, Moses!" (See Exodus 20:19.)

The result was that the Israelites had the privilege of seeing the deeds of God, but only Moses had the privilege of knowing His ways. (See Psalm 103:7.) Anyone can observe God's deeds, but only those in relationship with Him can get to know His ways. This is one of the reasons why Jesus said that there would be those on the Day of Judgment who declare, "Lord, Lord, did we not prophesy in your name and in your name drive out demons and in your name perform many miracles?" These people knew His deeds, but they didn't know His ways. They had no relationship with Him. Jesus said He would respond to these ones, "I never knew you. Away from me, you evildoers!" (See Matthew 7:21-23.)

Longing Fulfilled

Let's finish the story of the African woman with poor eyesight. After about twenty minutes of ministry in front of everyone, she could suddenly read the large-print headings in the Bible I was holding. At this point, I said, "Good! That means it's working!" I turned to the onlookers and added, "I'm going to continue ministering to her until her vision is completely clear, but I think you see now how this works. Speak to the person's condition in Jesus' name, and if you don't see results, do it again. Keep going until things change."

I asked those who needed healing to line up across the front of the room, and then I had the other Christians come minister healing to them. To prove a point, I told the ten pastors who were present to stay in their chairs and watch how God was going to use average people to minister with power.[3] The people took their places, and I returned to the woman with the failing eyesight. Almost immediately, she was reading the small print of my Bible with a big smile on her face.

But the story doesn't end there! What happened next is my favorite part!

The woman started to return to her seat, and I stopped her. "Where are you going? You should go find someone in the line and pray for them!"

She went to the one man who didn't yet have anyone ministering to him. It was divinely orchestrated: The man was almost completely blind. She placed her hands on the man's eyes and said, "Be healed in Jesus' name."

Of all the people in that line receiving ministry, he was the first one healed!

When I was ministering to the woman, my hope was deferred. I could have backed off and allowed it to make my heart sick, but instead I feasted my mind on a "tree of life." I reminded myself of the six "eye healings" I had already witnessed in the past couple weeks. The natural outcome was sustained perseverance. I had boldness. I ministered with "shameless audacity." I refused to allow circumstances to redefine what Jesus has already revealed about God's will. My mind was renewed regarding eye problems, and the result was that I could "test and approve" God's will.

Not only was that woman healed, but she found herself with a "tree of life" fueling her own faith. Her ministry worked even faster than mine!

The rest of the people caught on too. Every sick, diseased, or injured person in that meeting was completely healed by Jesus—and I only ministered to one of them.

Faith is the substance of things hoped for. Have faith in God. He is the object of your desire—the focal point of your hope. And as you learn to trust in Him, feast your mind on the testimonies of what He has done in the past. These testimonies can be your own personal experiences, they can be from the lives of people you know, they can be stories from total strangers, and they can be from the Bible. Whatever the case, a longing fulfilled is a tree of life. Continue to nourish yourself with the stories that reveal God's true nature. Remembering testimonies and having faith in God work hand in hand to fuel hope.

Endnotes:

1. Of course, the obvious exception is "blaspheming the Holy Spirit," which Jesus called an unpardonable sin. But that's not what we're talking about here. The context here is about the typical sinner coming to Jesus for salvation.

2. I want to reiterate for the sake of clarity that I'm not talking about those who are not healed lacking faith. If a sick person *must* be any part of the equation for healing, then Jesus could not have had 100% results. The only way a lack of faith in a sick person keeps them from being healed is if it causes them to avoid ministry. To explore this topic deeper and see the biblical case for it, see my article "Who Needs to Have Faith for Healing?" at http://supernaturaltruth.com/who-needs-to-have-faith-for-healing/

3. In Luke 10, Jesus sent out the 72 "others" to preach the Kingdom and heal the sick. When the others came back rejoicing, He said privately to the 12 disciples, "Blessed are the eyes that see what you see. For I tell you that many prophets and kings wanted to see what you see but did not see it, and to hear what you hear but did not hear it." (See verses 23-24.) The disciples' eyes were blessed because they witnessed average people ministering the Gospel of the Kingdom. So I made the African pastors remain seated because, I said, "I want your eyes to be blessed!"

Chapter 4:

Limitless Hope and Living Sin-Free

In the previous chapter, I showed you the difference between a sickened heart and a renewed mind. As I briefly mentioned, this sickened heart—afflicted with the deferred fulfillment of hope—tends to expect disappointment.

As a father, I can't imagine how sad I would be if my boys only ever expected to be disappointed. I would much rather they trust me implicitly and anticipate good—even if I'm delayed in responding to their needs. Why do we think that our heavenly Father is any different?

Nevertheless, when our hearts are sick, we expect to be disappointed. We lower our expectations and back off in our boldness.

In this chapter (and every chapter through the end of this book), I'm going to offer you maxims—or concise statements—that contrast between limitless hope and "expected disappointment." The purpose is to expose any sickness that might exist in your own heart and awaken you to the Truth, which is Jesus Christ Himself. Brace yourself, though, because you may be surprised how much "expected disappointment" has crept into your own mindset, church-culture, and theology.

Sin-Free Living

To sin is to miss the mark. What's the mark? I suppose it's different in every situation, but let me simplify it: The mark is the best possible action that is only possible to hit when we actively trust in Jesus. This active trust is called "faith." Romans 14:23 says that "everything that does not come from faith is sin."

Faith and sin are opposites because whenever we truly partner with Jesus, we end up doing the right thing (since Jesus always does the right thing). But whenever we drift from Jesus, even our best actions are performed apart from Him. No matter how hard we try or how well we behave, even our good deeds are sinful apart from a faith-filled relationship with Jesus. (See Isaiah 64:6.)

The actions we consider to be "sins" are actually just evidence of one's deviation from a healthy relationship with God. When we have truly surrendered completely to the Lord, and when we truly live out of our identity in Christ, we are no longer separated from God. His life becomes our life, and our actions follow suit.

Before sin is an action, it is a state of being. People don't perish in hell because of their actions. People perish in hell because of the vast chasm between them and God that started thousands of years ago. (See Romans 5:19.) As a Christian, if you find yourself behaving sinfully, this doesn't mean you aren't saved, but it is an indicator that you need to move back to a place of simple trust in Jesus. Our sonship is realized and expressed through simple faith, and this simple faith produces the ability to live free from sin. Jude 1:24 calls Jesus the One "who is able to keep you from stumbling." If you maintain your trust in Him, you will maintain a sin-free life.

> **1 John 5:18 —** We know that anyone born of God does not continue to sin; the One who was born of God keeps them safe, and the evil one cannot harm them.

It is possible to live sin-free!

> **Limitless hope produces the capacity to live sin-free. Expected disappointment says, "I'm only human."**

Our typical response to our sinful actions is to excuse them away. And one of the classic excuses is, "I know it's wrong, but I'm only human."

There's a problem with that: Jesus was also a human! Jesus was both fully God and fully man, and He lived sin-free. Hebrews 2:17 says that Jesus was "fully human in every way." And Hebrews 4:15 adds that He was "tempted in every way, just as we are—yet He did not sin."

If you want to be "fully human," then you need to

be like Jesus. Anything short of His example is less than human. God didn't create sinners in the Garden of Eden; He created innocent, perfect children. Sin is subhuman.

Partnering with Christ

I can remember being a child and getting into a verbal fight with a friend of mine. As our emotions escalated, my opponent said, "I'm gonna get my brother, and he's gonna beat you up! He's fifteen years old!"

Naturally, I responded in kind, "Yeah, well my brother is twenty-five, and I'm going to go get him to beat your brother up!"

Neither of us actually wanted to get into a physical tussle, but both of us wanted to win. And the only way to win such a fight without injury is to find someone bigger than you to do your dirty work!

Jesus doesn't do dirty work—only clean work—and His "clean work" is to destroy the devil's dirty work! (See 1 John 3:8.)

As we find ourselves in altercations with the kingdom of darkness, we have the privilege of partnering with our Savior. We experience the joy of being part of destroying the devil's work. And since our older Brother has already taken every blow that the enemy has to dish out, we are able to destroy the devil's work without any fear of retaliation. The devil can't touch us when we partner with Jesus! (See Luke 10:19, John 14:30, and Ephesians 6:16.)

Furthermore, our partnership with Jesus is deeper than mere brotherhood. We actually become one with Him. (See 1 Corinthians 6:17.) We enter into Him and He enters into us. Read carefully these words of Jesus:

John 14:20 – On that day you will realize that I am in My Father, and you are in Me, and I am in you.

John 15:4-5 – Remain in Me, as I also remain in you. No branch can bear fruit by itself; it must remain in the vine. Neither can you bear fruit unless you remain in Me. I am the vine; you are the branches. If you remain in Me and I in you, you will bear much fruit; apart from Me you can do nothing.

Jesus has welcomed us to a place of unity with Him. In this way, Jesus lives in us and through us. He allows us—through His empowerment—to speak with His authority. He allows us to sit on His throne with Him—a place of authority and intimacy with our Father in heaven! (See Ephesians 2:6.)

Partnership with Jesus produces a lifestyle that actually looks like Jesus. Independence only produces sin. Apart from Him "you can do nothing."

The Path to Partnership

If all this is new to you, you may be wondering: "How does this work in practice, though? Is it actually possible to be free from sin?"

Let me ask you something: Did Jesus ever sin? No. Never. (See 2 Corinthians 5:21 and Hebrews 4:15.)

"But that was Jesus," you say.

Notice what Paul said:

Galatians 2:20 – I have been crucified with Christ and I no longer live, but Christ lives in me. The life I now live in the body, I live by

faith in the Son of God, who loved me and
gave Himself for me.

The Bible gives us the prescription for living sin-
free: it's death. Dead people don't sin.

> **Romans 6:6-7 –** For we know that our old self
> was crucified with Him so that the body ruled
> by sin might be done away with, that we should
> no longer be slaves to sin—because **anyone
> who has died has been set free from sin**.
> (emphasis added)

Do you see? If you want to live sin-free, you need
to crucify your old way of life.

We don't literally go to the cross; Jesus already did
that for us. Even though Jesus never sinned, He actually
became sin-in-human-form when He hung on that cross,
dying a criminal's death. (See 2 Corinthians 5:21 and 1
Peter 2:24.) Sin itself was crucified so that we could be
reconciled to God and become His righteousness. When
Jesus died, your sin died. When Jesus died, you died.

To be partners with Christ begins with partnership
in His death. But there is more! Jesus didn't stay dead in a
tomb. Death couldn't hold Him! Three days after Jesus
physically died on the cross, the Holy Spirit physically
raised Him from the dead. And that same resurrection
power of the Holy Spirit will give you new life as well.

> **Romans 6:5 and 8 –** For if we have been united
> with Him in a death like His, we will certainly
> also be united with Him in a resurrection like
> His....Now if we died with Christ, we believe
> that we will also live with Him.

2 Corinthians 5:16-17 — So from now on we regard no one from a worldly point of view. Though we once regarded Christ in this way, we do so no longer. Therefore, if anyone is in Christ, the new creation has come: The old has gone, the new is here!

Something fundamentally changed about the identity of Jesus between the moment He died and the moment He rose. When He died, He was sin-in-human-form. But when He rose again, there wasn't a speck of sin associated with Him. Jesus had transformed from His temporary role as a personification of sin into the perfect, risen Son of God. When Jesus rose again, sin stayed in the grave, and He emerged from the tomb victorious. If you have partnered with Jesus in His death and resurrection, then the same fundamental transformation has happened to you. Sin is no longer your identity. You are a son.

The good news doesn't stop there, though. When Jesus rose from the dead, He didn't sit around in the tomb for the next couple millennia. If you have a vacation booked for Jerusalem, I have bad news for you: Jesus isn't there!

Actually, that's good news! The reason Jesus isn't there is because He has ascended into heaven to sit at the right hand of the Father. That's a place of intimacy with the Father where Jesus has face-to-face fellowship with Him at all times. And the throne He has been given at the Father's right hand is the throne of highest authority! (See Ephesians 1:18-23 and Philippians 2:9-11.) There is no power or authority in heaven or on earth that can remotely challenge the position of Jesus Christ.

Here's where things become especially interesting. Many years ago, the Lord gave me a vision where I saw the ocean of angels that encircles the throne—thousands upon thousands and ten thousand times ten thousand. You couldn't see the end of them. But I became frustrated! As amazing as that vision was, I cried out, "Jesus! I don't want to see your angels; I want to see You!"

That's when He spoke softly, yet intensely in my ear, "Stop straining to see Me. We're already sitting together! Your place is not out there—lost in the ocean of angels. Your place is here on My throne with Me!"

The vision ended, and I wrote down what I saw. But I became afraid because it seemed prideful or even blasphemous. I had never heard anything about sitting on Jesus' throne.

That's when I came across this Scripture:

> **Ephesians 2:4-7** — But because of His great love for us, God, who is rich in mercy, made us alive with Christ even when we were dead in transgressions—it is by grace you have been saved. And God raised us up with Christ and seated us with Him in the heavenly realms in Christ Jesus, in order that in the coming ages He might show the incomparable riches of His grace, expressed in His kindness to us in Christ Jesus.

Do you see? We died with Him, and He raised us to new life with Him. But the unity never stopped: we have also been seated with Him!

> **Revelation 3:21 –** To the one who is victorious, I will give the right to sit with Me on My throne, just as I was victorious and sat down with My Father on His throne.

Those who are victorious are invited to rule and reign with Jesus. And what victory is there apart from the resurrection life of Christ? This is not about us striving to be victorious; it is about us dying to our old ways of living and allowing the Holy Spirit to triumph through us. Victory only comes through Jesus. When we abide in Him—when we live faith-filled lives of actively trusting Jesus—we are considered "more than conquerors!"

> **Romans 8:31-35,37 –** What, then, shall we say in response to these things? If God is for us, who can be against us? He who did not spare His own Son, but gave Him up for us all—how will He not also, along with Him, graciously give us all things? Who will bring any charge against those whom God has chosen? It is God who justifies. Who then is the one who condemns? No one. Christ Jesus who died—more than that, who was raised to life—is at the right hand of God and is also interceding for us. Who shall separate us from the love of Christ? Shall trouble or hardship or persecution or famine or nakedness or danger or sword? …No, in all these things we are more than conquerors through Him who loved us.

Living from Heaven to Earth

This is salvation. Christ's victory did not merely purchase us a one-way ticket to heaven. It also procured new life for us on earth. And part of this new life is that we live now from a heavenly perspective. We may be physically on earth, but we are spiritually in heaven.

Notice what Jesus said about Himself to Nicodemus (before this reality was available to the rest of us):

> **John 3:13 –** No one has ascended to heaven but He who came down from heaven, that is, the Son of Man who is in heaven. (NKJV)

Jesus said that He had been to heaven; but more importantly He implied that He presently resided there. The same is now true of us in Christ!

As we have already seen, hope is our anchor in the throne room of God. Hope is what helps us to live from heaven's perspective. But we have also seen that faith and love spring from hope. (See Colossians 1:5.) Hope by itself is not enough.

My father-in-law has a small fishing boat with an electronic "fish-finder" built in. The device has a screen that not only alerts him to fish but also measures the distance to the bottom of the lake. From the side of the boat, it is impossible to see the bottom of the lake, but the fish-finder offers an accurate measurement.

Suppose his anchor line is fifty feet long. It's not going to do any good if the lake is seventy feet deep! He is not going to go to the work of lowering his anchor by hand unless he is certain that it has a destination. That's where the fish-finder helps him. When he has a depth of less than 50 feet, he knows there is a place to secure the anchor.

Faith is the fish-finder of our salvation. Faith

allows us to know that our anchors will not drift aimlessly in the seas of life. Faith ensures that we are secured to the Rock.

> **Hebrews 11:1 –** Now faith is the assurance (title deed, confirmation) of things hoped for (divinely guaranteed), and the evidence of things not seen [the conviction of their reality—faith comprehends as fact what cannot be experienced by the physical senses]. (AMP15)

This salvation—this place on the throne with Jesus—is not secured by aimlessly drifting in life, hoping our anchors will bump into something. This salvation is secured by faith! (See Ephesians 2:8.)

By faith, we know who Jesus is. We cannot see heaven, but our faith assures us that Jesus is there, that His presence there procures for us a relationship with God, and that this love-relationship will sustain us from this world into eternity. When people ask me how I know I'm going to heaven, I tell them that I know because I'm already there!

Your salvation is a free gift, but faith is how you open and experience the gift. Faith is the way we become everything the Bible says we are. And who does the Bible say we are? That's a big answer in detail, but at its core, the answer is simply this: Jesus.

Jesus is my identity. No, I'm not literally Jesus. Jesus is in heaven, physically seated at the right hand of the Father. But I am there too, spiritually dwelling inside of Him! And since I am in Him and He is in me, I can't help but be just like Him. "I no longer live, but Christ lives in me…" (See Galatians 2:20.)

If I put a sponge in a bucket of water, the water is in the sponge and the sponge is in the water. The water in the sponge takes on the shape of the sponge while the sponge takes on the nature of the water (wetness, temperature, etc.). They are distinct yet unified. The water enables the sponge to do things that it could not do without it, and the sponge enables the water to go places that it would not otherwise go alone.

If I live by faith—drawing my identity from Christ—then I will live differently than the world around me. I am the sponge who takes on the nature of Jesus. And He is the water that goes with me everywhere I go.

This is the truth about you as well if you are in Christ. Whatever God says is actually true about you trumps anything false that you may think is true about you.

Salvation is Summed Up in Relationship

Faith is trusting what God says more than trusting what you see. "We live by faith, not by sight." (See 2 Corinthians 5:7.) If God's word says that I'm sinless because my sin-nature died and the sinless Jesus lives in me, then I need to believe Him and willfully live accordingly with His help. If God says that I'm sinless, and yet I sin, then I've forgotten who I am. I have forgotten what I look like to God.

> **James 1:23-24 –** Anyone who listens to the word but does not do what it says is like someone who looks at his face in a mirror and, after looking at himself, goes away and immediately forgets what he looks like.

God's word (whether through Scripture, direct communication to us, or right preaching or prophetic messages from someone else) tells us what we look like to Him. He sees things that we cannot see. We may see imperfection, but He sees Jesus because we are clothed with His Son. (See Romans 13:14 and Galatians 3:27.) That's what you look like. If you live differently, then you've forgotten what you look like!

Sin-free living isn't based on our perfection. It is only possible because Jesus is sin-free, and we are unified with Him through faith—first through partnership in His death, then His resurrection, and thirdly His ascension and current place at the right hand of the Father.

"As He is, so are we in this world." (See 1 John 4:17, NKJV.) I am free from sin because of my union with Jesus. I believe the words of my Father more than I believe the mistakes I occasionally make.

> **Limitless hope focuses on relationship. Expected disappointment focuses on personal gratification.**

As a married man, every decision I make is done with my wife, Robin, in mind. I do not want to grieve her heart or squelch her dreams. She does the same for me. That's a real relationship. As a married man, I do not make life-decisions apart from this context.

Relationship with God is even deeper. Your identity is more profound than merely being a married person. Your identity is one of constant intimate union with the Savior of the world. Look at Jesus, and that's what you look like to the Father. Just as a sinner would have to rebel against his own nature to live righteously, you—in Christ—have to rebel against your own nature to sin. Why? Because your sinful nature died at the cross, and you are now a new creation. You now have self-control from the Holy Spirit. (See Galatians 5:22.) This means that any sin you commit as a Christian is done knowingly and decisively. You are no longer a slave to sin. (See Romans 6:6.) You're not allowed to say, "I couldn't help it."

Accept it by faith. "Without faith, it is impossible to please God." (See Hebrews 11:6.) The only way to live a sin-free life is to consider your sinful nature dead, ask the Holy Spirit to make you a new creation, believe God about who He says you are, and then trust Him to do the work.

You Are a Child of God

I've learned that the key to a sin-free lifestyle— outside of salvation itself—is knowing your identity now that you're saved. If we believe that we are sinners and that sin is our default position, then we will respond to temptations with earthly strength. But if we believe that we are united with Jesus as He presently is in heaven, then we will respond to temptations with heavenly authority. Consider what Solomon said about the fruit of one's thoughts: "For as he thinks within himself, so he is." (See Proverbs 23:7, NASB.)

If I am united with Christ, then everything about His identity is somehow true about me. This is possible because a spectacular exchange took place on the cross. Everything that was once true about me (wretched sinner, lost, spiritually blind, bitter, addicted, wounded, etc.), Jesus became on the cross. He put all that garbage to death. And since everything that was once true about me died with

Him, the only identity left for me is the one He has given in exchange: His own. Jesus is no longer on the cross. He is the risen and exalted Conqueror of death.

That which is true of Jesus' identity is now somehow true of your identity (as a Christian) because you are united with Him and seated with Him:

- ❖ Jesus is God, and while you are not God, you are a partaker in His divine nature. (See John 1:1 and 2 Peter 1:4.)
- ❖ Jesus is the light of the world, and so are you. (See John 8:12 and Matthew 5:14.)
- ❖ Jesus is the Lord our Righteousness, and you are the righteousness of God. (See Jeremiah 23:5-6 and 2 Corinthians 5:21.)
- ❖ Jesus is seated at the right hand of the Father (a place of intimacy and authority), and you are seated at the right hand of the Father. (See Mark 16:19, Ephesians 2:6, and Revelation 3:21.)
- ❖ Jesus is the Son of God, and you are adopted as a son of God. (See Mark 1:1, Romans 8:14, and Galatians 3:26.)
- ❖ Jesus is the King of kings. If your King is King of kings, that makes you a king! (See Revelation 17:14 and 1 Peter 2:9.)

The list could go on and on. Jesus shares Himself with us. He grants us His identity. The only stipulation is that we must receive Him and remain in Him by faith.

> **John 1:12-13 –** Yet to all who did receive Him, to those who believed in His name, He gave the right to become children of God—children born not of natural descent, nor of human decision or a husband's will, but born of God.

Sonship vs. Slavery

In Luke 15, Jesus told a parable about a man who had two sons. One of the sons approached his father and demanded his share of the inheritance. In essence, he was saying, "I wish you were dead!"

The father granted the son's request, and the young man left to squander his fortune on wild living. Once he had lost everything, he went to work for a man who let him take care of his pigs.

The son's wake-up call came as he found himself hungry enough to eat the pigs' slop. He thought, *Even a slave in my father's house is treated better than this!*

The son hurried home in hopes that his father would at least receive him back as a slave, even though he was no longer worthy to be called a son.

This is where the story takes a surprising twist. The father noticed a blurry speck rising over the distant horizon. As he shielded the sun from his squinting eyes, that speck took the form of his runaway son.

What did the father do?

He ran! Without delay, he raced to his son, threw his arms around him and kissed him. Rather than begrudgingly receiving this rebel as a slave, the father joyfully embraced him as a son. The son immediately received a robe, sandals, and a ring; and a big party was thrown in his honor!

Many of us seem to connect with this first half of the story because it's such a vivid depiction of the sinner who comes to repentance and is met by Father God's open-armed reception. But the story doesn't end there.

The father had a second son. This one continued to work diligently in the father's fields while his rebellious brother burned through their father's money. To many of us, this son is the picture of the good and faithful believer—perhaps raised in church and never wandering too far. That sounds nice, but this brother actually suffered from the exact same heart-issue as his sibling.

When the older son returned home from the fields, he heard the commotion of his brother's celebration. Confused, he approached the walled courtyard cautiously. A servant exited, and the older son grabbed him by the arm. "What's going on in there?" he asked.

"Your brother came home," replied the servant, "and your father decided the throw a feast in his honor!"

"Honor?" demanded the enraged brother, "What honor? I'll have nothing to do with this! Tell my father that his *faithful* son will be waiting outside for his own party!"

The father came outside to the older son and begged him to come in.

"Not a chance!" shouted the son. "All these years I have obediently served you, and you've never even killed a scrawny goat to honor me! But when this other son comes home—the one who devoured your estate with wild partying and immorality—you killed your fattest calf to celebrate him!"

The father's response is fascinating to me:

> **Luke 15:31-32** – "My son," the father said, "you are always with me, and everything I have is yours. But we had to celebrate and be glad, because this brother of yours was dead and is alive again; he was lost and is found."

Do you see the similarity between the two

brothers? Each was looking for his own limited share of the father's wealth rather than realizing that their sonship afforded them the fullness of the father's entire estate!

"Everything I have is yours," said the father. The older son could have eaten that fatted calf at any time while his brother was gone. He could have thrown his own fatted-calf party! Instead, he continued slaving away in the fields, proud of himself for being a better son than his brother yet never enjoying the privileges of his sonship.

Neither son knew what it was to be a son. Both sons thought that their place in the father's house was as mere servants. Both lived their lives looking forward to a limited reward from a dead father rather than embracing the one-hundred-percent ownership granted to them through right relationship with their living father.

> **Limitless hope lives from the perspective of grace and sonship. Expected disappointment lives from the perspective of guilt and slavery.**

Sons are treated differently than slaves. Slaves receive rations while sons share the entire estate. Slaves labor while sons reign. And in times of failure, slaves are disposed of while sons are disciplined.

Many of us live our Christian lives assuming that we need to perform well to earn our Father's favor. We strive to accomplish great things to win His smile. What we don't realize is that He already favors us and smiles brightly upon us.

When I first wrote this chapter back in 2011, my first son, Josiah, was about twenty months old, and my younger son, Jeremiah, was a newborn. Neither one knew how to do anything to please me. The only thing they really knew how to do was make messes that I had to clean up! But even then, I was wildly, madly in love with them! Even today as Josiah is five and Jeremiah is on his way to turning four, they may have learned ways to bring me extra joy, but they have also learned ways to make bigger messes. And yet I love them even more now than I did back then.

My sons can't buy me a car or mow my lawn. They can't pay me rent money or cook me dinner. But I don't love them because of what they can do for me; I love them because they're my sons.

I don't have a housecleaning service, but if I did, I wouldn't have any problem firing a maid who didn't do an adequate job. But if my sons—as they grow older—fail to fulfill my expectations, I won't throw them out on the street. I'll lovingly come alongside them and correct their behavior. There's a difference between a servant and a son. Servants live in fear of termination. Sons live in the security of relationship.

This is another key to sin-free living. We must see that not every mistake we make is an affront to God. Not every wrong action jeopardizes our salvation—in fact, very few do. On the contrary, God is a loving Father who would rather shape us through discipline than kick us to the curb.

> **Hebrews 12:7-11 –** Endure hardship as discipline; God is treating you as His children. For what children are not disciplined by their

father? If you are not disciplined—and everyone undergoes discipline—then you are not legitimate, not true sons and daughters at all. Moreover, we have all had human fathers who disciplined us and we respected them for it. How much more should we submit to the Father of spirits and live! They disciplined us for a little while as they thought best; but God disciplines us for our good, in order that we may share in His holiness. No discipline seems pleasant at the time, but painful. Later on, however, it produces a harvest of righteousness and peace for those who have been trained by it.

Verse four places this passage within the context of struggling against sin. Clearly, God's preferred response to sin is discipline rather than judgment and destruction. Lamentations 3:33 says that God "does not willingly bring affliction or grief to anyone."

Our loving Father would rather discipline us to make us more holy than send us to hell for the slightest infraction. We're His children, not His slaves. It is possible to willfully throw away your salvation, but that's much less common. More often, we encounter sin that does not lead to death.

1 John 5:16-17 – If you see any brother or sister commit a sin that does not lead to death, you should pray and God will give them life. I refer to those whose sin does not lead to death. There is a sin that leads to death. I am not saying that you should pray about that. All wrongdoing is sin, and there is sin that does not lead to death.

Let me pause to point out the Scriptural fact that there is sin which does not eliminate our salvation. The verses immediately following that passage continue to expound on this subject with emphasis on our identities in Christ.

> **1 John 5:18-20 –** We know that anyone born of God does not continue to sin; the One who was born of God keeps them safe, and the evil one cannot harm them. We know that we are children of God, and that the whole world is under the control of the evil one. We know also that the Son of God has come and has given us understanding, so that we may know Him who is true. And we are in Him who is true by being in His Son Jesus Christ. He is the true God and eternal life.

If you're born of God, then you're no longer part of this world—you're a part of heaven. You're now considered a stranger here. (See 1 Peter 2:11-12.)

The world is under the control of the devil, but heaven is under the control of God. He has granted this authority to His Son, Jesus Christ, and we are invited to share in it as we sit with Him on His throne. By being "in Christ," we are also "in God." Colossians 3:3 tells us that "you died, and your life is now hidden with Christ in God."

That's who you are. You are hidden with Christ in God. It's your true identity. When God looks at you, He sees Jesus. When the kingdom of darkness looks at you, they see Jesus. And this should affect both how the world sees you and what you see when you look at yourself.

> Limitless hope believes that Jesus' sacrifice
> makes us sons and daughters of God.
> Expected disappointment believes that
> Jesus' sacrifice paid only for our former way
> of living and that we must now strive
> to live flawlessly.

The Sin That Does Not Lead to Death

When I first read John's words about the sin that does not lead to death, I became fixated. I wanted to know what was the difference between sin that leads to death and sin that doesn't. I began to ask the Lord to reveal it to me, and that's when a thought came to me: If you want to see sin that does not lead to death, find the first sin that did lead to death, and see if any sins were committed prior to that.

The answer seemed really simple at face value, but then it took some thoughtful examination of Scripture to carry out.

We all know that the first sin to lead to death was when Adam and Eve ate the fruit from the tree of the knowledge of good and evil. We aren't given much information about their lives prior to this event, but I believe there are three things we can extrapolate from what is written.

Remember that the word "sin" means to miss the mark, and it always comes from a lack of faith. If I am living disconnected from God, then I am living in a place where sin is likely to happen. But if I am living by faith, then I am living in a relationship with God where He enables me to do what is right.

Faith and sin are opposites. You're either in faith or you're in sin. Remember, "everything that does not come from faith is sin." (See Romans 14:23.)

It is impossible to do both. Faith is full trust. You cannot fully trust a person in percentages. You either trust Him or you don't. If you fully trust Him, you'll hit the target. But if not, it will be impossible to do what God wants. (See Hebrews 11:6.) Apart from Jesus, you can do nothing. (See John 15:5.)

When Adam and Eve ate the fruit from the tree of the knowledge of good and evil, they willfully disobeyed God for the sake of pride (to be like Him). Eating of the tree was not an accident; it was not an addiction; and it was not impossible to avoid. This bite of the fruit was the sin that led to death. Deliberate, willful disobedience born of pride and defiance against God does result in death.

As they stood at that tree during Eve's chat with the serpent, they were not actively engaged in relationship with God. We know this because God came looking for them after the fact. But more importantly, we see that they didn't trust God. The serpent led them to believe that God was hiding something good from them, and their trust in Him wavered.

It should be noted though that Adam and Eve still could have turned back at this point and been okay. Everyone's faith wavers from time to time. All of us slip in and out of perfect trust from time to time. If we don't catch it, our lack of trust will lead to sinful actions, but we can still turn back.

Prior to eating the fruit, Adam and Eve still missed a few of the targets God gave them. I can find three in the Genesis account: (1) They fell short of God's vision, (2) they deviated from a healthy thought-life, and (3) they missed the mark of God's order.

Falling Short of God's Vision. God's vision for Adam and Eve was clearly defined in His first command: "Be fruitful and multiply, fill the earth, and subdue it." (See Genesis 1:28.) Yet Adam and Eve did not have any children until after they were kicked out of the garden. (See Genesis 4:1.) Adam did not even name his wife "Eve," which means "mother of all the living" until after they sinned. (See Genesis 3:20.)

In other words, for however long it was that Adam and Eve were in the Garden, they were technically sinning against God's vision for their lives—not in willful disobedience, but simply through neglect. They should have been subduing the earth through their God-given authority rather than allowing the serpent to subdue them. They missed the mark of their only mission. It was sin. But did this cost them their home in the Garden? No.

Deviation from a healthy thought life. This sin came during the serpent's cunning questions that planted seeds of doubt. They began to believe the lie of the serpent over the love of their Father. They separated themselves from thoughts of truth and embraced thoughts of falsehood and unholy curiosity. Nevertheless, this was not the sin that caused their eviction from the Garden. Yes, it ultimately led to that, but they still had not eaten the fruit.

Missing the mark of God's order. According to God's order, man was designed by God to be a spiritual head for his wife. (See 1 Corinthians 11:3.) Nevertheless, the entire time Eve was being deceived by the serpent, Adam stood by quietly and did not stand up for her. How do we know this? Because immediately after Eve ate the fruit, it says, "She also gave some to her husband, who was with her…" (See Genesis 3:6.) In other words, Adam was there all along and did not guard the spiritual door of his household. At any point, Adam could have said, "Hey, Sweetheart, I don't think we should be listening to this thing. Let's go talk to Dad about it." But he didn't. Adam and Eve sinned against the order of God.

The interesting thing about these "sins that do not lead to death" is that each of them did eventually result in such a sin. But if you really think about it, Adam and Eve could have repented at any moment up to the second their teeth sunk into that fruit. Perhaps they even could have spit it out before they swallowed. God, the loving Father, would have been happy to remind them of His vision, His thoughts, and His order for their lives. He would have guided them and corrected them as a loving Father because He never expected mankind to be totally perfect.

Children are not perfect, but with proper fathering they grow into obedience. Even Jesus "learned obedience" and was "made perfect" over time, which implies that His earthly life was not flawless, although He certainly never sinned. (See Hebrews 5:8-9 and Hebrews 4:15.)

And this is one of the keys to living sin free: If I can recognize my lack of faith (by noticing little ways in which I miss the mark of God's perfection) before it leads me to a sin that does lead to death, I will never commit such a sin. Let me put this another way: If I can recognize that I'm not living according to God's vision, thoughts, or order for my life before it's too late, then I'll be able to repent before my sinful condition gives birth to sinful action.

These things are still "sin" in the sense that they

miss the mark of God's ideal, but they are not outright, willful rebellion against Him. It is possible to still have a relationship with God while He lovingly disciplines these things out of me as my good Father. Left unchecked, they will eventually lead to willful, relationship-breaking, sinful action; but if submitted to the cross in their early stages, it will never escalate into deliberate sinful action.

This is why it is possible for John—in the same letter—to say both (1) that those born of God do not continue to sin and (2) that "if we claim to be without sin, we deceive ourselves and the truth is not in us." (See 1 John 5:18 and 1:8.) None of us is so perfect that we never miss God's mark on some level (though that is something we can and should desire and live toward); but if we are truly born of God, then we will not allow our shortcomings to produce sin that leads to death. Rather, we will delight in the Lord's discipline as He purges such things from us.

One last thought on this point: Lest you think that committing willful rebellion against God is unforgivable, remember that this too can be surrendered to the cross. The prophet Jonah committed such a sin by running from God's instruction. But God brought a solution, and that solution spoke prophetically of Jesus Christ's death and resurrection. (See Matthew 12:40.)

> **1 John 2:1 –** My dear children, I write this to you so that you will not sin. But if anybody does sin, we have one who speaks to the Father in our defense—Jesus Christ, the Righteous One.

Partnership with Christ still holds the power to set

us free from sins that lead to death. But that is no way to live. It's not your identity. Recognize and address any sinful condition in you before it produces sinful action, and you'll find yourself living sin-free.

Being vs. Doing

> **Limitless hope is about "being."**
> **Expected disappointment is about "doing."**

It is impossible to "do sonship." My boys are not my sons because they behave like sons. My boys are my sons because I fathered them. And son-like behavior is nothing more than an outflow of their realization that I'm their father and I love them. Josiah doesn't run and jump into my arms because someone taught him that this is what good little boys do with their fathers. He does so because he loves me and knows I love him.

The Bible doesn't tell us to "do holy;" it tells us to "be holy." (See 1 Peter 1:16.) It doesn't tell us to transform ourselves; it tells us to "be transformed." (See Romans 12:2.) God doesn't instruct us to behave as a royal priesthood; He tells us that we are a royal priesthood. (See 1 Peter 2:9.)

Our perception of Jesus shapes who we are. The more clearly we can see Him, the more we are made like Him. (See 1 John 3:2.) If we abide in Him and He abides in us, we will not sin simply because He does not sin.

> **1 John 3:6, 9 –** Anyone who continues to live in Him will not sin. But anyone who keeps on sinning does not know Him or understand

who He is.…Those who have been born into
God's family do not make a practice of
sinning, because God's life is in them. So they
can't keep on sinning, because they are
children of God. (NLT)

The Christian life is not difficult for those who are
born of God. But the opposite is also true: If a person is
still living according to his or her old nature, then the
Christian life is impossible.

It is impossible for a mouse to be a lion, no matter
how it behaves; but it is very easy for a lion to be a lion,
and its behavior is natural for a lion. Likewise, it is
impossible for a sinner to be a saint—unless, of course,
that sinner brings his or her sinful nature to death at the
cross and allows the Holy Spirit to make him or her into a
new creation—no longer a mouse, now a lion.

This new identity looks like Jesus. We're not
slaves; we're sons. Jesus no longer calls us servants; He
calls us friends. (See John 15:15.) Servanthood is all about
doing; friendship is all about being. You have been granted
the spirit of sonship, not slavery. (See Romans 8:15.)
Actions naturally follow identity.

1 Peter 1:13-16 – Therefore, with minds that
are alert and fully sober, set your hope on the
grace to be brought to you when Jesus Christ
is revealed at His coming. As obedient
children, do not conform to the evil desires
you had when you lived in ignorance. But just
as He who called you is holy, so be holy in all
you do; for it is written: "Be holy, because I
am holy."

Chapter 5:

Limitless Hope and Hearing God's Voice

Have you ever wished that God would open the heavens and speak loudly and audibly to you? If you're anything like me, the reason for this wish is probably because we would love to have that sort of clarity from Him. It would be unmistakable!

Or would it?

So far I have never heard the audible voice of God; although I hear His voice in other ways every single day. I hear from Him in ways that could be easily unnoticed or ignored if not for my desire to hear Him. As a matter of fact I have learned that even the audible voice of God can be misunderstood and excused away.

Don't believe me? Check out how a crowd

responded when God spoke audibly from heaven:

> **John 12:28-29** – [Jesus prayed,]"…Father,
> glorify Your name!" Then a voice came from
> heaven, "I have glorified it, and will glorify it
> again." The crowd that was there and heard it
> said it had thundered; others said an angel had
> spoken to Him.

Even the audible voice of God was easily
overlooked! I believe this happened because hearing God's
voice—in whatever form—is actually incredibly natural.

You were created to have a relationship with God.
In His infinite wisdom and creativity, God designed every
part of you—body, soul, and spirit—to recognize His
voice in some way. Hearing God is part of your original
purpose. Therefore, hearing God is the most natural thing
you may ever experience.

This is why so many of us miss God's voice and
assume that He never speaks to us. The truth is that He
was speaking all along, but we didn't notice anything
supernatural to imply that this was so. God's voice rarely
feels supernatural because your natural self was designed
by Him to commune with Him.

Hearing God's voice is natural.

**Limitless hope looks for the subtle voice of God.
Expected disappointment assumes that when
God speaks, you'll know.**

Admittedly, there are those circumstances when

God's voice is incredibly obvious—perhaps the appearance of an angel who declares a message on His behalf, or an open-eyed vision that interrupts your current range of sight, or maybe a voice from a burning bush like Moses encountered. God can indeed speak in these startling and obvious ways, and He does when absolutely necessary. Nevertheless, these tend to be exceptions— usually reserved for extreme circumstances, thickheaded listeners, or preparation for ministry. The rest of the time, God seems to speak with more subtlety.

The Subtle Voice of God

Dramatic revelations of God's voice seem so frequent in the Old Testament. Consider the burning bush, the writing of the Ten Commandments, the pillar of cloud and fire, and the many vivid visions of prophets like Ezekiel and Isaiah (to name a few). What we don't realize is that the scope of the Old Testament spans a few thousand years, which means that these encounters were actually very rare on average. In fact, there were even seasons when people barely heard anything at all from God. (See 1 Samuel 3:1.)

Then comes the New Testament, which only spans a few decades. Here we have God's greatest revelation of Himself: Jesus Christ. (See Hebrews 1:1-3.) And yet the New Testament is also filled with visions, dreams, miraculous signs, prophecies, and more. When divided evenly across a timeline, the voice of God appears to have exploded during the few decades of the New Testament.

But the New Testament believers appear to follow God's voice a little differently than those of the Old

Testament. Rather than waiting for an absolute, dramatic revelation of God's will before they act, these men and women of faith consider Jesus to have fulfilled that need and now give weight to subtler revelations. Jesus is the only "absolute, dramatic revelation" we need. (See John 14:8-9.) Once you've surrendered to Him, His voice becomes as natural as your own thoughts. As Paul said, "we have the mind of Christ." (See 1 Corinthians 2:16.)

In Acts 15:28, the Jerusalem Council offered insight to the new Gentile believers by saying, "It seemed good to the Holy Spirit and to us…" That's a new way of doing things! Can you imagine if Moses returned from Mount Sinai with the "Ten Good Ideas" and said, "These seem like a good way to live"! In the Old Testament, the people needed God's clear revelation to reveal their sin. In the New Testament, sin has been dealt with, and our Father would rather us learn to grow in a present relationship with Him than rely on things He said previously to someone else.

I've had some dramatic encounters with God including open-eye visions, visits to heaven, and prophecies that shook me to the core; but I'm not interested in telling you about those things—I simply want you to know that I am not ignoring these things. The ways God most often speaks to me are much more subtle. Usually His voice is more like the Jerusalem Council— things just "seem good" to the Holy Spirit—and I'm left to discover through trial and error if that is in fact true.

"It seemed good to the Holy Spirit and to us…" The word "us" could be personalized as "me, within the context of community." God no longer speaks to individuals in a vacuum. He has given us the Body of

Christ for support, discernment, fellowship, and implementation of His words. Paul wrote regarding church meetings, "Two or three prophets should speak, and the others should weigh carefully what is said." (See 1 Corinthians 14:29.) In other words, even the gift of prophecy can come with such subtlety that we may need the entire group of Christians present to discern whether or not it was the true word of God.

Does this mean that God never speaks to us individually? No. In fact, His personalized communication is what most often happens during our ministry to others. For example I was once praying for a woman and saw a mental picture of an empty warehouse. I felt a subtle fear associated with the image. I mentioned the picture to the woman and the accompanying feeling and asked if that meant anything to her. I didn't run the thought by the other Christians in that church service because it wasn't called for. God spoke to me, and I immediately put it to use in ministry.

When the woman said "yes," I knew that the accompanying message would also have meaning. I spoke to the woman what I felt the Lord was saying: "I was with you in the warehouse, but I never intended for you to be there." The woman began to weep. Through that simple picture and the associated message, the Lord brought much healing to this woman's heart from a painful experience in her past.

Another example would be the occasional body ache or pain that doesn't seem consistent with my normal experience. Generally, I have learned that this is God's way of speaking to me about pains that other people are currently experiencing (and ultimately His desire to physically heal them).

In one such case, I was preaching at a church about holiness and loving God rather than the world. Suddenly my neck and shoulder began to faintly hurt. I asked if anyone had the same problem, and a man in the second row said, "That's me!"

I brought him to the front of the church and asked if anyone had a twenty dollar bill I could borrow. Another man handed me the banknote, and I proceeded to rub it all over the shoulder of the man who was standing.

"Are you feeling any better?" I asked.

The man, very confused, answered, "No."

"Apparently the god that our country worships doesn't have the power to heal!" I joked. "Tell me: How much money would we need to pile on top of this man before his shoulder will feel better?"

The man chimed in, "You're welcome to experiment!"

As the laughter died down, I handed the twenty dollar bill back to the seated gentleman and returned to my object lesson. I placed my hand on the man's shoulder and said, "Neck and shoulder, be healed in Jesus' name. There. How does that feel?"

The man began moving his shoulder and neck with a big smile, "That's a lot better!"

Not only did these people witness an object lesson they'll never forget, that man was miraculously healed by Jesus. But I would have never thought to take such an action if it hadn't been for that subtle tinge of pain that I felt while I was preaching. If I hadn't been looking for the subtle voice of God, we would have all missed out.

These subtle impressions happen rather often—

probably every day, though I'm not perfect at always noticing them. Several times now I have posted a status to my Facebook page asking if someone was dealing with a specific condition (which I faintly felt), instructing them to place their hand on the place of that problem, and then commanding healing in Jesus' name. Multiple people have told me that they've been healed in this way.

I believe that if every Christian would pay attention to the subtle impressions that the Lord gives, we would see more miracles and salvations every day than we could count!

> **1 Corinthians 14:24-25 –** But if an unbeliever or an inquirer comes in while everyone is prophesying, they are convicted of sin and are brought under judgment by all, as the secrets of their hearts are laid bare. So they will fall down and worship God, exclaiming, "God is really among you!"

In today's social and technological culture, unbelievers and inquirers no longer need to enter our meetings in order to hear what we're saying—they just need a smart phone or an internet connection. Whether in meetings, in public, or even on social media, if every Christian lovingly conveys what they feel God is speaking, imagine how many will come to repentance!

God has Good Things to Say

Many of us are afraid to listen for God's voice. Our concern is that He might demand something unreasonable or uncomfortable of us. We're afraid that He will make fools of us or ask us to do something we don't want to do.

On one hand that's a problem because Christianity is not about living for your own wants and desires. Christianity is about focusing on the wants and desires of God (which allows Him to fulfill the wants and desires of your heart—but that's another topic for another time). The point is that when we surrender to God, we place our lives in the hands of a loving Father who only wants the best for His children.

We're not pawns; we're sons. A king does not send his son to war with the first line of infantry. He gives his son rank and position in his army in an effort to guard the throne. Our Father loves us and is not interested in giving us orders that make us miserable! He will send His angels ahead of you to protect you and secure your victory.

Allow me to clarify: The Father has no problem making people miserable in their sin (which is why He allows demons to do what they do), but He has no reason to make people miserable in their sonship. He is a loving Father who only has good things to say to His children— words that shape us, encourage us, comfort us, and strengthen us. (See 1 Corinthians 14:3.) If you are a child of God, then you have no reason to fear what He might have to say. Even His discipline is good and beneficial.

> Limitless hope is based on a firm understanding of God's character and will.
> Expected disappointment stems from fear and questioning God's intentions.

Jesus told Peter to get out of the boat and walk

with Him on the water—not as a joke but as a lesson in faith. God told Noah to build an ark—not so he would be ridiculed but for his preservation. God told Moses to confront Pharaoh—not so he would be shamed or exiled but so his people would be free.

When I went to Africa for the first time, I didn't do so because of a shocking encounter with God. I did it because it seemed good to me and the Holy Spirit, and no one in my life was saying not to go. Even though I was traveling alone to a continent I had never been to, I had a lot of support from friends and family who believed that God would protect me. And while I was there, I didn't always know what God wanted me to say or do until the moment came that I was saying or doing it. Even then I wasn't always sure that I was bringing the right message, but God always backed up His word with miracles, signs, and wonders. Hundreds were healed, and hundreds received salvation within a mere seventeen days.

Relying on the subtle voice of God should never be done at the expense of following the revealed voice of God. What I mean is that Jesus has already clearly revealed His will, and we do not need to wait for Him to speak it to us specifically before obeying what He has already said.

For example, Jesus has already said, "Go into all the world and preach the Gospel…" I don't need God to nudge me into evangelism. My standing orders are always, "Go!"

On the contrary, the subtle voice of God is usually more useful in helping us rightly deviate from our standing orders. Paul was all about action until the Holy Spirit stopped him from going to Asia and pointed him in a new direction. (See Acts 16:6.) Jesus was still trying to fly under the radar in His early ministry until He was moved with compassion for the lame man at the pool of Bethesda. (See John 5:1-9 and 13.) The revealed commands of Jesus should be our default actions, and His subtle voice should be our priority—again, within the context of community. We will talk more about this in later chapters.

The Context of Community

> Limitless hope is not afraid to confirm a word with fellow Christians. Expected disappointment assumes that you are the only one who can hear accurately from God.

The Spirit-filled New Testament Church is a prophetic community. Every one of us has the capacity to hear the voice of God. Paul told the Corinthians, "For you can all prophesy in turn so that everyone may be instructed and encouraged." (See 1 Corinthians 14:31.)

We fulfill the dream of Moses, who mused, "I wish that all the LORD's people were prophets and that the LORD would put His Spirit on them!" (See Numbers 11:29.) Today, God has poured out His Spirit "upon all flesh" so that prophetic utterance would become the common practice of the people of God. (See Joel 2:28-29.)

Even the apostle Paul—who could easily be mistaken as a sort of "Lone Ranger" in the Kingdom— submitted himself to the Spirit-filled scrutiny of his peers. Despite his miraculous, open-eyed encounter with the resurrected Jesus during which he was called into ministry, Paul still performed his ministry in the context of fellowship with other believers. (See Acts 9:26-28.) When a question arose that Paul couldn't settle through debate, he went to the apostles and elders in Jerusalem for counsel. (See Acts 15:2.) And when the riot broke out in Ephesus, Acts 19:30 tells us, "Paul wanted to appear before the crowd, but the disciples [ordinary Ephesian believers] would not let him."

According to Paul's example, even the apostle is subject to the common believers. It doesn't matter if you've had open visions of Jesus or if you are having revelations worthy of becoming Scripture—you're worthless outside the context of community. "If I have the gift of prophecy and can fathom all mysteries and all knowledge…but do not have love, I am nothing." (See 1 Corinthians 13:2.) Paul didn't say the prophecy was nothing without love; he said that he was nothing apart from it.

This has ramifications for the ways in which we share what we believe the Lord is saying. One of the men who has had significant influence in my life is Pastor Dan Vander Velde. He taught me to be very careful about the phrase, "God told me." To use that phrase is to silently imply that the listener is not allowed to discern for himself. Who among us would dare to reply, "Well, I guess I disagree with God!"?

The truth is that "we know in part and we prophesy in part." (See 1 Corinthians 13:9.) We don't always perfectly nail everything God wants to say. In fact, I'm very rarely certain that God told me something until after the message has produced good fruit that proves it was Him. Until then, I would be better to use phrases like, "I feel like God is saying…" or, "I think I'm sensing that the Lord is saying…" In this way, the audience is invited into the listening process. And my experience proves that if the message is truly from God, no amount of verbal cushioning will make it any less powerful.

Once a message comes to pass, we can be sure that it was from God. That, I believe, is one of the reasons the Bible is called "the prophetic word made more sure." (See 2 Peter 1:19-21, NASB.) Until the message comes to pass, it's up to the discernment of God's people.

> **Deuteronomy 18:21-22 –** You may say to yourselves, "How can we know when a message has not been spoken by the Lord?" If what a prophet proclaims in the name of the Lord does not take place or come true, that is a message the Lord has not spoken. That prophet has spoken presumptuously, so do not be alarmed.

If I ever emphatically say that the Lord once told me to do something, it is because I have already seen the fruit of that message, and it was proven true. But in the moment that He speaks, I am typically careful to submit the message to other believers in a way that welcomes their own engagement with God's voice on the matter.

Some of the Ways God Speaks

God speaks to different people in diverse ways; and as I stated in the beginning of this chapter, they usually seem very natural and normal. In fact, if you're a Christian then you have already heard God's voice!

> **John 6:44-45 –** "No one can come to Me unless the Father who sent Me draws him; and I will raise him up on the last day. It is

written in the prophets, 'And they shall all be
taught of God.' Everyone who has heard and
learned from the Father comes to Me."
(NASB)

When you came to salvation, did the sky rip open
as God bellowed from heaven, "Follow Me"? Probably
not. It's more likely that as you heard the message of
salvation, something settled in your heart that "this is
right." You may not have realized it at the time, but that
was God's voice. You heard the Father and responded by
coming to Jesus. This may have been your first encounter
with the voice of God, but it was never intended to be
your last!

Again, God's voice to us is typically very natural.
A great example is "visions." Perhaps I'm being too
inclusive with my definition, but I am convinced that
visions are not only defined as interruptions to our
physical field of view. I believe they can also be subtle
mental pictures in the visual centers of our brains. If I tell
you to picture a pencil, you can "see" a pencil even though
there is not a pencil hovering in front of you. That's the
part of your physical brain that God gave you so that He
can speak to you in pictures. Most often, this is how I
receive visions from God. If I'm praying for someone, I
pay attention to any pictures that might pop into my mind,
and I make constant judgments about which images were
obviously from my own mind and which might be from
Him.

A similar example would be dreams. Some dreams
seem incredibly ordinary until we discover that God is
speaking to us in parables while we sleep. And, by the way,
when God speaks to you in symbols, it is not because He's

hoping you'll run to a "dream interpretation manual" to figure it all out. Rather, when God speaks in symbols, it is because He wants you to ask Him what they mean! The riddles of God are always meant to draw us into deeper relationship with Him.

There are also external ways God speaks—things like the difficult situations through which He disciplines us. (See Hebrews 12:7-11.) He speaks through nature. What could seem more "natural" to us than nature! (See Romans 1:20.) Another subtle way He speaks, which is actually very clear, is through the Bible. It seems so ordinary because it's a physical book printed on a press somewhere; but this does not change that it is the proven recorded message of God to man. (See 2 Peter 1:20-21.)

God also speaks through the Church—and not just to the world, but also to the entire spiritual realm!

> **Ephesians 3:10-11 –** His intent was that now, through the church, the manifold wisdom of God should be made known to the rulers and authorities in the heavenly realms, according to His eternal purpose that He accomplished in Christ Jesus our Lord.

God is declaring His multifaceted wisdom through the Church! But it seems so natural because the listeners are not physical beings who visibly react to what we reveal; rather they are invisible spiritual beings in the heavenly realms. The evil ones shudder at the name of Jesus and respond to the Church by surrendering their territory. The good ones rush to the throne room of heaven and erupt in praise to God for the wisdom they've seen displayed in His handiwork. This produces changes in the natural realm that often seem more like interesting coincidences than miracles. I assure you: When the influence of darkness shifts to the light of Christ in a region, it is no small thing!

God also speaks through signs, wonders, miracles, and spiritual gifts. (See Hebrews 2:4.) These things are usually less subtle (though not always), so I'll let them be the exception to the principle.

We may also have physical sensations that alert us to what God is doing. Jesus felt power go out from Him and thereby knew that someone had just received a touch from His Father. (See Luke 8:46.) The book of Hebrews talks about "those who by reason of use have their senses exercised to discern both good and evil." (Hebrews 5:14, NKJV.) This could be like the subtle pains I described earlier that led to healing, or it could be even more subtle than that—perhaps a gentle warmth or tingling sensation. If I'm praying for someone and my feet become hot or tingly, I typically take that to mean that God wants to encourage that person to preach the Gospel with boldness. (See Ephesians 6:15 and Isaiah 52:7.) If I'm ministering to someone and I suddenly feel afraid, I begin to pray for them to be free from a spirit of fear. Many people have been set free from night terrors, nightmares, and addictions to horror movies in this way. There are many ways God speaks in this way, but I'll allow you the joy of discovering them.

Even subtler than that, we may also have a sense, an impression, or a perception of something. How many times have you felt like something good or bad was about to happen, and then it did? Perhaps this was God (I like to give Him the credit). During his journey to Italy, Paul warned, "Men, I perceive that this voyage will end with

LIMITLESS *hope* — Art Thomas

disaster and much loss, not only of the cargo and ship, but also our lives." (See Acts 27:10, NKJV.) They went anyway and, sure enough, were shipwrecked. (See Acts 27:41.)

God can also put a person into a trance as He did with Peter and Paul to convince them to preach the Gospel to the Gentiles. (See Acts 10:9-17 and 22:17-21.) We tend to shy away from talking about trances because of the way the word is used in Eastern mysticism. The main difference between Christian trances and the trances of Eastern mysticism is this: One is initiated by a human in an effort to empty oneself, and the other is initiated by God to fill a person with truth. Two of my most life-altering encounters with God happened through unexpected trances in which the Lord revealed things to me that I would probably not have learned any other way.

As you can see, God speaks in many different ways. He is not limited to the audible voice—although He does speak that way. And I have not even mentioned other ways He reveals His voice like preaching, teaching, music, prophecy, angels, and more. This is nothing more than a simple overview to help you open your expectation to a wide variety of ways to hear God. Look for Him in everything. He won't be hard to find because He already "fills everything in every way." (See Ephesians 1:23.)

Look for God's Voice

Limitless hope anticipates that God could be speaking through absolutely anything. Expected disappointment fears presumption.

When you expect that God can speak through

anything, you maintain an open awareness of the world around you, looking for anything God might have to say. With this mindset, God has spoken to me through movies, sunsets, songs, paintings, meals, and simply watching people at work (just as He spoke to Jeremiah while he watched a local potter making a pot in Jeremiah 18).

Some of us might think such an active searching for God's voice is a little hokey. We might think that we run the risk of falling into deception if we assume God is saying something that He isn't. Don't worry about that. That's why we have the Scriptures as a measuring rod and our fellow believers as a sounding board.

There is nothing wrong with being childlike enough to see some measure of your Father in everything. Take a look around you right now. What could He be speaking that you would miss without searching?

I'm not saying that every little thing that happens is God's voice. All I'm saying is that it can be; and if we don't actively watch for it, we'll miss it. I would rather try to see God in everything than ignore the world and see Him in nothing.

Similarly, God often speaks through unlikely people. If we're not careful, we can make judgment calls against people, assuming that God would never speak to us through them. I can't tell you how many pastors I've heard say that they don't receive prophetic words from just anyone but only have a couple people they allow to speak into their life. In my experience, these folks are often also emotionally unhealthy and may even have tendencies of a potential cult leader.

In my travels as a minister, I often run into complete strangers who believe God has given them a prophetic word for me. Having no relationship with these people, I don't know whether or not they're credible. And to be honest, many times—at face value—these folks don't look like they are!

But Paul instructed us not to treat prophecies with contempt, saying that in doing so we may quench the Holy Spirit. (See 1 Thessalonians 5:19-22.) I refuse to shrug off these prophetic words just because they come from unlikely sources.

At the end of a small meeting in Ohio, a man approached me and said, "I had a vision of you while you were preaching. You were on one of those moving walkways like they have at the airport," then his eyes widened to the size of grapefruits, "but you were going the wrong way." He stared at me and then eased his head back as if to say, "Wasn't that profound?"

I thanked him and promised to pray about it.

To be honest, my initial gut reaction was that this was the devil's way of throwing me off my game and discouraging me in ministry. I took it like the word was accusing me of being in sin that I knew wasn't happening. I almost shrugged it off completely, but I didn't want to miss God.

During the following days, I treated that man's message as though it was indeed from God and sought the Lord about what it might mean. I brought it up to my wife and some friends, hoping they might have some insight about what it applied to or even if it was actually from God.

A couple weeks later, I was ministering in India. In my downtime, I was reading a book, and the word "Pakistan" was in the book. As soon as I read it, something stirred in me.

A few weeks earlier, I was invited to travel to Pakistan with a friend of mine the following year. He was going to buy my ticket, pay me $1,000 for photographing his trip, and also give me several opportunities to train a couple hundred pastors there in healing ministry (which is what I'm most often invited to do around the world). He was even going to arrange an opportunity for me to film interviews with Christians who had been persecuted, which would have been perfect for one of my upcoming films.

It all looked great, and I was excited to go. I put Pakistan on my itinerary and carried on with my life.

But when I read the word "Pakistan" in that book, I knew the Lord was telling me that I was going the wrong way, and I decided not to go.

A couple hours later, my ministry partner—James Loruss—and I were discussing upcoming trips and filming opportunities for movies we were planning. We really wanted to film some friends in South America, but I realized my ministry itinerary was completely booked. That's when I remembered the vision again and realized I had two weeks blocked off for Pakistan. God wasn't telling me not to travel; He said I was going the wrong direction. We decided to replace Pakistan with South America, and I started trying to figure out a way to break the news to my friend that I wouldn't be able to photograph his trip.

But on the way home, during a layover in Paris, I received an e-mail from that friend. He had decided to split the cost of his event with another minister, and they were going to use a photographer they had both used before. He said I was still welcome to come if I paid my own way, but the cost of the trip was going to be about twice as much as South America would turn out to be.

If I had shrugged off that one guy's vision, I might not have known what to do next. I might have even forgotten about South America and tried to honor my original commitment (since that tends to be more my style). But because I honored a possible prophetic word from an unlikely vessel, I found myself comforted, strengthened, encouraged, and even knowing what I was supposed to do next before I even knew that the original plan wouldn't work out.

Like any person, God loves to speak to those who are listening to Him. If you will listen, He will speak. Look for Him in the subtle things. And if you're faithful with the little things, He may begin to speak bigger things.

Chapter 6:

Limitless Hope and Prayer & Fasting

Why would anyone in his right mind spend hours or even days without food, speaking to an invisible person who might not be listening and isn't likely to do anything in response? It doesn't make sense. Yet many Christians today have become convinced that prayer only changes us (not circumstances) and that fasting is little more than a "discipline."

Is this how you would like to have a relationship with your spouse? I can't imagine if every time I lovingly asked my wife to make me a sandwich, the result was only that I became more capable of making my own sandwich (though she might like that). I can't imagine if my wife never had a conversation with me but rather stared at me without response. I can't imagine if my wife were invisible and silent, requiring me to do everything for my family. That wouldn't be a marriage; it would be me—all alone with an imaginary friend.

Yet this is what many of us believe to be true about God. As a result, we pray things that require little faith to expect—things which, when they do happen, could have easily had a natural explanation. We say things like, "God only helps those who help themselves," and then we merely ask God to help us with our own plans rather than asking Him to do something only He can do. We unload all our thoughts in prayer and rarely wait for a verbal response. We feel better because we vented, but the circumstances remain unchanged. And when it comes to fasting, many of us have never even tried.

How do we move from "talking to an imaginary friend" to relationally engaging a limitless God who is passionate about us? As you may have guessed, the answer is limitless hope.

Pick a Target and Expect Results

> Limitless hope causes us to fast and pray with the expectation that we are being effective. Expected disappointment causes us to fast and pray religiously with the thought that "Maybe this will mean something personal for my life."

I remember the first time I fasted. I was eight years old, and our church had rented a big tent for a week in which to hold a series of outdoor meetings. People were being saved, healed, and set free. Lives were being changed for the better. And in the midst of this focus on God, I felt stirred in my young heart to fast for a day.

I didn't even know how to fast, and my parents weren't sure if I could do it. My mom was instantly tossed into coaching me through it: "You can have water; and if you start feeling lightheaded, drink some fruit juice. If you can't make it all day, that's okay; God still loves you. Some people will eat salad while they're fasting so that they get a little bit of nourishment…" Her advice went on and on—and it was great advice. The funny thing was that I still didn't know what I was fasting for!

My mom and I went to lunch with the female evangelist who was part of the event. When the woman saw that I wasn't eating and learned from my mom that I was fasting, she became so excited! Her face beamed. Then she looked at me sweetly and asked, "Are you fasting for me?"

Of course I didn't know what I was fasting for, so I just answered shyly, "Yes."

"Praise the Lord!" she squealed, "What are you asking God to do for me?"

It's not that I felt caught in a lie. By this point, I actually felt like she was the reason God asked me to fast and pray. But since I had only just discovered that she was the subject, I certainly hadn't thought about these bigger questions.

"Umm…I guess that He would help you talk?" I answered quizzically.

I don't remember exactly what the woman said after that—perhaps because of my lack of food—but I remember something shifting in my mindset after that day. This evangelist already had God helping her talk. I didn't need to pray for that (though I'm sure she appreciated it). If I was going to fast and pray, then it needed to be aimed at something that wasn't happening already. I could have prayed for more people to attend the meetings. I could have asked for greater effectiveness in the ministry—more salvations, healings, and such. And what I especially didn't realize is that I should have been fasting in such a way that actually brought me into the plan of what God wanted to do.

In my young mind, I somehow figured out that there was no sense fasting and praying blindly or for things that we already had. I needed to be asking for something that only God could do and fasting to align myself with Him and His plan.

> **Romans 8:24b –** ...hope that is seen is no hope at all. Who hopes for what they already have?

Fasting, Humility, and God's Grace

It's not enough to simply make a spiritual discipline out of fasting. While it is not a bad thing to routinely fast, we must do it with purpose—otherwise its just legalistic anorexia with a spiritual title.

Jesus and His disciples didn't participate in the expected, disciplined fasts of the Pharisees and John the Baptist because there was not a present need.

> **Luke 5:33-35 –** They said to Him, "John's disciples often fast and pray, and so do the disciples of the Pharisees, but Yours go on eating and drinking."
>
> Jesus answered, "Can you make the

> friends of the Bridegroom fast while He is
> with them? But the time will come when the
> Bridegroom will be taken from them; in those
> days they will fast."

Yet we do know that Jesus fasted. (See Matthew 4:2.) According to the principle Jesus shared with His questioners, fasting is necessary whenever we cannot see the presence of the Bridegroom. When Jesus is clearly present, it is a cause for celebration; but if you cannot see Jesus at work in a situation, it is the perfect time to fast.

Now allow me to seem to contradict myself for a moment so that you can see the full meaning of this. The fact is, Jesus—through the Holy Spirit—is present everywhere. How can He not be present? That's impossible. He also promised to never leave us nor forsake us. (See Hebrews 13:5.) Furthermore, it's not as though fasting is a means of convincing Him to do something He doesn't want to do. So why fast?

The truth is, the fundamental purpose of fasting is to humble ourselves so that we can come into alignment with God's purposes in our lives. Humility causes us to become smaller so that Jesus can be revealed in a greater measure through our words and actions. Fasting prioritizes God's kingdom above our own kingdoms. The purpose of fasting is not to convince God to act but to bring us into sufficient alignment with Him so that we can effectively act in His name. By humbling yourself through fasting, you place yourself in a position where God can use you to speak into a situation with authority.

> **Matthew 23:12 –** For those who exalt
> themselves will be humbled, and those who

humble themselves will be exalted.

When we humble ourselves, God exalts us. The word "exalt" means to lift up, to promote, and to grant authority. Thayer's Greek Dictionary says that the original word used here means (1) "to lift up on high, to exalt;" and (2) metaphorically speaking, (a) "to raise to the very summit of opulence and prosperity" or (b) "to exalt, to raise to dignity, honor and happiness." In other words, when we humble ourselves in the sight of the Lord, He picks us up and allows us to speak from His throne. Authority flows from humility, and fasting is a means of humbling our flesh.

As we have already seen, faith is a necessary component for all of the Christian life. Apart from actively trusting God, we can't please Him. The only thing that pleases God is partnership. Whenever we partner with God, He empowers us with undeserved grace—not because we earned it but because we trusted Him. Grace does the work, and faith gives us access to it. (See Ephesians 2:8.)

But there's another component. Real faith only works in conjunction with humility. Faith and humility bring us into alignment with God's enabling grace. If we do things apart from that humble trust in Him, our loving Father disciplines us by opposing us.

> **James 4:6-7** – But He gives us more grace. That is why Scripture says: "God opposes the proud but shows favor to the humble."
>
> Submit yourselves, then, to God. Resist the devil, and he will flee from you.

I have experienced times in ministry where my pride rose up, and God refused to send results until I humbled myself. While I know Jesus never left me, you could say that, in a sense, the Bridegroom was taken from me because our union was no longer evident to the world. God was humbling me.

I once traveled to India with an older evangelist to film him in action and minister in some hard-to-reach places. But since I was with this seventy-nine-year-old man who had been ministering in these places for decades, many of the locals treated me like I was nothing more than his bag-boy.

One church had over a thousand members. On Sunday morning, my elder friend spoke a spectacular message. During that time, the Lord spoke to me through a word of knowledge that there was a woman present who had a tumor under her left arm. I waited for someone to offer me the microphone, but it never happened.

That night, though, I was offered an opportunity to speak. I was thrilled! These people were finally treating me like a minister too!

But as it turns out, one of the church members was having a wedding reception that night (a really big deal in Indian culture), and there were only about 20 people present at the meeting.

I thought to myself, *I'll show this pastor. I'm going to preach a spectacular message, and then I'm going to give that word of knowledge about the tumor because I feel that woman is still here tonight.*

The message was mediocre. But when I gave the word of knowledge, sure enough, the woman came.

There in front of everyone, I commanded the

tumor to dissolve. I wasn't at all concerned because I had seen God's power dissolve tumors plenty of times before.

But deep in my heart, I was excited to have that pastor see my ministry in action. I couldn't wait to be validated in front of him and have him wish he had given me the meeting with a thousand people instead of the meeting with twenty.

After five awkward minutes of ministering to the woman without results she wanted to sit down, and I was left scratching my head. It wasn't until later that the Lord showed me He was disciplining me for my pride. It wasn't the woman's fault that she wasn't healed; it was my own.

When Jesus' disciples asked Him why He could cast out a certain demon and they couldn't, some of the ancient manuscripts tell us, "This kind only leaves when you pray and fast." (See Mark 9:29.) Other manuscripts just say, "pray." Since the principle is that we must acknowledge our own inadequacy, I don't have a problem including fasting in this verse—it's just good to know that fasting is not necessarily required.

What's interesting to me is that when you read the account of Jesus casting out that demon, He neither prays nor fasts beforehand. He doesn't say, "This is a tough demon. Wait here while I go fast for a couple days." And He didn't ask the Father to take the demon out of the boy. He simply said, "You deaf and mute spirit, I command you, come out of him and never enter him again."

Again, no prayer and no fasting. The implication is that Jesus had already been maintaining a lifestyle of humility before the Father through an ongoing prioritization of prayer and fasting.[1]

Partnering with God through Fasting

Prayer and fasting have nothing to do with convincing God to do something that He doesn't want to do. Rather, they have to do with humbling ourselves so that we can effectively partner with Him in what He already wants to do. Prayer and fasting involve humble recognition that we cannot meet a certain need on our own.

Luke's account of the above story happens in chapter nine (verses 37-45). In verse one of that chapter, Jesus gave these disciples His own power and authority to "drive out all demons and to cure diseases." Yet here we find ourselves in the same chapter with the same group of disciples being unable to cast out a demon. They had power and authority over "all" demons, but they lacked the humility needed to be effective. This is proven in verse forty-six, in which "An argument started among the disciples as to which of them would be the greatest."

Humility, expressed through prayer and fasting, invites the power of God in a situation. The prophet Joel spent a couple chapters calling all of Israel to a solemn fast, and it is in this context that he prophesied the famous words, "And afterward I will pour out My Spirit on all flesh..." (See Joel 2:28). After what? After fasting! And what would this outpouring of the Holy Spirit look like? It would be revealed as God spoke prophetically through average people:

> **Joel 2:28-29 –** And afterward, I will pour out My Spirit on all people. Your sons and daughters will prophesy, your old men will dream dreams, your young men will see visions. Even on My servants, both men and

women, I will pour out my Spirit in those days.

As Christians, we pray and we fast with an expectation that God will invade a situation where He is not currently expressing His victory—and that He will likely use us to do it! Humble prayer and fasting position us as representatives of God who can enact His will.

Yes, God is always present everywhere, but His will is not always done. The Bible says God wills that "none should perish," and yet people perish. (See 2 Peter 3:9.) His will is not always done. If the Father's will were always done, then why would Jesus teach us to pray that His will would be done? (See Luke 11:2.) Why would Paul tell us to "test and approve what God's will is" if everything is God's will? (See Romans 12:2.)

In Acts 14, we read about Paul and Barnabas visiting Lystra, Iconium and Antioch. There they encouraged the believers—none of whom had gone to Bible college or even grown up with the same Jewish history lessons as Jesus' disciples. These were Greeks with a raw belief in a God whom they just met. And do you know what Paul and Barnabas did? They "appointed elders for them in each church and, with prayer and fasting, committed them to the Lord, in whom they had put their trust." (See Acts 14:23.)

Who were the elders? Not scholars from another town! The elders they appointed were mature people from among their own ranks who were just as new at this faith as the rest of the believers. Paul and Barnabas (1) fasted and prayed for something only God could accomplish, (2) established leaders with the authority they received from Jesus, and then (3) moved on to the next city.

When you fast and pray, don't assume that the

result will be nothing more than a personal experience or a mediocre change that has a natural explanation. Rather, expect God to invade the situation. Expect Him to empower you for the task. Pray and fast until you have humbled yourself before your heavenly Bridegroom so that you can walk in true union with Him. Rest assured, you are being effective.

Changing Circumstances

> Praying and fasting with limitless hope changes circumstances. Praying with expected disappointment only influences our own perspective on the unchanged circumstances.

I was once staffing a camp for children in the foster care system who had histories of abuse and neglect. The first night is generally considered the most important because it is the basis for these kids' impressions of the entire camp and how it will go. But on that first night we found ourselves hurrying the kids indoors as a monstrous storm loomed in the distance, stretching across the entire horizon as far as we could see in either direction.

We had all been fasting and praying for this camp to be a success, and I had an intense feeling in my heart that this storm was not in line with God's will. Not every storm is God's plan. Some are—like the storm that nearly destroyed Jonah's boat. Others, however, are not—like the one Jesus calmed. Jesus worked in harmony with the Father's will; not at odds with it. If the Father desired a destructive storm, then Jesus would not have been correct in commanding, "Peace. Be still." Instead, Jesus was consistent in only doing what He saw His Father doing. (See John 5:19.) The Father's will—peace—was done on earth, just like it is done in heaven.

I knew in my heart that this storm wasn't right, so I grabbed my walkie-talkie and radioed the camp director: "Get the kids inside, but I'll be late. I'm going down to the campfire site to pray."

As the ominous clouds billowed closer, I ran as fast as I could to the ring of stones where we were supposed to eat marshmallows and sing camp songs later that night. It was right at the edge of a pond, so I had an unobstructed view of the storm from there.

When I arrived at the campsite, I thought, "What now, God?" To be completely candid, I felt totally helpless against this storm. Looking at the clouds, I felt so small and insignificant. In fact, the longer I looked at the massive storm, the more I wanted to run back to the shelter! I prayed, "Father, I'm not big enough for this! I desperately need You to do something here that only You can do."

Then God came through with something that was entirely unnecessary except to give me the boost of faith that I needed. Out of the corner of my eye, I noticed a small rowboat turned upside-down on the shore of the pond. It had nothing to do with my authority in Christ, but God knew it was just what I would need to ignite my faith. The thought immediately occurred to me that Jesus calmed a storm while standing on a boat, so I would too!

With my eyes set firmly on the storm and with newfound boldness from God stirring in my heart, I marched over to that boat, stepped up on top of it, and confidently stared down the storm.

"You are not of God," I said to the storm, "and you are not allowed to ruin this camp or scare these children. In Jesus name, I command you to come no further."

At that instant, I saw with the eyes of my spirit as a massive angel—hundreds of feet tall—rose up from one of the distant corners of the camp on the other side of the pond. Two huge wings stretched out to either side, and with my physical eyes, I watched as the storm parted and started to flow around the camp.

Right away, I radioed the director and said, "We're going to have a campfire tonight! The storm is going around us." A few of the camp staff quickly looked out the window and also witnessed the miracle taking place.

Sure enough, by the time the children were coming out of the building, the storm was visible in a full circle around the camp; but we had a perfectly clear, starlit sky above us. Thunder and lightning loomed at all four borders, but we were all dry and safe. In fact, we found out the next day that this was no small storm—there was flooding in the next city.

This is not a story about my abilities or authority—only that Jesus used me. It is a story about a weak believer humbling himself before an all-powerful God and receiving authority for the task at hand.

I have nothing apart from Christ. Any Christian at that camp could have worked the same miracle, but for some reason God chose me—maybe so I could write this example into this book or maybe just because I was the only one out there standing on that boat. Who knows? The point is simply that I was able to express the authority that Jesus currently has, and it was simply because I asked for His help.

When we have this position of relationship with God, we have opportunities to see circumstances change. Remember what I said in Chapter Two about the anchor of hope: As the waters rise, the solution is not to let out more line. The solution is to command the waters to recede. And if your current level of authority in Christ is somehow insufficient, keep humbling yourself before God, and ask Him to intervene. God won't allow you to be tested more than you can handle, so the water will not overtake your boat. The water will go back down if you persevere. James said to consider it pure joy when we "face" trials—not when trials merely happen, but when we actually face them. (See James 1:2.) Lock into your relationship with God and stand your ground against the devil's schemes. Circumstances will change.

Praying God's Will

Whenever I share things like this, I normally hear someone respond, "Yes, but you have to ask according to God's will. If it's not His will, then it won't happen. You can't go asking for just anything!"

Yes and no. First John 5:4 does specify, "This is the confidence we have in approaching God: that if we ask anything according to His will, He hears us." In other words, we can have unshakable faith that God will respond when we ask for something in line with His will. For example, God doesn't want anyone to perish and everyone to come to repentance. (See 2 Peter 3:9.) So if we ask God to destroy a city, He won't do it. (See Luke 9:54-55.) But if we ask Him to enable us to speak the Word with boldness, and if we ask Him to heal and perform mighty signs and wonders, then He will indeed respond! (See Acts 4:29-31.)

On the other hand, we are still allowed to ask for anything! If God answers "no," then that's His decision. But what we tend to do is not ask because we're afraid of what might happen if we ask Him to do something that He doesn't want to do.

When I'm out to eat with my wife, I might say, "Hey Honey, could you please pass the salt?" Then my wife will naturally respond in her best evil villain voice, "You fool! Can't you see that I'm enjoying my food? How dare you interrupt me to give you salt! It isn't my will!"

Of course you know that isn't true! Passing the salt is a piece of cake for my wife. She gladly puts down her fork and passes the shaker. In this case Robin's will was simply to love me. If her will was specifically to pass the salt, then she would have passed it without my asking. But if she willed to love me, then my asking was the sole reason for the salt being passed. Whether she wanted to pass it or not is irrelevant—her love for me responded with action when the salt was requested. The salt wasn't the point. She "willed" to love me!

While Moses was on the mountain receiving the Ten Commandments, the Israelites became restless. Moses had been gone a long time. Left to their own devices, the people convinced Aaron to make an idol—a golden calf—that they could worship. Moses knew nothing of what was transpiring below, but God saw it all. He basically told Moses, "These people make me so angry with their stubbornness! I'm going to go destroy them all and restart the nation of Israel through you." (See Exodus 32:1-10.)

But Moses wouldn't settle for that. Even though it

was God's will in that moment to destroy those people, His greater will was something different; and Moses knew it:

> **Exodus 32:11-14** – But Moses tried to pacify the Lord his God. "O Lord!" he said. "Why are You so angry with Your own people whom You brought from the land of Egypt with such great power and such a strong hand? Why let the Egyptians say, 'Their God rescued them with the evil intention of slaughtering them in the mountains and wiping them from the face of the earth'? Turn away from Your fierce anger. Change Your mind about this terrible disaster You have threatened against Your people! Remember Your servants Abraham, Isaac, and Jacob. You bound Yourself with an oath to them, saying, 'I will make your descendants as numerous as the stars of heaven. And I will give them all of this land that I have promised to your descendants, and they will possess it forever.'"
>
> So the Lord changed His mind about the terrible disaster He had threatened to bring on his people. (NLT)

The King James Version actually says that God "repented." This doesn't mean that He had been sinning—it simply means that He decided to stop going one direction and instead went another. God's immediate will may have been to destroy the sinful people, but His greater will was to live in relationship with Moses.

My wife may want to eat her food, but her greater will is to show me love by passing the salt when I ask for it. The things we ordinarily ask God for—like healing, provision, wisdom, and miracles—are as easy for Him as passing the salt. He does them because He loves us. And we can have confidence in asking because we know He truly does desire to do these things! Jesus proved that through the price He paid at the cross.

We should not be afraid as we approach God. Rather, we should "come boldly to the throne of our gracious God." (See Hebrews 4:16, NLT.) He invites us into this form of relationship. To waste that relationship is to waste the cross. The price Jesus paid in His suffering and death were to bring you into an intimate relationship with Father God. Ask the Lord for whatever you need. And you can even feel free to ask Him for whatever you want, simply because you know He loves you. He's allowed to say "no" because He is God, but you will probably be surprised how often He says "yes"!

Praying Heaven into Earth

Hope has nothing to do with coming to terms with a fallen world. Hope is about seeing who God is and what He wants to do and then bringing those realities into the earth.[2]

We have a tendency in our flesh to decide what God's will is (apart from Him revealing it). Our criteria for this decision is usually very simple: whatever requires the least effort, persistence, or sense of risk on our part. If we ask for something and it doesn't happen, then the outcome must have been God's will (or so we assume).

In Luke 11—as we have already noted—we see that God invites us to pray with "shameless audacity." And this is what we do, but we often do it according to our own made-up, risk-free, earthbound version of "God's will."

"Please pass the salt; unless, of course, it isn't your will to pass the salt. May your will be done." Can you imagine the puzzled look that would be on my wife's face? Of course she wants to pass the salt—cushioning my statement with all this fluff just makes it seem like I don't trust her to love me. Yet this is how we pray. Even though God wants to heal—enough to have His own Son pay the price that He paid—we add these little phrases like, "Not my will, but Yours be done."

We like to think that we pray this way in humility. In reality, it is often our pride. We often pray this way so that when nothing happens we can shrug it off and simply say, "Oh well. I guess it wasn't God's will."

Can you imagine if the disciples had that mentality when they couldn't cast the demon out of the epileptic boy? "Oh well. We prayed that God's will would be done, and the boy still has epilepsy. Clearly, that's what God wants." Such a mindset is utterly unbiblical and theologically absurd.

If, on the other hand, I ask God to do something that I know is in His heart to do, then I know I don't need to cushion my request. I can simply ask Him to pass the salt. The only reason I would cushion a request is if I really don't know what God wants to do.

When Jesus prayed, "Not My will, but Yours be done," it wasn't because He didn't know what the Father wanted to do. It was because He did know. And Jesus knew that what the Father wanted to do was going to cost Him everything. Biblically speaking, praying "not my will, but Yours be done" is supposed to be a means of self-sacrifice. It is not a means of "giving God an out." That's how we tend to use this phrase. Assuming that He doesn't really want to heal or provide or empower, we try to set things up so that we feel better if He says "no." We use the phrase because we are unsure of God's will, whereas Jesus used the phrase to surrender to the plan God had already revealed.

God's will is not based on our comfort or our assumptions. God's will is based on Him alone. And He has revealed His will to us in the life of Jesus who healed everyone who came to Him (not everyone He saw but certainly everyone who came to Him), worked mighty miracles, proclaimed His message with boldness, and loved extravagantly.

Strangely enough, we don't read about the disciples asking Jesus, "Lord, teach us to heal," or, "Teach us to multiply bread and fish," or, "Teach us to preach like You," or, "Teach us to love the way You do." But what they did ask was this: "Lord, teach us to pray." (See Luke 11:1.)

The disciples observed that all these things— healing, miracles, boldness, and compassion—flowed from Jesus' prayer life. They flowed from His relationship with the Father. (See John 5:20.) When Jesus then taught His disciples to pray, He started with words of relationship: "Our Father in Heaven…" Then He continued, revealing why it is important to note that this Father of ours is in Heaven: "May Your kingdom come and Your will be done on earth just like it is done in heaven…"[3]

This scripture tells us what God's will is. His will is done in Heaven! For example, no one in heaven has cancer, so we know that God's ultimate will is for no one to have cancer. No one in heaven is hungry, so we know that God's ultimate will is to feed the hungry—even multiplying food when needed. Everyone in heaven believes God and has a relationship with Him, so we know that God's ultimate will is for us to persuade people everywhere with the Gospel and invite them to salvation. We therefore have every right—and are actually commissioned by God—to pray persistently that cancer be obliterated, that the hungry be fed, and that entire nations be saved. We are taught to look at the condition and reality of heaven and then pray for that reality to invade the earthly circumstance before us.

We don't need to beg God for it because He wants it more than we do.

We aren't generally willing to be whipped with a "cat of nine tails," but He was. We aren't generally willing to be nailed to a cross, but He was. He paid the price; we just reap the reward. Randy Clark, of *Global Awakening Ministries*, once said, "To beg God to heal is to imply that we have more mercy than He does." We don't need to beg God to do what He has already paid for in full. We simply need to pray that His will would be done. And until that will is done, we need to humble ourselves with prayer and fasting so that we can be used by Him to bring the change.

> Limitless hope looks into the perfection of heaven and believes that the same can be true on the earth. Expected disappointment looks at earthly circumstances and assumes that nothing will change until the person dies and goes to heaven.

To put it another way, expected disappointment waits for you to go to heaven, whereas limitless hope brings heaven to you.

Addressing Our Needs

> Limitless hope causes us to spend more time praying than telling people about our problems. Expected disappointment causes us to spend more time talking about our problems than praying.

When I was growing up, I attended an interdenominational Christian school. While the biblical teaching and spiritual atmosphere was great, I noticed something troubling around the time of my seventh grade year. Every day, we had a time for prayer requests, after which we would pray. Sometimes this process would take nearly an hour as all twenty or so students unloaded their cares to the class. It was tremendously therapeutic!

But that was the problem. Over the years, many of my classmates stopped expecting God to actually change their circumstances. If God is going to change things when we pray, then it isn't necessary for everyone to feel sorry for us and "really understand" every detail of our problem. If, however, God is not going to do anything, then we need to get as much sympathy as possible from people so that we can feel better in our mess. I started to wonder if Jesus would have said of us—like He did of the hypocrites who prayed only to be seen by men—that we had "already received our reward in full." (See Matthew 6:5.)

You have to decide which reward you want: either

the life-altering response of God, or the false comfort of mere people. Of course, there is a difference between complaining and letting people know your needs. Complaining (or fishing for sympathy) is all about eliciting a response from a person on earth. Expressing our need with faith is about eliciting a response from our Father in heaven. When you have a need, let people know what they need to know in order to pray, but do so knowing that you don't need anything from them. Rather, you need something from God.

Prayer and fasting are first about asking God to do what only He can do. Second, they are about humbling ourselves and thereby being in the proper position to speak with His delegated authority and become part of the answer. Third, they are about inviting heaven to invade the earth, changing circumstances and revealing God's love.

At the center of it all is our relationship with Him. In the context of limitless hope, praying and fasting bring us into partnership with the God who loved the world enough to send His only Son.

If you're just beginning a prayer life, consider this: God isn't interested in the quantity of your prayer. He is not even interested in the quality of your prayer. He is simply interested in the fact that you pray. Start with something, and He will grow it.

James 4:10 – Humble yourselves before the Lord, and He will lift you up.

Endnotes:

1. We also learn something from this story about the will of God. When the disciples ministered without results, their response was not to tell the boy's father, "I'm sorry. It looks like it's God's will for your son to have epilepsy." No way! Instead, the boy was brought to Jesus, and the disciples asked, "Why couldn't we do what you did?" (See Mark 9:28.)

2. I want to give honor and credit to Pastor Bill Johnson for blazing a trail in this topic. His book *When Heaven Invades Earth* dramatically impacted my Christian walk and is the basis for much of what I share in this section.

3. The Greek words here are written in the imperative sense—actually implying a command as though you were literally calling heaven to earth. While not the proper translation, the oft recited words, "Thy kingdom come, Thy will be done," could be awkwardly rendered, "Come, Thy kingdom! Be done, Thy will!" God invites us into the process of seeing heavenly realities become earthly realities.

Chapter 7:

Limitless Hope and Studying Scripture

What are some of the activities we typically consider to be indicators of "being a good Christian?" You know what I'm talking about: pray, go to church, give generously, be kind, read your Bible, and the list goes on. Every one of these things can be done religiously, or they can be done out of relationship.

It's a fine line. Both motivations—religion and relationship—can look the same on the outside. If you were to meet someone on the street who said, "I read my Bible everyday," you might be impressed; but you wouldn't know if that man had a genuine relationship with God or if he were merely religious.

I imagine this happens because we often focus too

much on the "how-to" and too little on simply "being." There are many people who have genuine, passionate relationships with God. When you ask these people what their Christian lives are like, they might tell you about how often they pray, how they share the Gospel with everyone they meet, or how they read their Bibles every morning— basically, they tell you all about "how" they live their lives. Naturally, if you want to have a Christian life that mirrors one of these amazing Christians, you might start by trying to imitate their lifestyles—doing the same things and striving with great effort to become who they are.

Unfortunately, that's all you would be able to do: imitate. While there's a place for imitation in our spiritual growth, the ideal is transformation. The reason these Christians pray, give, evangelize, and read so regularly is that they are wild about the Jesus they love and serve. Having a relationship with God is first about "being" a son or daughter. Out of that comes the action. Going through the motions of Christianity is not the mark of true Christianity. But if you are a true Christian, then the right motivation will be present to produce the right actions.

Paul was clear that we are saved through faith and not via works. (See Ephesians 2:8-9.) Then we find James teaching the church that faith without works is dead. (See James 2:26.)

Which is it?

Both! You are saved because of faith. It is not because of anything you have done but rather because of what Jesus has done on your behalf. Remember that faith is a relational word, and relationships motivate us to do extraordinary things. The activities of Christianity are genuine when they flow from faith and love.

This is especially important when it comes to this topic of studying Scripture. I used to read my Bible every day for purely religious reasons. Yes, I would occasionally hear from God during those times, but it was generally a chore.

One could say that I was doing the right thing—making an opportunity for God to speak to me and maintaining a discipline—but there was a problem: If I forgot to read my Bible one day, or if I simply chose not to read it, then the next day I would feel horrible. I would feel like I failed my Lord and that He was displeased with me.

What was the fruit of these nagging thoughts? Only that I would start to avoid God, which naturally led to additional days of not reading. I felt like God was disappointed with me, and that certainly didn't make me want to enter into His presence. The more days I missed, the guiltier I would feel. Trying to read religiously actually drove a wedge between God and me rather than bringing us together.

Then one day I entered into a thriving relationship with Him. I rested in the fact that He loved me, and I accepted the reality that I am His son. The result? I started devouring my Bible! I carried a pocket-sized New Testament with me wherever I went, and I would pull it out whenever I had the opportunity. I was doing volunteer work at a school during that time, and I would look for any spare moment to sneak away and pray or read—sometimes in the elevator or while waiting for the copy machine to print worksheets.

Today I don't read quite as constantly throughout the day, but I needed that season in my life to jumpstart my walk with God. Whereas I used to feel guilty for missing a day of reading my Bible, I now feel like I missed something valuable. Rather than thinking about how I failed God, I wonder what I might have missed. The old way caused me to distance myself from Jesus whereas the new way compels me to dive into the Scriptures as soon as possible so that I can find out what I missed the day before.

This relationship with God is what generates limitless hope. Our faith-filled expectation is directly related to how we read the Bible, interpret the Bible, and apply the Bible.

Reading the Bible

> Limitless hope causes us to be excited about what God wants to reveal to us in the Scripture. Expected disappointment causes us to forget or even avoid spending time reading it.

Expected disappointment causes us to say things like, "It's always boring and dry," or, "I can't focus when I read," or, "Reading the Bible always puts me to sleep." With this expectation, it's no wonder some people stay in such a rut!

If you read with an expectation of disappointment, all you can focus on is the fulfillment of that disappointment. But if we read with an expectation of encountering God, we will dig into the text in search of the gems He has buried there.

An archaeologist doesn't focus on the mountains of dirt that need to be painstakingly removed from an excavation site. Rather he or she focuses on the treasures and unseen artifacts that are hidden in that dirt. The difference between archaeology and studying Scripture, though, is that you don't dig through dirt looking for treasure—you dig through treasure looking for treasure!

Limitless hope causes us to look at our Bibles as infinite resources for connecting with a limitless God—a God who has hidden treasures in piles of treasure. Not only that but we see that our loving God hid those treasures for the sake of our own delight in finding them. He loves when we pick up one of those treasures and run like little children to show Him what we found. He delights in it because it opens the door for Him to show us new facets of that gem. This strengthens our relationship with Him.

When I was a young boy my mother would often take me with her to visit the homes of ladies from our church. One of those ladies—an eccentric musician and artist—would let me investigate her attic, looking for old toys while she and my mother talked. I loved it! The attic was full of toys, puppets, books, and more. Occasionally, I would find something that looked fun but that I didn't know how to use. I would bring it downstairs to ask her about it. She always smiled, "Oh yes! Watch this…" Then she would teach me how to use what I found—whether it was a top that spun with a crank or a marionette puppet with strings.

I learned something from those adventures in the attic. Everything up there was valuable, but only some of it had meaning for me at my stage in life. If I were to go up into that same attic today, I would probably overlook all the toys and start looking at things more meaningful to my new stage in life—things like old books, tools, and paintings. It would be the same attic with the same treasures, but now I would be discovering new things that weren't relevant to me before. Everything in the attic was a treasure, but some of those treasures have more meaning at different stages in life.

The Bible works the same way. Every word of it is a treasure, yet it seems that we can read it a thousand times and still find new things. Sometimes we can even pick up things we discovered previously and still find new features and details. In every case the greatest level of revelation comes from running to the Owner of the "attic treasures." Only He can reveal how to properly use the truths we discovered. Father God loves to unveil application to His kids!

Sometimes I feel like everything I read is a new revelation—as though every sentence holds fresh insight that I never saw before. Other times I can read page after page and see nothing but the obvious. Either way, I make it a practice to read until I receive a revelation. Why? Because the purpose of reading the Bible is not to learn information but to encounter the Author of the message! As Paul said, "Knowledge puffs up, but love builds up." (See 1 Corinthians 8:1.)

I have known people who say that the New Testament is full of relevant revelation, but the Old Testament has no present-day meaning for us beyond setting the prophetic context for Christ. I disagree! The author of the book of Hebrews certainly received a lot of revelation from reading the Old Testament! What matters is that we filter everything we read through Christ and His finished work on the cross. If what we read in the Old Testament doesn't line up with Jesus' example and His grace revealed in the New Testament, then it is not for us to embrace today (even though it is true). But if what we read reveals and reinforces the Biblical revelation of Christ and His heart, then it certainly contains revelation that is relevant to us today. And this brings us to our next topic: interpretation.

Interpreting the Bible

> Limitless hope causes us to interpret Scripture according to the truth about God. Expected disappointment causes us to interpret Scripture according to our limited life experiences.

The truth about God is that He is good and that He passionately loves us—that His heart and His will are perfectly revealed in the life of Jesus Christ.

Jesus is called "the exact representation" of the Father. (See Hebrews 1:3.) When we interpret Scripture according to this reality, we receive a right understanding of God's will and intentions. But when we base our interpretation on limited life experience, then we wind up with limited hope, limited results, and erroneous perspectives on life.

A great example is the topic of spiritual gifts. When Jesus walked the earth, He demonstrated many spiritual gifts—prophecy, miracles, healing, word of knowledge, leadership, encouragement, and more. Then His disciples received the same Holy Spirit with the same supernatural power. (See the book of Acts.) This continued through the centuries until certain historical events caused Christians to let spiritual gifts drift into hibernation.[1]

Eventually, the Church was pressed with the inevitable question of why our present experience did not line up with the Bible. To solve this problem, theologians like B. B. Warfield wrote texts promoting a perspective called "Cessationism."[2] They purported that spiritual gifts were necessary in the Bible to prove right doctrine but that they were no longer needed since we now have the canonized Bible.

Around the same time as Warfield wrote, though, an unorganized fringe group known as "Pentecostals" was emerging. These people looked at the same Scriptures as Warfield and came to an utterly different conclusion. They saw what the Bible said, took it at face value, and received the power of the Holy Spirit along with a spiritual gift known as "speaking in tongues." Healings and miracles began happening as part of the package. While Warfield and his colleagues interpreted Scripture based on their religious predisposition and limited life experiences, these Pentecostals interpreted Scripture according to its face-value meaning and the truth of God's consistency and goodness.

Nowadays I have heard that Pentecostalism accounts for roughly a quarter of the world's Christians and is one of the fastest-growing branches of Christ-followers. The largest denomination of Pentecostals, The Assemblies of God, is today one of the largest missionary-sending organizations in the world. These men and women who interpret Scriptures about the Spirit's power with limitless hope have experienced over a century of blessing, spiritual gifts, and multiplication—proving that the God of the Bible is still alive and well today.

I was raised in an Assemblies of God church and currently hold credentials with this fellowship. What I've noticed, though, is that perspectives built on expected disappointment have crept into even our Pentecostal churches. For example, we believe in physical healing, but we often have a hard time believing that God will actually heal a person for whom we are praying.

I grew up around people who argued that God doesn't always heal and that it's usually because He is teaching us a lesson or trying to make us better Christians. I found this perspective incredibly logical at the time—especially since healing miracles seemed to be somewhat rare. But our interpretation of Scripture was based on frail human logic and expected disappointment. We didn't expect a person to be healed, and so we rarely persevered long enough in ministry to see that person healed. Then, when the person wasn't healed, we assumed that it must have been God's will.

But there was a big problem with this. Any "suffering" we see promised in the Bible specifically has to do with persecution—not sickness. In forty-six different New Testament passages where "suffering" is viewed positively, the context is always persecution. And in the mere eighteen cases where suffering is treated negatively, the context is always sickness, disease, or tragedy, and the most common next step is healing.[3]

Beyond that, we never once see Jesus saying to a blind man, a leper, a paralytic, or otherwise, "I'm sorry. I can't heal you because My Father gave you this disease to strengthen your character."[4] Our perspective was usually based on obscure passages in the Old Testament, ignoring the example of Christ and the purchase made by His blood. We'll talk a lot more about this in a few chapters, so I won't belabor the topic here. What we need to see, though, is that our interpretation of Scripture must be based on what we know to be true of God according to the example of Jesus Christ—not according to our limited experiences or our lack of faith in His limitless love or limitless power.

Expectations of disappointment caused the Jewish leaders of Jesus' day to miss the fact that He was the Messiah. There had been too many false Messiahs and false hopes leading up to that point. They overlooked the hundreds of Scriptural prophecies that were fulfilled in Jesus' life. They couldn't comprehend the "suffering servant" foretold by Isaiah. Jesus had seemingly let them down by failing to set them free from Roman domination. By misinterpreting Scripture and misunderstanding the heart of God (who wanted to suffer the torment that His children deserved), these men put to death the One who came to save them—and they thought they were doing God's work. Thankfully, God didn't condemn them but recognized their actions were nothing more than ignorance of the truth. (See Acts 3:17.)

Admittedly, these men were ultimately doing the will of God, but not in the way they thought they were. They thought they had relationship with Him when in reality they were opposing Him. They thought they were children of Abraham, but Jesus called them children of the devil. (See John 8:31-47.) They were not obeying God; they were murdering Him.

Without the anchor of limitless hope, these men were tossed by waves of fear, religious prejudice, and peer pressure. They could not correctly interpret Scripture because they did not have a relationship with Scripture's divine Author. They had wrongly placed their hope in an inferior revelation of God and rejected the most perfect revelation: God in the flesh.

> **Hebrews 1:3a** – The Son is the radiance of
> God's glory and the exact representation of
> His being...

Jesus embodied limitless hope. Everyone who came to Him for healing was healed. He had a knack for messing up funerals by raising the dead. He calmed storms, multiplied food, and generally did the impossible. He taught, "All things are possible for the one who believes." The limitless hope of Jesus shows us what our own hope can and should look like. Jesus gives us the right interpretation of Scripture because He perfectly reveals the will of the Father.

When we have the right interpretation of Scripture, we find ourselves living like Jesus. The right interpretation leads to the right application.

Applying the Bible

> Limitless hope enables us to let the Christ of Scripture live in us and reveal His nature through us. Expected disappointment, on the other hand, fears true surrender.

Surrender is a necessary component for the person who desires to live like Jesus. There was once a time when I asked God for a ministry like some of the faith-filled heroes of the past—men like Smith Wigglesworth, Watchman Nee, and Charles Finny. He said to me, "Many people want the anointing of those who have gone before, but few want their cross." What He meant was that these heroes walked in victory that came in the midst great trials. If I wanted their ministry, then I also needed to practice their faithful endurance in the midst of great hardship. It's the only way to withstand the weight of their ministry without being crushed by the responsibility.

Consider, for instance, the seven churches in the book of Revelation. Each church is promised something different as a reward for those who "overcome." Likewise, Jesus promised blessing to His disciples, but He was clear that it would come along with sacrifice—first forsaking everything for the sake of the Kingdom and then enduring persecution. (See Mark 10:29-30.) With faithful endurance comes blessing from the Lord.

The point is not that we earn our blessings—that would render grace meaningless. The point is that trials produce in us the character necessary to carry our blessings well.

God will sometimes bless people who don't have good character, but they typically burn out quickly. The greater the blessing, the more intense will be our struggle to remain in love with the Lord.

Trials will come—first because the enemy wants to oppose us and second because God knows that those trials will help keep us focused on Him. The greater our endurance, the greater our rewards will be. Again, this is not because we are somehow earning something—all the hard work in the world would not be enough to earn one ounce of favor from the Lord. Yet in His love for us, the

Father takes joy in blessing the endurance of His children.

When I talk about blessings from God, I'm not referring to a distant experience in heaven that takes place after we die (even though those future rewards are very real and will indeed be given). Jesus was very clear that rewards and blessings would even be given to His disciples "in this present age." (See Mark 10:30.) Limitless hope sees that God's heart is to lavish His love on us through provision and power. Limitless hope causes us to step out in faith, knowing that the cost will be great and that the reward will be even greater.

> Limitless hope causes us to decide that the historical accounts of Scripture are attainable and worth pursuing. Expected disappointment causes us to believe that the cost of such a lifestyle is too great.

People generally want to serve their own individual concepts of Jesus. A well-fashioned imitation relieves us of personal cost. The Muslims want Him to be a mere prophet because this costs them nothing. The Buddhists want Him to be an enlightened being because this costs them nothing. Historians want Him to be an obscure religious cult leader—again this costs them nothing. Yet even we Christians tend to invent our own ideas of who Jesus is—usually in a subconscious effort to lessen the cost of discipleship detailed in Scripture.

We want to ignore the Jesus of Scripture who requires our total and undivided devotion. We want a Jesus who loves us "just the way we are" and doesn't expect us to change. We want a Jesus who won't cost us our jobs, our relationships, our reputations, or our comfort. But when we rightly understand the God of Scripture, we become convinced that our lives are nothing compared to loving and serving Him.

People do amazing things because of love. Before my parents were married, they lived a few hours away from each other. My dad would gladly drive the entire way just to see my mom. Once, my mom baked my dad some muffins and mailed them to him. By the time they reached him, the muffins were as hard as rocks. But because of his love, Dad ate them anyway!

Throughout history, men and women have risked and sacrificed their lives, their health, their reputations, their friendships, their careers, and more for the sake of love. Yet we often look at the cost involved in loving God and decide that it's just too great. In reality, this is just evidence that we don't truly love Him the way we think we do.

When we really love Him there is no cost too great. When we really love Him the things we read in the Bible about abandoning sin, crucifying the flesh, and valuing the Kingdom of God above our friends and family seem miniscule. We joyfully lay down our lives for our King—not out of duty but out of love. After all, that's what He did for us.

Again, right interpretation leads to right application. When we truly comprehend how much God loves us, and when we understand to what lengths He is willing to go on our behalf, our own love for Him is stirred and reinforced. No cost is too great. He deserves everything.

152

Limitless hope gives us a clear perspective of eternity. Having an anchor of hope in the throne room of God reminds us that the discomforts and inconveniences of this world will be over in the blink of an eye when compared to eternity. But expectations of disappointment cause us to doubt that Jesus is truly worth the cost. We then fear that we might be wrong. And so we go through our earthly lives living comfortably just in case the whole "eternity" thing doesn't pan out. Those of us who live this way have received our rewards in full.

In Luke 9, Jesus encountered three people who He challenged to consider the cost of discipleship. One wanted to follow Jesus, but the Lord replied by saying that the man could expect to be homeless if he became a disciple. Another wanted to stay with his father until the old man passed away, but Jesus made the point that preaching the Gospel is far more important. The third man wanted to say goodbye to his family before following Jesus, but Jesus was clear that the Kingdom of Heaven requires immediate, focused, decisive action.

These are the things we learn from the Word of God, and without limitless hope they are difficult—if not impossible—to follow. Without limitless hope we look at the cost of discipleship described in the Bible and interpret it away with meaningless rhetoric until Jesus is nothing more than a friend who is content to have you just the way you are. When we don't have limitless hope anchoring us to the heart of God, we do more than misinterpret Scripture; we misunderstand God Himself.

When approaching the Word of God, our greatest need is to walk in relationship with the Author of that Word. What some Christians tend to do is read the Bible, formulate a concept of God, and then worship that concept. But this can all be done without an actual relationship, and it often results in a skewed concept of God based on misunderstandings of the Old Testament rather than the clear revelation of Jesus.

What we should rather do is enter a deep spiritual relationship with this loving God through knowing Jesus Christ; and then as we read the Scriptures we can discover new facets of who He is and what lengths He has taken to love us.

We should allow the Scriptures to challenge us to act on who Jesus is today—exalted to the right hand of the Father and dwelling within us and through us by the power of His Holy Spirit. Jesus is Lord.

> **Expected disappointment causes us to approach the Bible from an earthbound, carnal viewpoint. Limitless hope, however, enables us to encounter God in the pages of the Bible and apply His words in such a way that Jesus is revealed all around us.**

Endnotes:

1. The subject and scope of this book does not allow for an adequate analysis or list of these historical events, but there are plenty of authors and teachers who have detailed them for the Church.

2. Much of Warfield's arguments are examined in the 1993 book, *On the Cessation of the Charismata: The Protestant Polemic on Post-Biblical Miracles,* by Jon Mark Ruthven, Professor Emeritus, Regent University School of Divinity. The second edition (2008) is currently available as a free PDF online at http://www.jon-ruthven.org/cessation.pdf.

3. **Here are the 46 passages that treat suffering positively and pertain to persecution:** Matthew 16:21; 17:12; Mark 8:31; 9:12; Luke 9:22; 17:25; 22:15; 24:26; Acts 3:18; 5:41; 9:16; 17:3; 26:23; Romans 5:3; 8:17-18; 2 Corinthians 1:5-7; 11:23-33; Ephesians 3:13; Philippians 1:29; 3:10; Colossians 1:24; 1 Thessalonians 1:6; 2:2; 2:14; 2 Thessalonians 1:5; 2 Timothy 1:8; 1:12; 2:3; 2:9; 3:10-12; Hebrews 2:9-10; 2:18; 5:8; 10:32-34; 13:12; James 5:10; 1 Peter 1:6; 1:11; 2:19-23; 3:14-18; 4:1; 4:12-19; 5:1; 5:9-10; Revelation 1:9; and 2:10. **And here are the 18 cases the treat it negatively, referring to sickness, disease, or calamity:** Matthew 4:24; 8:6; 15:22; 17:15; Mark 5:26-34; Luke 4:38; 14:2; Acts 7:11; 28:8; 1 Thessalonians 5:9; Jude 1:7; Revelation 2:22; and 9:5.

    For a more thorough examination of suffering (specifically the Greek word "*astheneia*"), see Chapter One, "Was Paul's Thorn in the Flesh an Eye Problem?" in my book, *Spiritual Tweezers: Removing Paul's Thorn in the Flesh and Other False Objections to God's Will for Healing.* This book is available wherever books are sold and at SupernaturalTruth.com.

4. Does this mean that God cannot use sickness and disease to strengthen character? No. But since we don't see it used this way in Jesus' ministry, it is clearly not God's preference. One could argue that this is what happened when Saul was blinded for three days after his encounter with Jesus on the road to Damascus. Nevertheless, he was still healed. And if we only have one possible case of it throughout many documented miracles, we must accept that this is the exception rather than the rule. Jesus only did what He saw

His Father doing; and if the Father was making people sick to build their character, then that's what Jesus would have gone around doing. But He didn't. Instead, Jesus "went around doing good and healing all who were under the power of the devil, because God was with him." (See Acts 10:38.) Many of us treat sickness and disease as though it is the only tool available for God to use. My encouragement to you is that we not limit God. He is far more creative than that and can come up with much better ways to shape character!

Chapter 8:

Limitless Hope and Evangelism

Pastor Paul Basuule Habib was working with an influential pastor in southeastern Uganda, planting churches all over the region and enjoying his life in the city. Then God called him to plant a church in the rural village of Wanenga—an area known for violence and drunkenness.

Pastor Paul left his home while still a very young man, found a place to build a small mud hut, and started his church in a "shed" made of sticks and banana leaves. The church consisted of him and three other Christians. The four crammed inside the little shed week after week to worship Jesus and study the Word.

Attempts were made to take his life. He was

arrested and questioned. He was persecuted regularly. He had confrontations with witchdoctors. The stories are amazing, but what is particularly impressive is that he has stayed in that same village for almost 20 years at the time of this writing.

Wanenga is a different place today. Violence and crime have essentially disappeared. Many of the people who used to persecute Pastor Paul now attend his church. And every witchdoctor in Wanenga has either died, moved away, or converted to Christianity. Today, *Wanenga Christ the Healer Church* is a large wood and mud structure with a metal roof. About 250 people call the church home with many more in the satellite churches he has planted.

What possesses a man to enter a city with so much spiritual darkness and devote his life to such a task? I believe the answer is limitless hope. People asked him, "Why would you waste your time in the bush? Why not use your spiritual gifts in the city where all the people are?"

Pastor Paul would simply answer, "Because God did not call me to the city." He knew that he could be successful in the city, but he valued his relationship with God more than the applause of man.

I spent half a month living in Pastor Paul's home during October of 2011, and I saw a man who was utterly consistent with this assertion. He cares for widows and orphans. He loves the poor. And he has devoted his life to spreading the Gospel in obscure regions without any significant fanfare or recognition.

Pastor Paul wasn't content to stay comfortable in the city. There were enough churches there. Rather, he needed to forsake everything and find the people who needed Jesus most desperately.

> *Limitless hope causes us to naturally live the Gospel and look for opportunities to express it clearly. Expected disappointment causes us to merely live a good life and "hope" people might ask us about it.*

The latter is what many Christians tend to do. We tend to spend our efforts figuring out the least we can do for Jesus rather than throwing ourselves completely into our faith and letting God pull back the reigns. Rather than looking for opportunities to share the Gospel and allowing God to stop us (like Paul in Acts 16:6), we look for opportunities to entertain ourselves while telling God that He's welcome to interrupt those plans if He likes.

We are soldiers sent to the frontlines who are sitting in our camp and commenting about how wonderful it is to be soldiers. Every now and then, one of our fellow soldiers goes out into the battle and returns with amazing stories of victory. The rest of us stay sitting in the camp, marveling at what that person experienced. "I wonder why I never have experiences like that? I sure wish God would send me to do something amazing."

Have you forgotten? You were sent to the frontlines of battle! Why are you waiting for another commission? The King has already commanded us to go!

We tend to look for the path of least resistance. When water follows the path of least resistance, it takes a very long time to produce changes. It gradually erodes at nearby surfaces until they're smooth. But the change is generally only surface-level. On the other hand, when something like a flash-flood or tsunami occurs, the torrent of water moves with too much speed and too much volume to merely follow the path of least resistance. Instead, it plows through everything. More than surface-level issues are changed. Trees are uprooted. Cars and trucks are thrown. Buildings are demolished.

First John 3:8 says that the reason Jesus came to earth was to destroy the devil's work. As ambassadors of Christ, we share this same mandate. If we're just "good Christians," then we'll visit people in the hospital and make them feel loved. If we're just "good Christians," then we'll mow our neighbor's lawn or shovel snow from their driveway as an expression of kindness. If we're just "good Christians," then we might gradually erode away at the surface until the person decides they want to change. But change into what? Mediocrity begets mediocrity.

If, however, we embrace our roles as commissioned soldiers—if we choose to move forward with the authority and power that have been granted to us—then things will change. The people we visit in the hospital will be healed. We'll stick around after mowing the neighbor's lawn and prophesy truth into their homes—possibly leading them to Christ. Rather than gradually eroding at the surface, we bring people to a crisis of faith—a point of decision. We place before them life and death, and we urge them to choose life.

Be Empowered by the Holy Spirit!

Many people thought I was crazy the day I decided to travel to Uganda. Two different men had invited me—one of whom I was certain was a scam artist (and he was), and the other of whom I wasn't sure. I had only met this other man through e-mail. But I knew I had to go, and the Holy Spirit wasn't stopping me. Much to the contrary, I felt like He was encouraging me! I reasoned in my mind that even if I was walking into a scam, it was only because God intended to save the scammers.

I traveled alone. There was nothing safe about it. But I knew that I had already been commissioned to go, and I knew that the Holy Spirit approved. This was the only assurance I had. I knew no one in Uganda except for Jesus, and that was sufficient.

Let me be clear that I'm not trying to guilt-trip you into doing the same thing. Putting your life on the line for Jesus is great, but we have to be sensitive to the Holy Spirit and know His voice. If we don't know His voice, then we won't know when He is telling us to stop or to change our plans. If you're not yet in a place where you have an active, dialogue-based, empowered relationship with the Holy Spirit, then don't go anywhere! This is why Jesus put the Great Commission "on hold" until the believers were "clothed with power from on high." He instructed His disciples not to go anywhere or do anything until they received power from the Holy Spirit. (See Luke 24:49 and Acts 1:4-5.)

I'm told that in some branches of the Chinese underground house church movement, the believers won't allow a new Christian to leave until they have been baptized in the Holy Spirit—not because they're spiritual fanatics but because they know that the person may be killed if they aren't led by the Spirit on their journey home. This lifestyle of being filled with the Holy Spirit is absolutely vital.

Until you have entered this dynamic relationship with Him, don't even share the Gospel with your next-door neighbor. Jesus' emphasis on this Baptism in the Holy Spirit is significant. In fact, it seems to imply that your personal empowerment is even more important than your neighbor's salvation. Why? Because if you launch into evangelism without this empowerment, then you'll be distracted from seeking the Spirit's power! And if you're distracted from Him, then you'll never receive His empowerment, which means your entire life will have less of an impact than God intends. Furthermore, the message you preach will be devoid of this empowerment theme, which means you will make disciples who are not empowered.

You cannot give what you do not have. There's an old adage in evangelism that says, "What you win people with, you win them to." Jesus doesn't intend for powerless Christians to win people to powerless Christianity. He intends for a Spirit-filled Church to multiply like wildfire throughout the earth!

If, on the other hand, you begin with seeking and receiving the Holy Spirit's empowerment, then your efforts in evangelism will be far more successful (and they usually won't seem like "efforts" at all). I like to say that the Baptism in the Holy Spirit is not what secures your ticket to heaven (salvation did that), but it sure does help you bring other people with you!

Limitless hope is dependent upon the empowerment of the Holy Spirit. A life of limitless hope is impossible apart from His life-saturating presence! But when we expect disappointment, we assume that the Pentecostal/Charismatic experience will not bring any meaningful change or improvement.

I believe the fault for this misconception generally

lies in the hands of today's Pentecostal and Charismatic Christians—at least in my home-nation of America. In many nations of the world, Spirit-filled Christianity is the fastest growing, most effective, and most revered; but here in America, typical "Evangelical Christians" barely tolerate us, and society at large considers us to be, at best, weird or, at worst, deceived.

The problem, I believe, is that our only identifying marker has for a long time been nothing more than speaking in tongues (and perhaps some weird manifestations like falling over or shaking), which I admit is weird to anyone who hasn't experienced it. For various reasons, we as a movement gradually drifted from demonstrative spiritual gifts such as healing and miracles. Thus, many Christians don't see any value in the Baptism in the Holy Spirit. They look at such believers and see nothing more than what they already have—except, of course, for the ability to "babble nonsense," fall over, and maybe feel goose bumps.

I'm not downplaying speaking in tongues. I speak in tongues all the time! All I'm trying to do is show what those on the outside see and then move us into purpose. The devil has succeeded in shifting our focus away from the Gospel's impact on the physical realm. We cannot allow the Baptism in the Holy Spirit to be divorced from the mission of God!

The Spirit's Work Within Us and Upon Us

Many have suggested that the evidence of the Spirit's work is spiritual fruit and character development. In a sense, they're right, but only in part. While these are great and necessary things that the Holy Spirit does, they aren't the purpose of His empowerment.

When a person comes to salvation, they receive the Holy Spirit as a seal upon their hearts—a guarantee of their eternal security. (See 2 Corinthians 1:22, Ephesians 1:13 and 4:30.) This particular work of the Holy Spirit is sufficient for salvation, character development, holiness, purity, and generally living the Christian life.

But this is only what the Holy Spirit does within us. There is more that He wants to do.

After Jesus rose from the dead, He appeared to His disciples many times during a period of forty days. On one occasion, we read about what I have already told you—that Jesus told His disciples not to leave the city, but rather to wait for the promised Holy Spirit. A casual reading of the book of Acts shows clearly that the day the Holy Spirit was poured out upon the church was the Day of Pentecost. This was ten days after Jesus ascended into heaven.

What many often miss is that Jesus already gave the Holy Spirit before He ascended:

> **John 20:19-22 –** On the evening of that first day of the week, when the disciples were together, with the doors locked for fear of the Jewish leaders, Jesus came and stood among them and said, "Peace be with you!" After He said this, He showed them His hands and side. The disciples were overjoyed when they saw the Lord.
>
> Again Jesus said, "Peace be with you! As the Father has sent Me, I am sending you." And with that He breathed on them and said, "Receive the Holy Spirit…"

I have to believe that if the resurrected Jesus literally breathed on me and said, "Receive the Holy Spirit," that something would have happened! I'm convinced that at this moment the disciples received the first "born-again" experience, which Jesus had purchased through His death and resurrection. The Holy Spirit entered their lives with resurrection life. If any of them happened to die before the Day of Pentecost (when the Holy Spirit came with power), I believe their eternity was already secure in Christ—sealed by the Holy Spirit.

Now that the Holy Spirit had taken up residence within the disciples, He would begin the work of sanctification—producing spiritual fruit in their lives and conforming them into the likeness of Christ. But even though the disciples had already received the Holy Spirit prior to Jesus' ascension, Jesus still commanded them to wait until they were "clothed with power from on high." (See Luke 24:49.) The Spirit's work "within" them was sufficient for their own salvation, but the mission of saving others would require the Spirit's work "upon" them.

> **Acts 1:8 –** But you will receive power when the Holy Spirit comes **on** you; and you will be My witnesses in Jerusalem, and in all Judea and Samaria, and to the ends of the earth." (emphasis added)

Biblically speaking, salvation and the Baptism in the Holy Spirit are two different things. Acts 8:14-17 tells us about the Samaritan believers who had been baptized in water after believing the Gospel, but they had not yet received the Holy Spirit. Verse 16 specifically indicates that the Holy Spirit had not yet come "on" any of them, but they had indeed been baptized in the name of Jesus. They believed the message and were saved, but they had not yet been empowered.

Conversely, in Acts 10:44-48, we read about some who were baptized in the Holy Spirit prior to being baptized in water. While Peter was still preaching, these people came to believe the message. And as if to imply that the Jesus simply couldn't wait to empower these new Gentile believers, He baptized them in the Holy Spirit without anyone laying hands on them.

Notice the use of the word "on" in reference to the Holy Spirit's work, and then notice the signs accompanying His work upon the new believers:

> **Acts 10:44-46 –** While Peter was still speaking these words, the Holy Spirit came on all who heard the message. The circumcised believers who had come with Peter were astonished that the gift of the Holy Spirit had been poured out even on Gentiles. For they heard them speaking in tongues and praising God…

Peter's next step was to form the logical conclusion that this proved God's approval of the new Gentile Christians, and so he arranged for them to be baptized in water as well.

Furthermore, have a look at what happened when the Apostle Paul encountered twelve Ephesian believers:

> **Acts 19:2-6 –** [Paul] asked them, "Did you receive the Holy Spirit when you believed?" They answered, "No, we have not even heard that there is a Holy Spirit."

So Paul asked, "Then what baptism did you receive?"

"John's baptism," they replied.

Paul said, "John's baptism was a baptism of repentance. He told the people to believe in the one coming after him, that is, in Jesus." On hearing this, they were baptized in the name of the Lord Jesus. When Paul placed his hands on them, the Holy Spirit came on them, and they spoke in tongues and prophesied.

Again, they spoke in tongues and prophesied in reaction to the Spirit coming "on" them.

Salvation and the baptism in the Holy Spirit are two different experiences because they have two different purposes and affect us two different ways. Salvation happens when the Holy Spirit comes within us, and empowerment happens when the Holy Spirit comes upon us. Salvation is all about you, whereas the Holy Spirit's power is all about others.

Yes, you can evangelize the lost without this Baptism. Many do. But they have limited effectiveness, and they do not produce empowered disciples. Only those who are already on fire can spread fire.

The Lord wants us to seek this secondary work of the Spirit because He wants to give us an opportunity to admit our own inadequacy and desperately cry out for His empowerment. Seeking empowerment does not require that we be "desperate" for the Holy Spirit—He already dwells within us in His fullness, without any limitation. (See John 3:34.) Seeking empowerment is about being desperate to accomplish the mission in partnership with God. And that requires power—an overflow of the indwelling Spirit.

If you think you don't need this baptism, then you are essentially rejecting God Himself. You're saying that the work of the Spirit within you is sufficient and now you can do the work of the Gospel in your own strength. To seek the baptism, however, is to say, "Thank You for transforming my life and making me a new creation. Thank You for planting the seed of Christ in me so that I can grow in character and holiness. But I want to spread this life to others, and I know that the only way to do this is to be saturated with You, both inside and out. I need more than Your indwelling presence. I need Your active empowerment."

It is the same Holy Spirit who enters a person at salvation as it is who clothes a person with power during this secondary experience. The difference is that at salvation, the Holy Spirit comes to live within you (internally), whereas at the baptism in the Holy Spirit, He overflows to clothe you with power (externally).

Empowered to Shine

When Jesus said in Acts 1:5 that the disciples would be "baptized in the Holy Spirit," the Greek word He used for "baptize" means to completely immerse something. It is the same word used when referring to cloth that has been soaked in dye. It implies total, transformative saturation. Jesus was essentially saying that it's not enough to merely have the Holy Spirit within you—people need to see Him on the outside too.

Purely for the sake of illustration (and not for theological significance) I like to say that if He's within you, then He can effectively influence your heart; but if He wants to touch anyone through you, He has to push His way through your imperfect flesh. On the other hand, if you are saturated with His presence—clothed with His power on the outside—then He doesn't have to push His way through flesh. He is readily accessible to the world.

Being saturated with the Holy Spirit doesn't make you perfect. Consider the Apostle Peter who—though baptized in the Holy Spirit—was far from perfect. Even after he received this empowerment, Paul had to publicly rebuke him for allowing Jewish laws and customs to be imposed on Christians. (See Galatians 2:11-21.) Nevertheless, the Holy Spirit had so saturated Peter that people only needed to get into physical proximity to him, and they would be healed! (See Acts 5:15.) He didn't even have to touch them!

Many Christians are content to live with expectations of disappointment. They preach the Gospel without demonstrations of Christ's power, and the results are limited. Such people often become jaded and gradually expect less and less from their ministry efforts—especially in evangelism. They blame their ineffectiveness on the darkness of the world's culture rather than taking responsibility and looking for solutions. If you think that the solution to your ineffectiveness is an earthly culture that looks more like Jesus, then you don't have faith in God; you have faith in culture.

John talked about the dangers of loving the world and the things of the world. (See 1 John 2:15.) He said that this happens when we give in to the lust of the eyes, the lust of the flesh, and the pride of life. One of the things our flesh lusts after is an over-abundance of comfort, and there are many overly-comfortable Christians in the world.

Likewise, the pride of life often makes us think that we're the only ones who matter (content to have the Holy Spirit within us for our own sake and perhaps even seeking empowerment but still for our own sake instead of for the lost and dying world around us).

"Loving the world" is not limited to living a life of sin or selfishness. We are equally as guilty of loving the world if we believe that the success of any aspect of the Christian life is dependent on the condition of the world.

For example, If we say that we can't live free from anger because the people in the world are so horrible to us, then we are putting our faith in the world, not God. If we say that we can't live free from lust because of the way most men and women dress, then we are putting our faith in the world, not God. If we say that we are ineffective in evangelism because the culture or the political environment is so dark, then we are putting our faith in the world, not God. This is love for the world, plain and simple; and John says that it proves that the love of the Father is not in us.

Don't wait for the world to change so that your Christian life can be easier. Live your Christianity in a way that changes the world.

> **Isaiah 60:1-3 –** Arise, shine, for your light has come, and the glory of the LORD rises upon you. See, darkness covers the earth and thick darkness is over the peoples, but the LORD rises upon you and His glory appears over you. Nations will come to your light, and kings to the brightness of your dawn.

Limitless hope is not intimidated by darkness in

the earth or thick darkness covering the people. Limitless hope expects the light of God's empowerment—the fiery glory of His presence—to overcome the darkness. I've never known a light bulb to chicken out because a room was too dark. And Jesus said that you are the light of the world. (See Matthew 5:14.)

We must be saturated with the Holy Spirit—not merely so that we can speak in tongues but so that we can shine brightly in this world through acts of love and demonstrations of power and authority. The Baptism in the Holy Spirit is necessary. It is vital. I make no apologies for emphasizing its value.

If you have received salvation, then the Holy Spirit dwells within you. But if you have not yet experienced a lifestyle in which His power and presence are actively demonstrated through you, then you have reason to seek something more. I plead with you: Cease all ministry activity until you are clothed with power from on high!

That may sound like a bold statement, and it is! But if you think it means you won't be sharing the Gospel for a few weeks, then I'm afraid you're expecting disappointment.

> Limitless hope expects to receive the Holy Spirit's power immediately upon asking. Expected disappointment assumes that God is reluctant, and it will take a long time.

Seek the Lord. Ask Jesus to baptize you in the Holy Spirit right now. Allow Him to saturate your physical body, both inside and out. Expect an encounter with God's power right where you are. Let the Holy Spirit overflow through your speech to produce an intimate language—enabling you to commune with God in a whole new way.[1]

Then arise. Shine. Your light has come. Don't be intimidated by darkness. Rather, go. Take the message of the Gospel to the darkest regions of society as you remain sensitive to the Holy Spirit.

Preaching is Not Overrated—Just Misunderstood

Many Christians have grown disenchanted with preaching the Gospel. They don't want to be considered "Bible-thumpers." They don't want to offend people. Really, what they don't want is the cost of following Jesus. They truly believe that they have noble motives in why they are so reserved with their faith, but the truth is that those so-called "noble motives" were planted in their minds by demons, and their carnal nature saw an escape route.

Our flesh doesn't like to die. It doesn't like to surrender. So when our flesh sees something that looks like a "good Christian excuse," it lunges for it. Our flesh is always looking for a justification for its dominance when in reality the only justification with any value (which is found through Jesus' sacrifice) is found when we consider our flesh to be dead.

The problem is not with preaching. The problem is with our methods of preaching. We think that preaching has to look a certain way. We imagine standing on a soapbox on the street corner.

I believe there are two reasons for this. First, there

are those in history who, led by the Spirit, actually preached on street corners and successfully led massive revivals. Consider, for instance, William Booth and the early days of the Salvation Army. The second reason, I believe, is that our fear of public speaking has caused us to relegate this form of ministry to professional clergy. As a result, our understanding of the word "preach" is based on the 45-minute discourse of a Sunday morning church service.

If that's what it means to preach, then I can understand why so many Christians are intimidated by the notion.

Yet preaching is absolutely necessary!

> **Romans 10:14 –** How, then, can they call on the One they have not believed in? And how can they believe in the One of whom they have not heard? And how can they hear without someone preaching to them?

Preaching doesn't have to look like a Sunday meeting—and it doesn't have to look like William Booth or any other historical "hero of the faith." Yes, it *can* look those ways, but it doesn't have to.

You have the liberty to be creative within the constraints of obeying the voice of the Holy Spirit and loving people. If both those things are happening, then you can preach in any way you like—through music, artwork, questions, well-timed comments, or general conversation. Preaching is nothing more than conveying the message of the Gospel in a clear, understandable way.

I loved attending college—not simply because I enjoy learning but because it opened so many easy opportunities for well-timed preaching. The easiest place to preach was my speech class, where I turned every assignment into an outlet for expressing my faith. When my first assignment was to tell about the three most influential people in my life, the third person I talked about was the Holy Spirit (I figured that would be less cliché and might grab more attention than saying "Jesus"). When a group of us were assigned to host a panel discussion about marriage, I presented the Christian perspective. Every assignment revealed Jesus, and as a result I spent many after-class hours having conversations in the hallway with people who wanted to know more. One particular man spent nearly every day asking me questions—specifically about the Holy Spirit.

Later I took an anthropology class. Here I didn't have the opportunity to speak in front of everyone, so I looked for relational opportunities. I looked for the people who seemed to have the wackiest beliefs. Every week after class, I would hang out with a young man and a young woman. The man was dabbling in Hinduism and Buddhism, and the woman had a self-invented religion that included paganism, Wicca, and various other perspectives. I would ask them about their beliefs and why they believed them. Naturally, this would lead them to return the question.

As far as I know, the young lady never changed. The young man, on the other hand, came to Christ and has now been a part of my life for over a decade. He now has a Master's degree in Pastoral Ministry and has helped plant a church in Garden City, Michigan.

A few years after leading that friend to the Lord, I attended an online university. After boldly writing about

Jesus in the first three classes, my academic advisor suddenly changed my course requirements to include a class he apparently thought I needed. It was called "Critical Thinking." I loved it! In every example I was asked to provide, I used Biblical "apologetics"—logical, scientific, and history-based arguments for the validity of Christian belief. Even the professor couldn't refute the cases I laid out in my assignments. I aced the class.

We need to look for any opportunity to share the Gospel—even if it seems like the worst possible moment. In Acts 4:1-21, Peter and John found themselves on trial in front of the same people who murdered Jesus only a few months earlier. If ever there was a time to keep their mouths shut and be discrete with their faith, this was it. But Peter preached boldly to them and was not afraid of the consequences. He refused to be intimidated by mere men. In fact, Peter and John went right back to the temple and began preaching all over again.

Likewise, consider what happened to Paul and Silas when they were imprisoned for preaching and demonstrating the Gospel:

> **Acts 16:25-32 –** About midnight Paul and Silas were praying and singing hymns to God, and the other prisoners were listening to them. Suddenly there was such a violent earthquake that the foundations of the prison were shaken. At once all the prison doors flew open, and everyone's chains came loose. The jailer woke up, and when he saw the prison doors open, he drew his sword and was about to kill himself because he thought the prisoners had escaped. But Paul shouted,

"Don't harm yourself! We are all here!"

The jailer called for lights, rushed in and fell trembling before Paul and Silas. He then brought them out and asked, "Sirs, what must I do to be saved?"

They replied, "Believe in the Lord Jesus, and you will be saved—you and your household." Then they spoke the word of the Lord to him and to all the others in his house.

First, Paul and Silas were presenting the Gospel to the other prisoners through prayer and song. They literally had a captive audience! That part was easy; the hard part came after the earthquake. If I were Paul, I would have probably tried to sneak away quietly. It would have been easy to let the jailer kill himself. But Paul took this awkward opportunity to preach the Gospel to the jailer and later his entire household.

> Limitless hope knows what it means to be unashamed of the Gospel. Limitless hope sees the worst possible moment as a golden opportunity. Limitless hope expects people to respond to the Gospel and isn't intimidated by the rank or influence of the listeners. Expected disappointment, however, avoids confrontation, risk, and personal cost.

Romans 1:16a – For I am not ashamed of the gospel, because it is the power of God that brings salvation to everyone who believes…

Offensive "Good News"

> **Limitless hope causes us to share the Gospel every time we see an opportunity. Expected disappointment causes us to fear offending or making people feel uncomfortable.**

Suppose I were a structural engineer who inspected buildings for safety hazards. Now imagine that I walked into an office building and saw that the entire structure was going to collapse and kill all the people inside. Admittedly, I don't know when it will collapse— perhaps five minutes from now or five years from now— but it would be evil of me to walk away and say nothing about it.

On the other hand, if I begin announcing the imminent destruction, I'll likely upset a lot of people. Some might be in the middle of important business transactions. Some might be discussing a merger with a larger corporation. Some might be simply eating their lunch, annoyed that I would interrupt their routine. The owner of the building would be upset about the potential cost of repairs or loss of renters. And since there's no proof (at least to the untrained eye) that the building will collapse soon, no one has any interest in allowing me to interrupt their work.

The flow of life taking place in that office building looks very important to the people caught up within it. And frankly, if all I do is announce that the building is going to collapse, most of them will probably continue with business as usual—unless, of course, I start waving around credentials. If they see that I am indeed a structural engineer, then they might take notice and believe me.

Maybe.

It's not guaranteed, but credentials do help.

Jesus had credentials too. Check out what Peter preached to the onlookers on the day of Pentecost:

> **Acts 2:22** – Fellow Israelites, listen to this:
> Jesus of Nazareth was a man accredited by
> God to you by miracles, wonders and signs,
> which God did among you through Him, as
> you yourselves know.

In a very real way, we as Christians are aware of a very real danger, and we exist in a world full of people who don't know about it. Some may heed your words, but many will want some sort of proof that you actually know what you're talking about. In the Kingdom our credentials are healings, miracles, and gifts of the Holy Spirit.

> **John 10:37-38** – [Jesus said,] "Do not believe
> Me unless I do the works of My Father. But if
> I do them, even though you do not believe
> Me, believe the works, that you may know
> and understand that the Father is in Me, and I
> in the Father."

When Jesus was confronted with unbelief, He pointed to the power of God. He validated His words. This is yet another reason why we so desperately need the power of the Holy Spirit. In today's culture, talk is cheap. Every direction a person turns, he or she is bombarded with advertisements and persuasive arguments. Words are necessary for sharing the Gospel, but they are not always sufficient. Even among the Jewish people who knew the stories of God's miracles in the past, Jesus knew this to be true. He sent His disciples with credentials.

> **Matthew 10:7-8** – "As you go, proclaim this message: 'The kingdom of heaven has come near.' Heal the sick, raise the dead, cleanse those who have leprosy, drive out demons. Freely you have received; freely give."

If miracles were necessary then, they are certainly necessary now! Miracles bring people to a point of decision. If all you share are words, then a person has the liberty to go home, consider those words, talk them over with a friend, or even forget what was said. But if the person was blind, and you said, "Eyes, open in Jesus' name," and now the person sees—it's hard for them to argue their way out of that experience. It's hard for that person's entire family to argue out of that experience! Encounters with the Kingdom force people into a crisis of faith. A decision becomes mandatory. You can embrace this message of love or you can run away from it, but you can't be indifferent. You can't pretend you never knew about it.

The Gospel ("Good News") is sometimes offensive. That may seem strange, but notice that immediately after Jesus offered miracles as His credentials, verse 39 says, "Again they tried to seize him, but he escaped their grasp." In general, people don't like good news. Actually, they do like good news; what they don't like is being forced into a decision by that news.

To the people in the building that is about to collapse, the warning of a structural engineer should be good news to those who are about to be spared from death. But if it interrupts important business, then it only frustrates people. The people have to choose between their current activities and living a longer life.

In Chapter Two, I told the story of an evangelistic meeting in a Muslim village overrun with witchdoctors. Before the meeting, I was scheduled to train pastors in the church across the street. But this being a church plant in an unreached village, the only pastors who came were the three or four who braved the muddy trails and came from other villages.

Since the church building only consisted of sticks and tarps, our music and singing rolled through the dirt streets of the town. A school was nearby, and since it was a Muslim fasting day, the children had nothing to do on their lunch break. Naturally, they ran to the church to see what all the commotion was about.

My meeting consisted of five Christians and about twenty Muslim school children between the ages of seven and sixteen. Obviously, I changed the focus of the meeting from training pastors to preaching to the children.

I told them about the goodness and the love of Jesus Christ, including His death and resurrection. Then I said, "If you don't know Jesus, raise your hand." The truth is, I knew none of them had a relationship with Jesus; I just wanted to see how they would respond. One little girl must have been caught off-guard because she threw her hand up.

"Would you like to know Him?" I asked.

The little girl glanced at her classmates, realized they hadn't raised their hands, and shook her head "no" as she yanked her hand back down into her lap.

"How about this," I said to the children. "How

about I show you how good and wonderful Jesus is?"

The kids smiled and sat on the edges of their seats, wondering what was coming next.

"If you have a problem in your body—like a sickness, an injury, a disease, or some other pain—and if you want that problem to go away, then come up here."

Six children lined up across the front—one of whom was the little girl who had raised her hand. One by one, each child was completely healed. As I was praying for them, a second crowd of children came running to the church. When the last child in the line was healed, I looked up, and every bench was filled. A large crowd of children were standing and craning their necks to see. There must have been forty or more.

"Did you just see that Jesus healed your friends?" I asked. "If you just came and you need to be healed too, come up here to the front."

Seven more children came to the front, and every one of them was also healed.

When the children sat down, I shared the Gospel once more. I told the children about the cost—including the reality that many of them might be thrown out of their homes for believing in Jesus. Then I made my second invitation.

About ten children came forward for salvation in front of all their friends. One of those children was the little girl who had raised her hand before and received healing in the first line of children.

The goodness of God is a wonderful message, but it is offensive. It wasn't politically correct for me to tell a group of Muslim children that Jesus Christ, God's Son, died on the cross and rose again so that they could have a relationship with God. It wasn't politically correct to tell them that Muhammad didn't demonstrate God's love and that the Koran wasn't telling them the truth about Jesus. Such words are offensive.

Furthermore, the message itself was not enough to bring the children to a point of belief. But after they saw the miracles—after they and their friends were healed—I couldn't talk some of them out of following Jesus! The message was just as offensive, and the risk of believing it was still just as real; but suddenly Jesus could be seen as a King worth following. The words came to life. God's love was tangible, and it convinced one girl in a way that mere words could not.

Combining Works with the Word

If you can't back up your message with some form of demonstration of Gods love and power (whether miracles, healings, encouragement, service, sacrificial giving, prophecy, etc.), then stop preaching and run to the Lord for empowerment. When you think you have received it, go back out and try preaching again. If there's still no power, return to seeking. Cry out to God in desperation for power from His Spirit. "Eagerly desire spiritual gifts." (See 1 Corinthians 12:31 and 14:1.) Crave the demonstration of the Gospel as a normal experience. Spare nothing in your pursuit of representing Jesus well. Let the Holy Spirit transform you inside, and let Him empower you to transform the world around you.

Again, preaching is not overrated—just misunderstood and often misapplied. Preaching must come with power. But the opposite is also true. If all we have is miracles but no message, then we are wasting everyone's time. Sure, we may have alleviated a person's physical problem, but we haven't offered them anything of eternal value. The message of the Gospel and the works of the Father must go hand-in-hand.

We must constantly look for opportunities. Some opportunities start with the message, and some opportunities start with works. The works may be profound (like a miraculous healing) or they may seem mundane (like raking dead leaves in your neighbor's yard). Either way, follow up with the message. Other opportunities start with the message—perhaps through conversation or a question. Follow up with proof that addresses the felt-needs of the person. (For example, if you talk about Jesus to your waitress or waiter at a restaurant, you had better leave a big tip!)

One of my favorite opportunities to seize is when someone starts complaining around me. Rather than letting them rant forever, I listen long enough to show that I care and then say, "Tell you what. I truly feel bad for you, but I know someone who can actually help you. How about I pray for you right now, and we see what God does." Then I pray. If I'm ministering healing, I have the person test it out right away. Sometimes I minister nine or ten times before we see results (I'll explain more about that in Chapter Eleven). If I'm praying for something like a financial miracle or a family issue, then I'll follow up as often as I can until there is change. If I'm able to give, I make myself part of the solution.

It is entirely possible to move any conversation into a spiritual discussion. Whenever I meet a new person and I know they're not a believer, I like to ask, "What's your biggest question about life?" This usually catches a person off guard, but they often come up with something. I listen and then ask if they'd like an answer to their question. Another favorite questions is, "What's your history with spirituality and things like church?" This often helps us deal with any wounds that the person received from people who misrepresented God in the past.

Look for an opportunity to ask a probing question. Look for an opportunity to pray. Look for an opportunity to share a testimony. Look for an opportunity to minister healing. If you actively look for opportunities, you will find them.

> **Limitless hope expects opportunities to appear every day. Expected disappointment waits only for divine appointments.**

How Many are Allowed to be Saved?

There seem to be two different perspectives on salvation trends in the last days. One group expects that salvations will increase while the other expects them to become less and less common. The first group points to Scriptures like Isaiah 9:7, which states that Jesus' kingdom will continue to increase without end. The second group points to verses like Matthew 24:12, which talks about the increase of wickedness in the "last days."

Setting aside age-old disagreements about "eschatology" (the study of what happens in the end), I personally think it's possible for both salvations and wickedness to increase, and that is what I anticipate will happen. In my observation, the people who do not expect the Kingdom to continue multiplying seem to be the ones trying to form excuses for why they aren't personally seeing results in evangelism. As for me, I will not form a theology based on disappointment. I must expect greater things. I must have limitless hope.

So let me ask you a question: How many people are allowed to be saved? I trust you answered "all of them!" After all, Second Peter 3:9 tells us that God does not want anyone to perish. Paul told Timothy that God "wants all people to be saved and to come to a knowledge of the truth." (See 1 Timothy 2:4.) And John 1:7 tells us that God's purpose in sending John the Baptist was so that "all men might believe." God's intent has always been for the salvation of the entire world.

> **1 John 2:2 –** He is the atoning sacrifice for our sins, and not only for ours but also for the sins of the whole world.

Unfortunately this doesn't mean that everyone will automatically be saved. We'd like that, but if it were true, then evangelism would be pointless. Martyrs would have lost their lives in vain. Missionaries would have abandoned their homes and sacrificed lucrative careers in vain.

No, the lake of fire is indeed real, and God doesn't want anyone to go there. Unfortunately His preferred eternity for us requires impossible perfection. But thankfully, with Jesus, there's no such thing as impossible.

I wish it weren't true (and God does too), but people do indeed go to hell.[2] I believe there are two reasons for this tragedy: (1) God has given mankind the gift of free will, and He allows each one to choose the destination of his or her life by receiving or rejecting Him,

185

and (2) we, the Church, could be more effective at presenting Him to the world. One of these problems cannot be changed, but the other is in our hands.

I wonder how many people have already gone to hell because I didn't take my role in Christ seriously. Thankfully, there is no condemnation for those who are in Christ. (See Romans 8:1.) The emotional burden of our failures can be surrendered to Jesus. (See 1 Peter 5:7.) And while I'm not judged by the opportunities I missed, they should still stir me to take my role seriously.

If the Gospel is available to everyone, then we need to take every opportunity we can to share it. If we fail, then we're not condemned; but that shouldn't stop us. Love frees us from the condemnation of the law. If we love the people of the world, then we will share the Gospel with them for their sake—not our own. We therefore do not need to feel guilty for missed opportunities. The love of Christ within us should be sufficient to compel us toward future ministry. Look forward, not backward. (See Philippians 3:13-14.)

Since God doesn't want anyone to go to hell, He will pull out all the stops to demonstrate His love to everyone we approach. For this reason I have tremendous confidence when praying for miracles and ministering healing in the presence of lost people. This, I believe, is why Jesus healed everyone who came to Him. The Father loves to demonstrate His love because He knows that it draws people to Him. His kindness leads us to repentance. (See John 6:44 and Romans 2:4.)

Evangelism with National Vision

While it is true that every person must make an

individual decision to receive Jesus Christ, we still have the privilege of expecting entire nations to be saved. If God truly wants to save everyone, and if He has empowered His people to make that possible, then we should work toward that end. God's idea of national transformation is not found in mere politics. Rather, it is found in the salvation of souls.

> **Limitless hope causes us to pray for entire nations to be saved. Expected disappointment causes us to merely pray that our own country will change its policies to make us more comfortable.**

I am not saying that Christians should not be involved in politics. On the contrary, the Scriptures are full of examples where God-fearing people helped point nations in the right direction by serving in positions of political influence—consider Joseph, Esther, and Daniel, to name a few. These people were intimately involved in political matters, and God's people benefitted.

My point is that we cannot become so focused on earthly matters that we forget about heavenly matters. It is too easy to become discouraged with the sinful direction of a nation and assume that nationwide revival is no longer possible. Such a mindset implies that God is incapable of such a thing.

Do you have limitless hope or not? Do you want to see lives transformed? Or do you merely want to influence enough political laws to ensure that you'll remain comfortable as a mediocre Christian?

Influencing laws and policies is great, but it does not send people to heaven. It might spare people from premature death (consider the ramifications of abortion being made illegal), but it doesn't save anyone for eternity.

The nations of the world where the Gospel is advancing fastest tend to be those that are the most politically hostile to Christians. We must be salt and light in this world while setting our minds on things above (not on earthly things). (See Matthew 5:13-16 and Colossians 3:1-2.) Entire nations can be saved, regardless of their political climate or direction.

All our efforts to influence the natural world are meaningless if they do not have eternity in mind. Jesus should be our focus—and He wants souls. His desire for the nations should stir us to do something. We should love our King enough to do whatever He asks of us.

Remember what the prophet Isaiah said. After commanding God's people to arise and shine, he said, "Nations will come to your light…" (See Isaiah 60:3.) Did God mean that or didn't He? We have to decide whether or not the Bible is true.

Consider what happened in Ephesus after some people had a confrontation with a demon:

> **Acts 19:17-20 –** When this became known to the Jews and Greeks living in Ephesus, they were all seized with fear, and the name of the Lord Jesus was held in high honor. Many of those who believed now came and openly confessed their evil deeds. A number who had practiced sorcery brought their scrolls together and burned them publicly. When they calculated the value of the scrolls, the

total came to fifty thousand drachmas. In this
way the word of the Lord spread widely and
grew in power.

Each "drachma" represented about one day's
wages. Fifty thousand "days wages" were burned up
because an entire city started to fear the Lord. It doesn't
say that everyone came to salvation, but we do see a
significant transformation take place on a regional scale. I
believe the same can happen today.[3]

Again, if you have not yet received the Baptism in
the Holy Spirit (as demonstrated throughout the book of
Acts), then stop everything and seek the Lord until you
have been clothed with power from on high. Find Spirit-
empowered Christians who will lay hands on you and pray
with you.

Then, once you have received His empowerment,
spare nothing to spread the message in whatever ways
possible. Don't let the enemy condemn you for
opportunities missed—simply ask for greater compassion
and greater love. Then move forward. With limitless hope,
expect the message of the Gospel to be followed with
signs and wonders. And do not think in terms of a small
impact; rather, expect entire nations to be saved.

God the Father said to Jesus, "Ask Me for it, and
I'll give you the nations." (See Psalm 2:8.) Jesus has asked
the Father, and we are God's representatives in the earth.
Will we fulfill our Lord's desire?

Matthew 28:19a – Therefore go and make
disciples of all nations...

Endnotes:

1. The focus of this chapter is evangelism, so I have not gone
    into much detail about speaking in tongues. The topic does,
    however, deserve a footnote for those who may have
    questions.

    Personally, I am convinced that "tongues" is a
    supernatural tool that is available to every believer. In Acts
    2:1-4, we discover that God's prototype for the first Church
    was that "all of them…began to speak in other tongues as
    the Spirit enabled them." This came along with the Baptism
    in the Holy Spirit.

    I have noticed three groups of people who argue against
    the idea of every Christian speaking in tongues. First are
    those who simply don't believe in it (but they probably
    aren't reading this book, so I won't address that issue).
    Second are those who believe in it but do not speak in
    tongues themselves. And third are those who do speak in
    tongues but are attempting to avoid offending other
    Christians who do not.

    For the second group, I would like to propose a
    scenario: Suppose a schoolteacher had a class of twenty
    students and brought a big box full of special, brightly-
    sparkling pencils, intending to give one to every student in
    her class. On the first day of the week, one little boy was
    absent, so he did not receive a pencil along with the rest of
    his classmates. The next day, when he came to class, he saw
    everyone with their brand new pencils and realized he didn't
    have one. Would it make any sense for the boy to conclude
    that his teacher never wanted to give him a pencil? Not at
    all! In fact, if you know anything about little boys, he will
    probably demand, "Hey! Where's *my* pencil?" In the same
    way, your lack is not evidence of God's will. Rather, take a
    look at what He has freely given everyone else and realize
    that He wanted you to have the same thing all along! Our
    Father in heaven loves to give the Holy Spirit to those who
    ask Him!

    And for the third group, I would encourage you not to
    apply to your faith the American habit of apologizing for
    abundance. As Westerners, we are reminded to be grateful
    for what we have because we live in a world where not

everyone has the same earthly blessings. Tongues, however, is not an earthly blessing. It is a heavenly blessing, and there is no lack in heaven. God saw fit to bring this empowerment and blessing of tongues the first time with a visible form: "They saw what seemed to be tongues of fire that separated and came to rest on each of them." Fire is not limited in its distribution. There is always enough fire. As long as there is fuel, the fire will spread, and in this case, the fuel was disciples. If you're a disciple, then the flame is for you. There is no lack. You do not need to worry about offending someone by telling them that the flame is for them too. If they're a disciple, then they qualify. This is not a Christmas party at an orphanage where some sponsors send many gifts while other sponsors send none. We're all children of the same loving Father who delights in giving good gifts to those who ask him!

If you're seeking the Baptism in the Holy Spirit, then seek Him as the wonderful, amazing Person that He is. You don't have to seek the tongues. Tongues are just part of the package. Shoes have tongues too, but when you go to the shoe store, you don't ask for a pair of tongues; you ask for a pair of shoes. Ask the Holy Spirit (who already lives inside of you) to overflow from your life so that you can touch the world around you. He'll then give you the sign that you're now empowered for this global mission by having you speak in a language you don't know (either an earthly or a heavenly language). It's just a sign, so don't get hung up on it.

What will it be like? Well, the Holy Spirit won't turn you into a puppet. The fruit of the Spirit includes "self-control." He never takes us over. Rather, He partners with us. "All of them...began to speak in other tongues as the Spirit enabled them." *They* began to speak; then the "other tongues" came as the Spirit enabled. You do the talking, and the Holy Spirit will do the language. Don't be afraid of doing it wrong; simply open your mouth and try. Start with what you think it's supposed to sound like, and let the Holy Spirit take over. You'll know if it's spontaneous or forced.

In Jesus' name, receive the Holy Spirit!

2. I recognize there is a lot of scholarly debate about what hell is and whether it exists or, if it does, whether people suffer

eternally or are burned up and destroyed there. It is beyond the scope of this book to lay out a case for why I believe what I do on this subject, but I feel it necessary to alert more learned readers that I am aware of the debate and have studied all sides.

Unfortunately the word "hell" comes with a lot of cultural baggage, and what most people think of in relation to that word is not likely what it actually is. But it is also beyond the purpose of this book to nuance every use of the word "hell" with disclaimers, descriptions, or obscure theological terminology. If you're the type of person who likes that sort of thing, I simply request that you forgive my simplicity and remain engaged in studying the main point of the text.

3. I wouldn't even limit the national impact of evangelism to mere social impact. I believe an entire nation could actually become Christian.

Think that's crazy? Let me ask you some questions: (1) Can an individual receive salvation? If so, can a husband and wife both be saved? If so, can their entire household be saved? If yes, what about their family plus their neighbors in the house next door. And if so, what about all the neighbors on their street? Is it possible? Of course. What, then, about all the people in their neighborhood? Could all of them be saved? Sure. And if so, what about all the people in their city? If a city can be saved, why not a county or state (as we have them here in the USA)? Yes again. So why not a nation?

If at any point in that progression you jumped off and said one of the steps was impossible, then I pray hope takes deeper root in you as you continue to read. I know the probabilities diminish with each successive step, but possibilities and probabilities are different things. In the Kingdom, while serving a limitless God, we deal less in probabilities and more in possibilities. Keep your mind in that place, and you're sure to see more results in your service of the King.

Chapter 9:

Limitless Hope and Spiritual Gifts

Spiritual gifts (like healing, miracles, encouragement, prophecy, and others) are found throughout the Bible—sometimes in lists with other gifts and sometimes on their own.[1] In short, they are all activities of the Holy Spirit, which means there may even be gifts that aren't mentioned in Scripture. If the Holy Spirit does something in partnership with a human being and beyond their natural skill or ability, it can be considered a gift.

The common thread that ties all the gifts together is a single passage in which Jesus explained how the Holy Spirit would work with believers:

John 16:13-15 – But when He, the Spirit of

truth, comes, He will guide you into all truth. He will not speak on His own; He will speak only what He hears, and He will tell you what is yet to come. **He will bring glory to Me by taking from what is Mine and making it known to you.** All that belongs to the Father is Mine. That is why I said the Spirit will take from what is Mine and make it known to you. (emphasis added)

Spiritual gifts are easy to define. Any time the Holy Spirit takes some aspect of Jesus and makes it known in and through a believer, a spiritual gift has taken place. For example, prophecy happens when the Holy Spirit makes known something that Jesus is saying. Whoever receives this gift from the Holy Spirit is then able to represent Jesus by speaking the message to the intended listeners.

There are many ways that this definition can be expressed. The Holy Spirit can reveal something Jesus knows (that's a "word of knowledge") or make known a nugget of Jesus' wisdom (that's a "word of wisdom"). He can reveal the words Jesus wants to speak (prophecy). He can reveal what Jesus clearly perceives and discerns in the spiritual realm (discerning of spirits). He can reveal the administrative genius of Jesus or His heart of a servant (administration and service).

The Holy Spirit reveals all these aspects of Jesus to the Church (and more), and when we each carry out our unique part in expressing Jesus, we literally act as His Body in the earth. That's why all the major passages about gifts of the Spirit in the Bible are always accompanied by a teaching about us being the body of Christ. Spiritual gifts enable us to become the physical expression of Jesus in the earth as though He were still literally walking among us.

Unfortunately, manmade arguments have crept into the Church that only serve to limit God's power. Rather than embracing spiritual gifts with limitless hope, we limit spiritual gifts by embracing an expectation of disappointment. In this chapter, I want to reverse this devious plan of the enemy. I want to plant seeds of limitless hope and show you what is possible.

Childlike Cravings

Limitless hope causes us to eagerly desire all spiritual gifts. Expected disappointment causes us to think that most gifts are only for other people.

Even though I was raised in an Assemblies of God church where prophecy, tongues, interpretation of tongues, and other spiritual gifts took place, I first started "eagerly desiring" spiritual gifts when I was seventeen-years-old. It began when a woman I knew came to me and prophesied that I would one day prophesy and minister healing to the sick. I went to my youth pastor, and he directed me to a book on spiritual gifts. I started reading and was instantly hooked. The idea that God could use me like the author of that book was mind-blowing.

Previous to reading that book, I thought spiritual gifts were only for special Christians. I thought you had to be somehow seasoned in your Christianity and hyper-mature in Christ before He would ever use you. What I learned was the exact opposite! There are even people in the Bible who demonstrated spiritual gifts without even being true servants of God![2] God isn't looking for people who are super-qualified. He is looking for able vessels with whom to partner.

I learned that as a Christian I have the privilege to "eagerly desire spiritual gifts." (See 1 Corinthians 14:1.) And I noticed that passage emphasized one particular gift: "Follow the way of love and eagerly desire gifts of the Spirit, especially prophecy." As soon as I saw that, I set to work "eagerly desiring" prophecy.

In the original Greek language, the term "eagerly desire" literally means to crave or even lust after something. In other words, spiritual gifts—especially prophecy—are the reason God gave you the capacity to lust. Lust is that deep inner drive which causes you to fixate on a thing and pursue it for your own enjoyment. The devil tries to pervert that inner drive by directing it toward people and the things of this world. But God gave you that capacity so that you would fixate on spiritual gifts and crave them—pursuing these things until your desire is fulfilled, and then longing for more.

Living with my parents at the time, I began spending my entire paycheck every week at the Christian bookstore, buying every book I could find about spiritual gifts and prophecy. I devoured those texts. Every night I begged God for a gift of prophecy. Every day, I wondered if it was the day that I would finally prophesy.

It wasn't long before I spoke my first public prophecy. It was a gift from the Holy Spirit—not earned but bestowed. The intense studying did not enable me to prophesy, but it did train me what to look for and what to expect when that prophecy finally came. The learning process made me eager and ready rather than passive and silent.

I used to attend my Pentecostal church and wonder if the one lady who sat in back would prophesy like she did almost every other week. But when limitless hope overtook my outlook, I began to wonder if I might be the one to speak the words of God that day. As it turned out, I started to prophesy even more often than the usual lady!

God can do the same thing through you. Don't sit around waiting for God to supernaturally take over your body as a sovereign puppeteer. It won't happen. He is looking for willing and able partners who look to Him with childlike faith.

I used to work as a childcare provider at a nursery school (that's actually what my degree is in). During that time, I also often entertained at children's birthday parties—singing songs, making balloon animals, and performing cheap illusions. It's quite comical (and sometimes a little frustrating) when you start asking for volunteers from an audience of children. Almost every child leaps from their seat and waves their arms frantically to gain your attention. And if a child isn't picked, it's as though their entire world has fallen apart.

Even though they might logically understand that not every person can be chosen for a task, children still honestly believe that they *should* and *will* be the one who is chosen.

Children love to be chosen as helpers, but adults love to blend in. Adults are afraid of looking too eager. If we have a desire to participate, we try to be subtle about it. When it comes to the topic of spiritual gifts, this sort of mindset can be crippling. God wants you to "eagerly desire spiritual gifts." And even though it isn't likely that every Christian in a gathering will always demonstrate a particular spiritual gift, a little part of you should have the desire and expectation that you're the one He does want to use. This isn't pride or selfishness (unless you're truly wanting such things for the sake of your own praise and glory). Rather, it is biblical desire. And it is right.

Nothing is Impossible

Jesus told His disciples, "Very truly I tell you, whoever believes in Me will do the works I have been doing, and they will do even greater things than these, because I am going to the Father." (See John 14:12.)

Some have interpreted this scripture to mean that we would do "more" works than Jesus ("greater" in quantity) because there are more of us on the earth to do these works. This interpretation sounds good in theory, but then we read the book of Acts. As I'll show you in a moment, Jesus meant what He said, and the disciples of the first century did things greater than Jesus did.

> Limitless hope believes that Jesus' earthly ministry set the bar low for what is possible. Expected disappointment believes that if Jesus didn't do a particular thing, then neither can we.

Not everything Jesus did during His earthly ministry is recorded in Scripture. (See John 21:25.) However, many scholars would suggest that the most significant things He did are indeed recorded. These acts would be the most memorable—things like raising the dead, touching lepers, casting out a demon the disciples couldn't, and rubbing spit-mud on a blind man's eyes. It is very likely that the things Jesus did that were not recorded were only left out because they seemed too ordinary to the disciples (at least for Jesus). Jesus healed so many people and cast out so many demons that the Gospel writers sometimes made broad, generalized statements about entire crowds coming for ministry.[3] These miracles became "ordinary" because of how common they were.

The reason I'm making this point is because the disciples probably would have remembered if someone was healed by touching Jesus' shadow. They remembered when people touched His clothes and received healing, and I would consider a "shadow-healing" to be even more amazing. Chances are, Jesus never did that; but Peter did. (See Acts 5:15.) Was Peter better than Jesus? Or was Peter simply doing what Jesus said would be possible? We also don't read about Jesus being supernaturally transported from one place to another, but Philip was. (See Acts 8:39-40.) Was Philip better than Jesus? Or was Philip doing what Jesus prophesied?

If we believe that we couldn't possibly do more than Jesus did, then we are discounting His own words. It may seem like humility, but it's actually pride because we are exalting our own opinion above His.

Today, many ministries draw large crowds just like Jesus did. But we don't read about Jesus declaring healing to the entire crowd and having hundreds of people testify of instant results. Yet many ministries today experience this very thing—like Evangelists Reinhard Bonnke and

Daniel Kolenda of *Christ for All Nations*. Tens of millions have been saved and healed in their large, open-air meetings. Are these men disobeying Jesus by doing greater things than He did? Or are they fulfilling His words?

I am convinced that the works of Jesus should be the bare minimum of what I carry in my ministry. First John 2:6 says, "Whoever claims to live in Him must live as Jesus did." Admittedly I haven't walked on water or multiplied food (yet), but that doesn't mean I see these things as impossibilities. If the need arises and the Spirit leads, I know He'll come through. Jesus said that "nothing will be impossible" for those who have faith. (See Matthew 17:20.) Do you believe Him? What do you think the word "nothing" means?

I have a friend who once fixed a lawnmower by laying hands on it and commanding it to be fixed in Jesus' name. I don't remember Jesus fixing lawnmowers. I have another friend who locked her keys in her truck, and after praying, the power-locks popped up on their own (her friend, who witnessed this, received salvation as a result and started attending our church). I don't remember Jesus miraculously unlocking truck doors. I have another friend—a missionary—whose computer, which he needed for ministry, broke. He laid hands on it over and over for a few hours, and suddenly it was able to turn on again without problems. Were these friends of mine dabbling in the occult? Or were they obeying Jesus?

Again, Jesus said nothing would be impossible. Where do we draw the line on that? At what point does your human mind kick into gear and begin to think an idea is crazy? What if I suggested to you that if the need arose, a Christian could possibly fly? Does that bother you? What if I suggested that God could use you to turn vinegar into Coca-Cola? Or what if I suggested that God could enable you to breathe underwater? I'm just dreaming here—I don't have any testimonies to back these ideas up. But does that make them impossible? If these ideas bother you, then it's probably because you think Jesus didn't mean what He said. Jesus said nothing would be impossible. And He said we would do greater works.

Abraham was willing to offer Isaac as a sacrifice because he believed God could raise the dead. What we often don't consider, however, is that Isaac was supposed to be a burnt offering. Abraham believed that God could raise the cremated! "Everything is possible for one who believes." (See Mark 9:23.)

Try to Excel in Spiritual Gifts

> Limitless hope causes us to actively attempt spiritual gifts. Expected disappointment causes us to merely refer people to others who have proven spiritual gifts.

As I mentioned, the same woman who declared that I would one day prophesy also said that God would use me to minister healing. In time, I reached a point where I had been prophesying for several years, but I had not yet seen even one person healed when I prayed for them. To make matters even more difficult, when my grandmother was on her deathbed, she too prophesied: "The Lord is going to make you into a well-known healing evangelist." About five years went by after she passed away, and I still had never seen the slightest inkling that

God had given me such a ministry. I prayed for hundreds of people, and they all stayed the same, became worse, or died.

Some "healing evangelist" I turned out to be!

It wasn't long before I started to expect disappointment. Deferred hope made my heart sick, and I wasn't feasting on the "tree of life" testimony about how God led me to the gift of prophecy. I accepted the possibility that my grandmother and the other woman who prophesied must have been wrong on this one. Grandma was heavily medicated, and the other woman probably ate some bad pizza.

So whenever someone came to me with a physical problem, I had my list of go-to people to whom I would refer the issue. My girlfriend (now wife), Robin, has a remarkable gift of healing. I had seen people healed of incurable diseases when she prayed. I knew God wanted to use her in this, so I sent people her way. Her sister also expressed this gift a number of times, so a couple times I sent people to her. But I knew *I* couldn't heal the sick, so I never even tried.

Eventually, God ambushed me on the topic of healing. To make a long story short, God cornered me into ministering healing to a church intern with a severe ear infection. He was instantly healed. Since then, I have seen more people healed than I can count—literally numbering over a thousand at the time of this writing—only a few years later. That's not a testimony of my own superiority; it's a testimony of God rescuing me from my unbelief.

As long as I lived with expected disappointment, I never even made opportunities for God to heal through my hands. Yes, I had made attempts for several years, but

I eventually started avoiding sick people and praying vague "if it be Your will" prayers when there wasn't another way out.

Today, though, the tables have turned. I now have such limitless hope where healing is concerned that I train others to do the ministry—even brand new Christians. Once, while ministering in Kenya, I preached to about three hundred schoolchildren who all received salvation and began to minister healing five minutes later. Every sickness, injury, disease, pain, and ailment in that room was completely healed by Jesus, and I only had the opportunity to minister to one of those children.

If three hundred newly-saved school kids can do it, what's your excuse?

Referring people to others isn't a bad thing. The disciples referred an epileptic boy to Jesus when they couldn't cast out the demon, but realize that they first tried to minister deliverance to the boy themselves. (See Mark 9:14-29.) You too should start by ministering, otherwise you'll never discover the gifts that God has made available to you.

If you try to minister and it doesn't work, then try again. I keep trying until either the person asks me to stop or I reach a point where I can tell that I'm striving in my own effort instead of resting in simple faith (because at that point it almost definitely won't work).

If there are still no results after giving it a good try, then you can feel free to refer the person to someone else. But also realize that the "someone else" doesn't necessarily need to be someone with a better track record. It could be a brand new Christian—even a child. We're not looking for the qualified; we're looking for the childlike and the humble. I was once ministering to a woman's ankle without results, so I flagged over an eight-year-old girl and asked if she wanted to give it a try. The woman was healed instantly and started dancing around the front of the church.

Before you refer a person who needs the ministry of a particular spiritual gift, ask God to equip you with that gift and then give it a try. There's nothing wrong with attempting a spiritual gift and missing it. What's wrong is sitting on our hands and never believing that God loves you enough to possibly use you.

First Corinthians 14:12 tells us, "Since you are eager for gifts of the Spirit, try to excel in those that build up the church." What does the word "try" mean? It means to actively attempt something. Allow yourself to become eager for spiritual gifts. And as you hunger for those gifts, take steps of action. You may be surprised how often God partners with you!

Deferring to Others

> Limitless hope causes us to trust and encourage others in the use and development of their spiritual gifts. Expected disappointment causes us to become one-man-shows.

I spent five years of my ministry life as a youth pastor. During that time, I purposely gave the students room to exercise more spiritual gifts than me. I regularly invited them to pray or minister even when I knew I had enough faith to address a situation. In love, I gave them the victories. Young people would receive prophetic words and physical healing through their peers rather than needing to look to a special minister on a stage.

I have also been involved in ministering to young adults for more than a decade. In recent years—since discovering the joy of sharing the work of ministry—I have done the same with the young adults. When people need healing, sometimes I minister to them; but more often I encourage members of our group to minister healing. I also share the teaching time, allowing everyone in the group an opportunity to share what God has been speaking to them throughout the week. It's a joy! Miracles happen, and lives are changed—not because the people encountered a professional minister, but because they encountered Jesus through His Body, the Church.

These young adults—within only a year or so of being involved in our group—have ministered in ways that would make some pastors jealous. One young lady led a man to salvation who she met at a dance class. A young man in our group led a homosexual couple to Christ, and they were both baptized within the week.

Another young man in our group went with his family to give a free Thanksgiving dinner to low-income families in a housing project. While there, he delivered food to shut-ins and started to pray for them along the way. One older woman was hunched completely over— her upper body was parallel to the floor. But within twenty minutes of ministry, she was walking upright without pain! One shut-in after the next was miraculously healed by Jesus!

When you have limitless hope, you truly believe that God can use anyone. You don't look for qualifications; you simply look for willingness. When we expect disappointment, we presuppose that others are going to do something wrong or misrepresent Jesus (the assumption being that you, on the other hand, would do everything right). But limitless hope sees through eyes of love and promotes others above oneself.

Even Jesus was of this mind, as evidenced when He said to His disciples, "Very truly I tell you, whoever believes in Me will do the works I have been doing, and they will do even greater things than these, because I am going to the Father." (See John 14:12.) If Jesus—the Master of our salvation—is willing to make His ministry vulnerable enough to share it with a bunch of roughneck fishermen, tax collectors, and ex-prostitutes, then I don't see any reason why we should hoard the treasures of ministry for ourselves.

In Luke 9:49-50, John was excited that he had stopped some "outsiders" who were casting out demons in Jesus' name. His reasoning was that these people weren't part of the "official group." They weren't disciples. They didn't have the specialized training. They didn't have as much relationship with Jesus as John and the other apostles. They weren't qualified. They were average. So John stopped them from ministering.

But Jesus corrected John by saying, "Don't stop them! If they're not against us, then they're for us!" In other words, "They may not represent Me as well as you think you would, but they're just as qualified. You're not the perfect representative yourself! Only a few minutes ago, you were arguing with the other disciples about why you would be the greatest in the Kingdom. Get over yourself!" (That's clearly a paraphrase. Jesus, I'm sure, was much more tactful.)

Spiritual gifts are available to everyone. Allow yourself to limitlessly hope for every spiritual gift. Be careful not to put a cap on the number of gifts you're allowed to practice. The Bible doesn't offer a limit, and we shouldn't invent one. Personally, I have at one time or another experienced every spiritual gift mentioned in the Bible—at least on some level—at some point in my life. This doesn't mean that I'm a super-disciple or anything. It simply means that I have a sensible reason for telling you that anything is possible!

Eagerly desire spiritual gifts. Actively attempt them. And make opportunities for others to practice the gifts of the Spirit in their own lives.

Endnotes:

1. This is a topic that deserves its own book; but for a cursory overview of some of these gifts, read 1 Corinthians 12 and Romans 12:3-8.
2. For example: Balaam prophesied (Numbers 22); Saul prophesied on his way to murder David (1 Samuel 19:22-24); Caiaphas, the high priest who ordered Jesus' execution, prophesied (John 11:49-52); and Gamaliel, a Pharisee, spoke what was arguably a word of wisdom (Acts 5:33-40).
3. For examples, consider Matthew 8:16 and 15:30; Mark 1:34, 3:10, and 6:13; Luke 4:40, 5:15, and 9:6. Healing, miracles, and deliverance from demons were very common in Jesus' ministry.

Chapter 10:

Limitless Hope and Physical Healing

J esus said, "And these signs will accompany those who
believe...they will place their hands on sick people, and
they will get well." (See Mark 16:17-18.) In other words, if
these signs do not accompany you, then there must be
something up with your belief.

This simple logical argument severely messed with
my head. It had been stated by Todd White, a healing
minister I saw on YouTube back in 2009. At the time, I
was skeptical about everything he said; but when he said
those words, I was rocked to the core. I couldn't argue
with Scripture. It was pretty clear: If you truly believe, then
it will lead to accompanying "signs." If the signs never
happen, then you have reason to question whether or not

your belief is correct.

This sent me on a quest for the truth. For about three months, I only read and listened to the perspectives of ministers who were actually doing the work of healing. I devoured the four Gospels and the book of Acts. I read classic authors like Smith Wigglesworth, F.F. Bosworth, and John G. Lake. I read the short biographies of healing evangelists compiled by Roberts Liardon in the *God's Generals* series. I listened to teachings from modern-day ministries like T. L. Osborne, Bill Johnson, Randy Clark, Heidi Baker, Todd White, Reinhard Bonnke, and many others.

What I found was that none of these people shared an identical theology on every point. Yes, they all believed in Jesus as the Son of God. They believed all the basic doctrines of Christianity. But I believed those things too and was still without results!

It didn't seem logical: If "these signs accompany those who believe," and I believe all the same doctrines as these people—and if all the fringe-issues these people believe don't have any common elements—then what's the difference? Why are they seeing results while I see nothing?

That's when I discovered something: There was indeed one common thread. Every one of these people from the first disciples to the healing revivalists to the modern-day ministers—every one approached healing ministry situations believing it was definitely God's will to heal. And while the early disciples may not have had all their theology articulated yet, the other common element I found—especially among everyone from the last hundred years—was that they believed healing would happen because Jesus had already paid for it with His own blood.

That's when I realized that Jesus' promise in Mark 16 wasn't about believing certain doctrines; it was about believing a Person. It mattered less "what" I believed; what mattered was "Who" I believed. Jesus is the healer.

Healing ministry is not about having perfect theology. Jesus doesn't need us to understanding everything. Your salvation is not accomplished through intellectual ascent. All Jesus wants is for you to have a deeply rooted relationship with Him. He wants you to take Him at His word and trust Him to work along with you. He wants you to believe what He says about the adequacy of His sacrifice. In this context of this relationship, Jesus partners with us; and that's how healing happens.

Immediately after Jesus' promise that signs would accompany believers, Mark writes this: "After the Lord Jesus had spoken to them, He was taken up into heaven and He sat at the right hand of God. Then the disciples went out and preached everywhere, and the Lord worked with them and confirmed His word by the signs that accompanied it." (See Mark 16:19-20.) Do you see? Even though Jesus was no longer on the earth—even though He was physically seated in heaven at the right hand of the Father—He still "worked with them and confirmed His word by the signs that accompanied it."

Jesus did the work. Jesus produced the signs. The disciples "went out and preached everywhere," and Jesus did the rest. He still does the work today.

The Difference Between Signs and Gifts

Back when I believed that healing was only sometimes God's will, I embraced a line of reasoning that didn't make sense. I believed that if I prayed for you and didn't see results, then it's because it wasn't God's will. But if you attended a healing meeting with a special evangelist and received healing, it was because he or she had a gift. What I didn't realize is that this would mean the evangelist's gift trumped God's will! When I prayed, God said, "No," but when the evangelist prayed, God changed His mind. Or, at worst, it would imply that God's hands were tied in the matter because He gave someone a gift and couldn't turn it off.

If we treat gifts as though they trump God's will or twist His arm into acting, then we will only pursue spiritual gifts so that we can manipulate God. But if we see that gifts are God's benevolent, grace-inspired actions through people who don't deserve to be used by Him, then we will desire such gifts for the sake of pleasing and obeying God.

Gifts of healing do not trump God's will; they illustrate it. Gifts are "for the common good." (See 1 Corinthians 12:7.) So when we see a gift of healing in action, we all benefit because we all learn that God's will is to heal.

The healing ministry "sign" mentioned in Mark 16 is for every believer. This is different from the gifts of healing mentioned in First Corinthians 12:9. Utilizing the definition from the previous chapter, a "gift" happens when the Holy Spirit takes from Jesus and makes it known to you.

Gifts are given by grace. We don't grow into them or learn them. In my experience, people who operate in a gift of healing typically can't explain to others how to do the same things whereas those who practice the sign can (because they have grown into their gift through experience with the Lord and learning to have simple faith in Him).

When I minister healing to people, it works a lot of the time; but not yet one-hundred percent. When Jesus ministered healing, it always worked. There was never a time when Jesus laid His hands on a leper, declared "Be clean," and then said with confusion, "Bummer. I really thought that would work."

I am convinced that a "gift" of healing is in operation when those "bummer" moments don't happen. I have been in meetings where every single sick person was healed. I can't credit that to my own faith, but I can credit it to a gift of Jesus' own unquenchable power through the Holy Spirit. I've also seen people have 100% results with a particular condition (maybe eye diseases or wrist pain) while other things are hit-and-miss when they minister. Perhaps this is why Paul uses the plural "gifts" of healing, identifying that there are a variety of ways it can function.

Nevertheless, as I mentioned in the previous chapter, I have seen 300 Kenyan schoolchildren minister healing after only five minutes of receiving salvation, and this was after I taught them the biblical basis for healing ministry: Jesus wants it, He paid for it, and He'll do the work if you trust Him. So put your hand on the person, speak with gentle authority, and have the person test things out to see what happened.

If those schoolchildren can do it without any fancy theological training or anything more than simply knowing Jesus and believing in His will to heal through them, then so can you!

Every child in that meeting was healed, but not

because an individual person practiced a gift. Everyone was healed because 300 kids simply acted upon their newfound relationships with Jesus and believed His sacrifice to be sufficient. The sign of healing accompanied the preaching of the Gospel. The Lord worked with us, confirming His word by the signs that accompanied it.

There is indeed a difference between gifts of healing and the sign of healing. Gifts of healing are a supernatural impartation of Christ's unstoppable healing power through a believer, whereas the sign of healing happens when Jesus works with us (in accordance with our faith) to confirm the message of the Gospel.

Every believer is commissioned to preach the Gospel throughout the world; and as we do this, Jesus will work with us to heal the sick. In this chapter, when I speak of healing, I am referring to healing as a sign, which works in tandem with declaring the Good News of the Kingdom of God. In other words, I'm referring to the sort of healing ministry that doesn't require a specialized gift of the Spirit. It simply requires that you believe.

Speaking with Authority

> Limitless hope causes us to command healing in Jesus' name. Expected disappointment causes us to pray for fast, gradual improvement and skillful doctors.

In today's world of medical technology, gradual improvement requires no faith at all. Most conditions will show gradual improvement on their own. When we pray for gradual improvement, what we're really doing is one of two things: either (1) demonstrating that we don't believe God can do anything better than that or (2) worshipping ourselves (I'll explain that in a moment). It's obvious that if we don't believe God can heal miraculously then we won't ask such a thing. That one makes sense; but what about "worshipping ourselves?"

Well, think about it: If you're praying for God to do something that you know will likely happen through natural circumstances, then what you're really doing is positioning yourself to look good when the prayer is seemingly answered.

We don't want to look bad if the person is not instantly and miraculously healed, but God needs people who are willing to risk themselves for the sake of His glory. He needs believers who will dare to believe that His Word is true and His sacrifice was sufficient. If we are self-worshippers and glory-seekers then we will limit our prayers to nothing more than asking for natural events to take place: "Lord, we ask that You give the doctors wisdom," or, "Lord, please help the recovery to go well." If the doctors didn't already have skill and wisdom, then they wouldn't be doctors! Stop wasting your miracle-working prayers on that which is already normal! This demonstrates more of a faith in natural events than a faith in God. Personally, I would call that "New Age"—attributing more power to creation than to the Creator.

While I'm making some bold, impassioned statements here, I should interject that in the moment of ministry, I don't have these arguments with people. There's a pastoral side to all this as well. When someone close to the sick person (or the sick person himself) is present, I have no problem praying for wise doctors or comfort—I just make sure I also address the situation with hope-filled healing ministry as well. It's okay to be pastoral with people and meet them where they are in the middle of their grief. What's not okay is settling for prayers of comfort when there's more available. Praying for comfort won't stop a miracle; but settling for comfort makes a miracle less likely. Limitless hope creates opportunities for our limitless God to do what He likes to do.

Years ago, my friend's mom was hospitalized with viral meningitis. When our small group of young adults gathered that Thursday night, we prayed for her. The prayers started in a way that requested "improvement," but then some people began to take the bull by the horns and expect the impossible. We rebuked the virus in Jesus' name, commanded her body to be restored to health, and prayed that God would make a way for her to come home from the hospital that night. Sure enough, there was nearly immediate change. Days before the doctors thought it would be possible, she showed remarkable improvement. Just a few short hours after we prayed, she was discharged and allowed to return home in the early morning.

This sort of thinking is found in the Bible too. For example, when Peter's mother-in-law came down with a fever, Jesus didn't kneel by her bedside and pray that the fever would eventually leave or that God would give wisdom to those who were caring for her during the sickness. Rather, He rebuked the fever and helped her up. (See Mark 1:30-31.)

When we have limitless hope, we expect things that do not have a natural explanation. Miracles seem normal to the reasoning of a renewed mind.

Furthermore, we realize that we are partners in the

ministry of healing. "The Lord worked with them…" Jesus never told His disciples to "pray for My Father to heal the sick." Rather, He said, "Heal the sick…" (See Matthew 10:8.) In other words, He placed that ministry in the hands of His disciples. But He also said, "Apart from Me, you can do nothing." (See John 15:5.)

It is equally true to say that we heal the sick as it is true to say that Jesus heals the sick. When Peter and John met the crippled beggar at the temple gate, Peter said, "…What I have, I give you. In the name of Jesus… walk!" In one sense, Peter was saying that he had healing virtue to offer; but when explaining his actions later, Peter presented the opposite, "Why do you stare at us as if by our own power or godliness we had made this man walk?....By faith in the name of Jesus, this man whom you see and know was made strong. It is Jesus' name and the faith that comes through him that has completely healed him, as you can all see." (See Acts 3:12,16.) Again, Peter was clear that he didn't have any special power or godliness that could work the miracle—Jesus did it. But it was Peter who administered the grace that was available in Christ. "What I have, I give you." If Peter never took the man by the hand and said what he said, that beggar would have remained crippled.

This is important to know because it means we have a responsibility in ministry. It is only Jesus who heals; but without our participation, He typically doesn't heal. Peter understood this principle and wrote about it later when he said, "Each of you should use whatever gift you have received to serve others, as faithful stewards of God's grace in its various forms." (See 1 Peter 4:10.) God is the one who has the grace, but we are the stewards of that grace. That's why after Jesus commanded His disciples to "heal the sick" in Matthew 10:8, He added, "Freely you have received, now freely give." Peter had received grace, so Peter gave grace.

If I sawed a wood plank in half, you could say that I was the one who sawed it. And yet, everybody knows that it was actually a saw that sawed the wood in half. Without the saw, I wouldn't be able to do the same job. On the same token, without me picking up the saw and moving it, it would just lay there without doing anything. So did I cut the wood in half or did the saw cut the wood in half? The answer is both. Just as the saw and the workman require partnership to be effective, so Jesus and the believer must work together. (Admittedly, Jesus is more like the workman, and we are more like the tools in His hand, but hopefully you get the picture.) You cannot heal the sick without Him, but He typically will not heal the sick without you.

For this reason, we are invited to command healing to take place—again, not because of our power or godliness but because we are partners with Jesus. There is no reason to pray for something you already have. If I give you a glass of water, it would be silly for you to then look at me and say, "I'm thirsty. Would you please bring me a glass of water?" I already gave it to you! And in the same way, Jesus has already given us the authority to speak on His behalf. We don't need to ask for healing when He has already made it available. You have freely received authority for healing, so freely give the healing virtue of Christ.

The Greek word for "freely" in Matthew 10:8 has a dual meaning. First, it means what we would normally think: to give unreservedly, without holding anything back. But the word also means for something to be "in vain" or "without cause." In other words, Jesus may have been saying that the disciples "freely received" because they did not do anything to deserve grace. In the same way, they cannot do anything to deserve or merit "giving" that grace. Both are effortless. Both are unmerited or undeserved.

Whenever we simply obey what the Lord has instructed us to do and avoid adding any sort of extra effort or human power to it, we are in line with God's grace. We humbly admit that no effort beyond placing our hands on the sick (and perhaps speaking with the authority you've been given) will accomplish anything of value, and God then "gives grace to the humble" and heals the person. If you try praying a perfect prayer, pushing power out your arm, thinking the perfect thought, or anything else beyond what the Lord has instructed, then you're no longer resting in grace and run the risk of missing the miracle that God wants. Grace is free and undeserved, but it goes to the humble.

We should also never question whether or not the sick person deserves healing. That seems to go without saying, but how often do we wonder whether or not the person has enough faith to receive? Or what about wondering if they have some hidden sin or bitterness in their heart that will hinder the healing? What we're actually doing is placing a stipulation on God's grace. It's an escape from our own responsibility to believe.

And don't worry about what the other person believes; if you believe then that is sufficient. You received grace without having a perfectly formulated theology or belief. In the same way, give it away.

Additionally, giving "in vain" could possibly mean "without effort." Just as we receive grace without any effort on our part, we are to give without effort. I have found that when I minister to the sick, the less I try, the more success I have. I used to try to feel power moving down my arm. I used to try to somehow push power into the other person. But now I just do what Jesus said: "they will lay their hands on sick people, and they will recover." All we have to do is lay our hands on the sick. Jesus didn't give any extra instructions because extra instructions aren't necessary. We don't have to figure out how to manipulate God's power. That's His business. Our job is simply to—without effort—lay our hands on the sick. It really is that simple.

Healing as a "First Resort"

> Limitless hope causes us to seek God immediately. Expected disappointment causes us to seek God only when medicine has failed.

My wife Robin and I only take medicine for a headache if prayer hasn't worked—not the other way around. That's our method with all medicine: we only take it when our faith doesn't get the job done.

In many cases, medication doesn't actually fix a problem; it merely masks the symptoms. So when people are on medication, they don't have an immediate way of knowing whether or not ministry has worked. Symptoms are often blessings in disguise, giving us tangible indicators that something is wrong and also when something has changed for the better.

Most of the time, I can pray for my wife's headache, and she will be completely fine. Other times, it doesn't work after a few minutes of ministry—at which point I give her a pill for the sake of her comfort.

I suppose someone could argue that this shows a lack of faith, but I have reason to question that. For one thing, the only thing that showed a lack of faith was when she wasn't healed. If my faith didn't get the job done, then there's no sense making her suffer and calling it faith. Faith moves mountains. If the mountain didn't move, then there was no faith.

As far as I can tell, the Bible doesn't condemn taking medication. It is true that the Greek root for the English word "pharmacy" is "pharmacopeia," which is more accurately translated "sorcery." But that's likely because the practice of mixing herbs and chemicals to treat illness did have its origin in ancient witchcraft. Modern medical history doesn't hide the stories of practices like bloodletting and other such methods that are now seen as scientifically meaningless. But at some point, science dominated over the metaphysical, and the practice of medicine diverged from sorcery to focus purely on the natural realm.

I'm not suggesting that this gives medicine the right to usurp the role of healing ministry. Science is not the enemy of faith. Science simply uses knowledge of God's creation to prolong human life in a fallen world and hopefully make it more comfortable while the Church is still growing into the faith necessary for the healing.

Sometimes our faith grows through prolonged persistence. If that's the case then I don't see any problem improving a person's comfort and quality of life while we persistently attempt to minister healing in anticipation of a miraculous breakthrough. Medicine will not disqualify you from a healing. I've witnessed many healings that have come to people who were presently taking medications (including myself).

James gives us one of the classic passages about physical healing:

> **James 5:14-16 –** Is anyone among you sick? Let them call the elders of the church to pray over them and anoint them with oil in the name of the Lord. And the prayer offered in faith will make the sick person well; the Lord will raise them up. If they have sinned, they will be forgiven. Therefore confess your sins to each other and pray for each other so that you may be healed. The prayer of a righteous person is powerful and effective.

For this reason, many ministers (following the example of old-time preachers like Smith Wigglesworth) carry around a little vial of oil, which they dab on their fingertip and spread on a person's forehead when ministering healing. I suppose there's nothing wrong with this, but I have seen far more healings that did not involve oil than I have seen healings that did.

The reason for this is likely found in the original purpose for that oil. Notice that James did not say that there was any healing purpose to the oil. He said that "the prayer offered in faith will make the sick person well"— not the oil. Historically, oil was smeared (or "anointed") on the person for medicinal and even cosmetic reasons.[1] In the parable of "The Good Samaritan," the Samaritan anointed the beaten man's wounds with oil and wine before bandaging them. (See Luke 10:34.) Anointing with oil would be the modern-day equivalent of giving a sick person some medicine and helping them wash and get dressed. In other words, our role as Christians is not merely to pray for the sick or even to command their healing in Jesus' name. Our role also includes caring for the practical, everyday needs of the sick until that healing takes place.

The problem only comes when we allow medical science to replace our hope in God. I believe it is utterly wrong for a Christian whose friend has cancer to carry on as though everything is just fine—as though medical science holds all the answers and Jesus is reserved for "only after all else fails." Our culture has developed a last-resort phrase for people with terminal illness: "All we can do now is pray." The problem is that this is what we should have been doing in the first place! Prayer is not a last resort—it is the first and constant resort. We should minister healing from the very beginning and welcome any treatment that will prolong a person's life while that healing is sought.

Think of it this way. According to the prophet Isaiah, "...by His wounds, we are healed." (See Isaiah 53:5.) In hindsight, we now understand that Jesus endured significant wounding, scourging, beating, and more for the sake of our physical healing. He purchased our healing with His own blood. But some people seem to think that Jesus purchased chemotherapy, wheelchairs, Prozac, and insulin. We say things like, "God gave the doctors the wisdom to invent these things, and therefore they are one of the ways God heals." I don't have a problem with giving God glory for something man invented, nor do I have a problem with Christians improving through medical treatment. But I do have a problem with placing more faith in the natural realm than we place in Jesus—as though He isn't as trustworthy as a bottle of meds.

In my mind, Jesus didn't go to the whipping post so that the hearing aid would be invented. He didn't endure sucker-punches while blindfolded so that blind people could receive white canes and trained dogs. He didn't carry the cross so that the crippled could receive leg braces, walkers, or wheelchairs. Jesus did these things so that the deaf would hear, the blind would see, and the lame would walk. Period. I have no problem with a person using any of these things while they seek God for healing. My concern is when we assume that these things are God's will for us—all the while limiting what He actually wants to do. Medical science should be where we turn only when we have discovered that prayer and the authority of Jesus' name have not yet produced the full results He desires.

When we expect disappointment, we rarely reach for anything unseen. We look for natural solutions, assuming that God probably isn't going to do the same things He did in the Bible. But limitless hope looks at the example of Jesus—that everyone who came to Him was healed—and it believes that He is the same yesterday, today, and forever.

> Limitless hope expects prayer and Christian authority to bring the change while medication brings comfort. Expected disappointment assumes that medication will bring the change while prayer brings comfort.

Healing in the Atonement

> Limitless hope causes us to trust that God wants to heal everybody. Expected disappointment causes us to pray "Thy will be done" without any conviction about what His will actually is.

As we have already briefly examined in this book, God's will is not always done. This is an important component in understanding healing ministry. If God's will is always done, then our assumption is that fruitless ministry is God's will. This mindset flies in the face of everything Jesus taught—especially in John 15. We are not victims of God's will; we are a freewill participants in carrying it out!

I want to look again at the epileptic boy whom the disciples couldn't heal but Jesus could. Until this moment, they had been having success in ministry. The demons submitted to the name of Jesus. But when this boy crossed their paths, they couldn't seem to accomplish the breakthrough. Today many Christians in the same scenario would look at the boy and his father and say, "I'm sorry it didn't work. It looks like maybe it's God's will for him to have epilepsy. Maybe there's a higher purpose. Just trust God, and He will receive the glory He deserves."

Instead the boy's father brought him to Jesus. Jesus was successful. Just because ministry doesn't always work the first time doesn't mean that healing isn't God's will. Healing is so much the will of God that He made it part of the atonement—that is, the price paid at the crucifixion with Christ's own blood.[2]

As I mentioned earlier, men like Smith

Wigglesworth, John G. Lake, T. L. Osborn, and other famous "faith healers" all had one bit of theology in common—that healing was paid for in the atonement of Christ. Those who believe that God sometimes doesn't want to heal rarely ever see people healed (I was one of them). But those who believe that God always wants to heal have a far greater track record. The perspective of limitless hope appears to have the best results.

Why are some not healed? I don't always know. It's different in every situation (except to say that the responsibility always falls to me as a healing minister), but it's not because healing isn't God's will. God wants everyone to be saved, but not everyone repents. When we lead someone to Christ and help them pray through their repentance, we don't add, "If it's Your will." We know it's God's will! Yet for some reason, many Christians add these words when we pray for healing.

Jesus has already revealed His will. If healing wasn't in the plan of God, then Jesus didn't have to pay for it. The wounds for our healing would have been unnecessary. (See Isaiah 53:5.) But our Lord paid the full price.[3]

I have found that most of my questions about God's will to heal can be answered when I replace healing with forgiveness. I can't imagine a sinner coming to God for forgiveness and God saying, "No," or, "Not yet." Jesus paid for it. As I mentioned in Chapter Three, when it comes to matters of the atonement, God's will is always "yes" and "now." Again, "Now is the day of salvation."

When the paralyzed man was lowered through the roof to the feet of Jesus, our Lord said, "Son, your sins are forgiven." Everyone looked at Him like He was crazy, and that's when Jesus verified His authority to forgive, saying, "...I will prove to you that the Son of Man has the authority on earth to forgive sins." (See Mark 2:10, NLT.) And the proof He offered was to tell the paralyzed man to get up, take his mat, and go home. If healing and forgiveness did not function on the same principle, then that wasn't proof!

We tend to be comfortable with God forgiving everyone. Jesus paid the price for all who believe. Whoever receives His salvation is welcomed to walk in His power— free from sin. And when it comes to freedom from evil spirits, even though there is debate throughout the Church regarding various aspects of "deliverance ministry," everyone seems to agree that God doesn't want anyone tormented by evil spirits. We're comfortable with this being purchased fully by Christ as well. Why, then, do we seem to struggle with the idea of God wanting to heal everyone?

The answer: Expected disappointment.

If God wants to heal everyone, then we will naturally feel like we've done something wrong when a person is not healed. But if it is only sometimes His will, then we can play the "sovereignty" card and sneak away with our reputations in tact.[4] We expect to be disappointed. We expect that "it probably won't happen." And so we prepare for such disappointment by creating a cushy theology that will cost us the least when that disappointment happens. Ironically, this wrong theology actually leads to more disappointment, and that makes us think it's correct (because we received the results we expected).

Limitless hope doesn't plan for disappointment.

Limitless hope sees the example of Jesus—one-hundred percent success—as an attainable possibility. Limitless hope prepares for the best.

While preaching in the rural African village of Bukiiri, Uganda, the Holy Spirit moved on me with boldness. I had taught the people of the church how to minister healing in Jesus' name. Then I decided to demonstrate how it is done. I wanted their faith to be built by witnessing healing with their own eyes. So I asked, "Is there anyone here who is deaf or partially deaf?"

The people finally pointed out a woman in the very back of the mud-wall church. We waved her forward, and she came. I wasn't satisfied with only one person, so I added, "Is there anyone here who is either blind or partially blind?" Four more people came forward (and eventually a fifth). I turned to the people and said, "I want you to see that Jesus Christ has power over everything." Then I turned to the deaf woman, placed my fingers in her ears, and began to minister. Within about a minute, she testified with joy that her hearing had been restored. Every person with eye problems was also healed. The people of the church then ministered to each other, and about thirty more healings took place.

God loves to respond when we—in true faith—create opportunities in which only He can produce results. Prepare for success. Expect the best-case-scenario, and see what happens.

Endnotes:

1. *The Jewish New Testament Commentary* (1992, David H. Stern. Clarksville, MD: Jewish New Testament Publications, Inc.) says of this scripture, "Anointing with oil is not merely a ceremony. In biblical times, olive oil was medicine (Isaiah 1:6, Lk 10:34), and being anointed with oil was considered physically pleasant (Psalms 23:5, 133:2-3)." Furthermore, When Jesus gave instructions about those who are fasting, He instructed the disciples to "put oil on your heads...so that it will not be obvious to others that you are fasting..." (Matthew 6:17-18). In this sense, its use was cosmetic.

2. The word "atonement" refers to the price Jesus paid to reconcile man to God and save us from sin, sickness, and the enemy. Because of sin, we deserve destruction. God's righteousness demands justice. But Jesus paid this price with His own blood, atoning for our complete wholeness. The atonement is God's payment for our forgiveness, our healing, and our freedom from the enemy.

3. Every once in a while, I meet a particularly astute believer who sees that when Peter quoted Isaiah's verse about healing, he did so in reference to our sins being forgiven. (See 1 Peter 2:24.) This, they say, proves that physical healing is technically not in the atonement—only spiritual healing. They say that Peter's words give us the right interpretation of Isaiah's prophecy.

   This may come as a surprise, but I don't disagree with them! However, if we're going to apply that sort of logic—that a New Testament author's interpretation applies right meaning to an Old Testament text—then we must also accept Matthew's interpretation of Isaiah's same words. In Matthew 8:16-17, we read, "When evening came, many who were demon-possessed were brought to him, and he drove out the spirits with a word and healed all the sick. This was to fulfill what was spoken through the prophet Isaiah: 'He took up our infirmities and bore our diseases.'" Matthew applies Isaiah's prophecy to the ministry of physical healing.

   The next argument I usually hear is that the Matthew 8 passage didn't happen during the crucifixion but rather during Jesus' ministry, and therefore—they say—it doesn't apply to the atonement. But they miss something. Isaiah 53 is all about the atonement in context. And putting all the scriptures together, we learn that the entire life of Jesus was part of the atonement—not just His crucifixion.

Philippians 2:6-8 describes Jesus' sacrifice in a way that begins with the incarnation. Hebrews 5:8 says that Jesus learned obedience through what He suffered. Are we to believe that Jesus didn't know what obedience was until He suffered at the cross? Or does it make more sense to believe that our Lord's suffering began when He set His Godhood aside, "taking on the very nature of a servant," born to a poor family with attempts made on His life even then?

Furthermore, Hebrews 9:22 says that without the shedding of blood, there is no forgiveness. But during Jesus' ministry—before one drop of blood was shed—Jesus forgave sins. (See Matthew 9:2; Mark 2:5; Luke 5:20; Luke 7:48; and John 8:11.) How could Jesus forgive sin without shedding blood unless He was already actively engaged in the work of atonement?

When we talk about the atonement, we point to the blood of Jesus because the cross is where Jesus declared, "It is finished." But the atonement was also a process that began all the way back at the incarnation with a stressful pregnancy. The entire life of Jesus atones for our sin. According to Peter, it purchased our forgiveness; and according to Matthew, it purchased our physical healing.

4.   The term "sovereign" is often misused. It simply means "supreme ruler." It's a noun. It does not mean that God is mystically manipulating the elements of the universe so that only His will happens at all times. God—our Sovereign— has chosen to place the ministry of evangelism in the hands of fallible people, even though He wills that none should perish and that all would come to repentance. (See 2 Peter 3:9.) In the same way, Our Sovereign God has chosen to place healing ministry into our hands. Of course He could do a better job of accomplishing His will on His own, but His greater will is partnership with us.

Chapter 11:

Limitless Hope and Extravagant Giving

Most of my experiences in ministry are great, but occasionally I run across something that sickens me. Very early in my traveling ministry, I was asked to lead a time of worship at an interdenominational gathering of Charismatic Christians. As I was carrying my keyboard into the banquet hall, a homeless man jumped off a bus and approached me.

"Hey man, you got any pop bottles or change on you?"

I was carrying a heavy piece of equipment, but I paused momentarily. Being the early days of traveling, I answered honestly, "I'm sorry, I wish I did. I've spent all my cash. I hope you can find some, though." I then proceeded into the building to set up the equipment.

Then I had this thought: *What if I invited him in as my "honored guest" and gave him my meal from the banquet? Not only would this guy enjoy a balanced meal, but he would have an opportunity to receive ministry.*

I hurried back to the door to find him; but when I arrived, the man was being escorted out by some of the greeters.

I thought greeters were supposed to greet!

They ignored the man's pleas and closed the door in his face.

To be completely honest, I wish I had acted on my previous thought and invited him back in anyway. I wish I could say I was that much like Jesus at the time, but I was unfortunately intimidated by the "bouncers" at the door. I've since repented, but I still wish I had handled it differently.

I did, however, run outside and apologize to the gentleman for the way he was treated.

"You know what I need?" He asked.

"What's that?" I replied as I chewed a piece of Trident.

"I need a piece of peppermint gum."

"That I can do!" But as I reached into my pocket to pull out my fresh pack of gum, I felt so wrong giving the man only one piece. And for that matter, as I looked at the fifteen pieces I had, I felt awkward holding onto any of it.

> **Matthew 5:40-42** – And if anyone wants to sue you and take your shirt, hand over your coat as well. If anyone forces you to go one mile, go with them two miles. Give to the one

who asks you, and do not turn away from the
one who wants to borrow from you.

I think Jesus might also say, "If someone asks you
for a piece of gum, do not withhold from him the entire
package."

"Here," I said, "I want to give you all of this. I'll
be praying for you!"

As I handed the man my pack of gum, I was
incredibly bothered about everything that was happening.
Here I was standing in a crowd of so-called "Christians"
who wouldn't give a homeless man the time of day.

As Pentecostals and Charismatics, we tend to
pride ourselves in being the ones who understand and
embrace spiritual gifts; but too many of us offer nothing of
substance to the world. If you read First Corinthians 12
and 14, you will learn about spiritual gifts. But the chapter
in the middle, chapter 13, is all about love. Without that
love in the middle, all we have is an empty sandwich.

That night I was bothered. As one minister after
the next came up to the front; as dancers waved their flags;
as people jumped, shouted, and clapped; I couldn't help
but think of Jesus' words: "Truly I tell you, whatever you
did not do for one of the least of these, you did not do for
Me." (See Matthew 25:45.) Did any of it count? Was Jesus
even present? Or was He busy walking that homeless man
back to his box?

> **1 John 3:17 –** If anyone has material
> possessions and sees a brother or sister in
> need but has no pity on them, how can the
> love of God be in that person?

I felt like many of the people present were feasting on empty sandwiches—no "chapter 13" in the middle. We celebrated the gifts of the Spirit, but we missed an opportunity to love someone. Not only was that homeless man deprived of an actual meal; he was deprived of a spiritual meal.

Limitless hope does not withhold anything from those who are in need.

Giving to Jesus

> Limitless hope causes us to give to the poor, knowing that we are ultimately giving to Christ. Expected disappointment causes us to avoid giving to the poor for fear that they'll waste the money.

I have noticed that many in the Church are cautious about giving money to the homeless. "Well," they argue, "What if he just goes back out and buys drugs? Then I purchased drugs!"

No. You're wrong. You didn't purchase drugs. Rather, you gave twenty dollars to Jesus. If that man wants to purchase drugs with Jesus' money, then he'll answer to God for that. Jesus didn't tell us to give to the poor unless we think they just want to get drunk. He said to give to the poor because when you give to them, you give to Him.

Matthew 25:37-40 – Then the righteous will answer Him, 'Lord, when did we see You hungry and feed You, or thirsty and give You something to drink? When did we see You a stranger and invite You in, or needing clothes and clothe You? When did we see You sick or in prison and go to visit You?'

"The King will reply, 'Truly I tell you, whatever you did for one of the least of these brothers and sisters of Mine, you did for Me.'

Our responsibility is not technically to the poor. Our responsibility is to Jesus. And if we love Him, then we will act on that love. How do we act on it? By loving the poor. By giving to those who are less fortunate. By considering others more highly than ourselves. By forsaking everything this world has to offer so that others can encounter the love of God.

Love the homeless. Don't waste all your resources on yourself. Limitless hope sees needs, meets needs, and trusts that one's own needs will also be supernaturally met.

We need to realize that for the Christian, this world is the worst that eternity is ever going to be; so who cares how much we give away? But for the person who doesn't know Jesus, this world is the best that eternity is ever going to be—unless they come to Jesus.

My encounter with that homeless man significantly impacted my feelings about many Christian conferences. I never want to attend another event where hundreds of so-called "believers" pay hundreds of dollars to pack auditoriums simply so they can experience or learn something "from God" that the homeless man outside is not permitted to attend. Is this what Jesus died for?

> **Luke 14:12-14 –** Then Jesus said to his host, "When you give a luncheon or dinner, do not invite your friends, your brothers or sisters,

> your relatives, or your rich neighbors; if you
> do, they may invite you back and so you will
> be repaid. But when you give a banquet, invite
> the poor, the crippled, the lame, the blind, and
> you will be blessed. Although they cannot
> repay you, you will be repaid at the
> resurrection of the righteous."

Limitless hope sees the highest potential of every person. Limitless hope causes one to associate with the refuse of society—like Jesus, who was ridiculed for being a friend of tax-collectors, drunkards, prostitutes, and sinners. Rather than prejudging the person's future actions, those with limitless hope give extravagantly with the eager anticipation that he or she will use that money (or whatever else) in the best way possible.

Stinginess only makes sense when we expect disappointment.

Giving in Faith

Limitless hope causes us to give beyond our means. Expected disappointment causes us to give only what fits our budget.

Paul praised the Christians in Macedonia for their lavish generosity. These people demonstrated such an inhuman generosity that Paul could only identify it as a gift of the Spirit. (See 2 Corinthians 8:1-7.) These men and women were giving with the generosity of Jesus—a generosity that gives beyond what is sensible for the sake of loving others.[1]

236

2 Corinthians 8:1-4 – And now, brothers and sisters, we want you to know about the grace that God has given the Macedonian churches. In the midst of a very severe trial, their overflowing joy and their extreme poverty welled up in rich generosity. For I testify that they gave as much as they were able, and even beyond their ability. Entirely on their own, they urgently pleaded with us for the privilege of sharing in this service to the Lord's people.

I know a man who for three years (before he was married) gave 25% of his income and three times emptied his bank account in obedience to the Lord (giving it all away). This man wasn't rich. In fact, he had an annual income between $10,000 and $14,000 at the time. He gave more than he could afford, but God always took care of his needs. (His lifestyle of generosity continued after marriage, but he had more income at that time as well.) In contrast, I know many people with more money than that man who give very little (if at all) yet struggle to make ends meet.

When our hope is limitless, we don't worry about how our love-filled giving is going to affect our budget. We simply give in full confidence that as we love others and follow the Holy Spirit, our Heavenly Father will take care of our needs.

When I entered into full-time traveling ministry, the Holy Spirit instructed my wife and me to empty our entire bank account and give it all away. Our first child, Josiah, was only three months old, our monthly bills were around $2,000, and we were going to be without a steady paycheck for the first time in our adult lives. Not only did we believe that the Lord wanted us to give away all the money we had, but I also sensed that the Lord did not want me to solicit any churches for speaking engagements!

The Lord was teaching me to trust Him—to detach from the luxuries of this world and prioritize His Kingdom. As it turns out, when Jesus said, "Seek first the Kingdom of God, and My Father will take care of everything else," He actually meant it. (See Matthew 6:33.) We were able to pay every bill. We had a few lean months, but people, led by the Spirit, gave us unexpected gifts that helped purchase groceries or pay bills.

During this season, the Lord provided a few web design jobs, and we received plenty of ministry opportunities. We cancelled our cable TV, stopped eating out as often, and cut back on other luxuries. At the end of one full year of living like this, the Lord supernaturally helped us to pay off nearly $10,000 in debt (completely paying off our small house).

All throughout this time, we continued to give. We helped take care of friends and relatives who had needs. We purchased extra food and drinks to bless the small group of Christians who gathered in our home every week. We gave to missionaries and to our church. Every week, we started afresh because the Holy Spirit had instructed me that any cash left in my wallet by Sunday was supposed to be given in the offering plate. Sometimes it was only a dollar, but usually it was more.

Now that I've shared all this, it's time to take a little self-test. Did you at any point feel like I was bragging? If so, then this goes to prove the point that this lifestyle is not as common as it should be among Christians. If I told you that I breathed every day of this past year, you would probably reply, "So what?" That's because breathing is natural. It would never occur to you that I might be bragging about how I breathed every day. That's natural and normal, so it's nothing to brag about. Do you see that extravagant giving should be as natural and expected in the Church as breathing? Stories like mine shouldn't make your jaw drop. They should simply make you happy. (I'm happy you're breathing, by the way.)

We live in a culture of expected disappointment. We assume that it's natural to focus on the things of this world and to separate the management of our money from the working out of our salvation. On the contrary, if you have surrendered everything to Jesus, then your finances are part of the picture.

Follow the Holy Spirit. If the Holy Spirit places it on your heart to give all your money away, then do it. If He commands you to save a certain amount, then you should do that as well.

In my early twenties, the Holy Spirit once instructed me not to spend any money for an entire month except on gasoline and my normal bills. At the end of that month, I had saved up $500. On the first day of the following month, I received a letter asking for donations to help a friend go on a foreign mission trip. I instantly knew why God asked me to save that money.

Serving the Right God

Even Christians tend to worship money. Before you think "not me," consider this: Do your emotions ever hinge on how much money you have or do not have?

Believe me: I'm not condemning you. I once slipped into a real depression because of a poorly thought-out business investment that cost me over a thousand dollars, which was all I had at the time. But the commonness of our emotional attachment to money does not justify or excuse it.

Why do we allow such an earthly thing as money to rule our emotions? Isn't that a role reserved for God alone? For this reason, I have to continually turn my eyes toward Him. When finances are at their worst, I do what I can to fix my mind on the all-sufficiency of God. The financial situation may not even change for some time, but I find myself looking at circumstances through the lens of limitless hope.

I once committed to purchase a motorcycle for Pastor Paul in Uganda—my plan being to use money from my tax return. When I finally received my money from the government, the IRS had corrected my accountant's work, making my refund about $1000 less than we had planned.

My wife said, "I think we should still buy that motorcycle."

Now I was in a predicament. I knew she was right, but I no longer had the money in my budget. I started to plan how I could possibly pay some bills on my credit card, and that's when the Holy Spirit convicted me. I felt as though God said, "Why do you have more faith in your credit than in Me?"

I believed my credit line could solve my problems rather than believing God would. My rationalizing would have resulted in ungodly debt, whereas God wanted to keep me debt-free. So I repented.

The next day, my wife and I were at the gas station, and a big truck pulled up to the pump in front of me. A visibly distraught woman jumped out, and with fear on her face asked, "Do you know where there's a hospital near here?"

To make a long story short, my wife and I ministered healing to her, and then she asked, "I hate to do this, but do you have a couple dollars for gas?"

I started thinking about how I needed to save my money for the motorcycle. I needed every penny—at least that's what my human mind thought. Then the Lord moved on my heart and said, "If I can provide you with a thousand dollars to pay for the motorcycle, what is to stop Me from providing a few extra dollars? Why do you live as though this money belongs to you?"

I gave the woman all the cash in my wallet. It wasn't much, but it was all I had for the rest of the week. Two days later, a couple men came up to me separately, each giving a check. The first check was for $1,000, and the second was for $500. The Lord gave me more than I needed—much like the 12 basketfuls of bread and fish that were leftover after multiplying the food for the 5,000. (See Mark 6:42-44). The extra money helped take care of my family a week later while I returned to Africa for a week of missionary work.

There is a reason that Jesus said you cannot serve both God and money. (See Matthew 6:24.) According to God's design, there is a correct hierarchy. At the top of the organizational chart is God. He owns everything. Under Him is you (and every other human being). Below your name on the organizational chart is money.

Service flows upward: Money serves you as you serve God. Those who serve money have positioned themselves a couple notches away from God rather than being directly under Him. Not only is this contrary to

God's design, but it cuts off the blessing of relationship that God intends. Money has nothing of real value to give you in return for your service. God, on the other hand, offers us eternal life and so much more!

> Limitless hope believes that our money's role is to serve God. Expected disappointment believes that God's role is to serve our money.

The typical message of "prosperity" is contrary to this design. It teaches that God wants to make you wealthy and financially successful. It tends to be very works-based: Give this ministry a certain amount, and God will multiply it and give you a supernatural return. In other words, God is the steward of your money, and all you have to do is give it to Him so that He can multiply it and make you rich.

That sounds great, but it's utterly wrong. God is not your servant. He is not the steward of your money. You are the steward of His money. You own nothing. He owns everything. Everything you have and everything you are belongs to Him. God does not serve money or you; money serves you as you serve God.

If my son had a computer and someone stole it, the insurance company and the courts would say that the computer was mine. That's because I'm the father and the head of my household. My son technically owns nothing— even if he is the only one who uses that computer. In the same way, childlike Christians realize that God owns everything they have. This is important because it means that we must consult Him about what He wants us to do with His stuff. God gives us His stuff so that it can serve us while we serve Him.

Sometimes God gives us very specific instructions about what to do with what He has given. He may tell us to spend or save a specific amount. Other times, He doesn't give us any direction at all. That's because He trusts us to make the right decision with the wisdom He has already given.

All that matters is that your heart is set on pleasing Him rather than pleasing yourself. I like to say that pleasing God is my job, and pleasing me is His job.[2] The trouble is that we expect to be disappointed. We don't anticipate that God will actually do anything to please us. So we use His money to please ourselves. As a result, we have already received our reward in full.

God doesn't need to please those who please themselves. But He does go out of His way to bless those who surrender everything they have to Him. Limitless hope trusts in God's joy toward His children and realizes that He truly does want to bless His kids. Limitless hope knows that God will bless us with pleasure even if we give away everything we have.

> **1 Timothy 6:17** – Command those who are rich in this present world not to be arrogant nor to put their hope in wealth, which is so uncertain, but to put their hope in God, who richly provides us with everything for our enjoyment.

You Have Everything You Need

There was one time during my first couple years of traveling ministry that we hit financial rock-bottom; and that, I'm sorry to say, led me to an emotional rock-bottom. I had taken my eyes off of Jesus and allowed money to rule my emotions.

I had a pregnant wife, a young son, looming bills, and only a handful of dollars in our bank account. To make matters worse, three very small purchases of some needed groceries—a couple of them costing only about three dollars—overdrew that bank account, and we were charged three $30 overdraft fees (one for each small purchase).

I was frustrated, depressed that I couldn't provide for my family as a minister, and I didn't know what to do next. I remember crying on the phone with the bank, begging them to reverse the overdraft fees, and not receiving any mercy.

Even though I had been crying out to God all along, I was still putting my hope in my money instead of in Him. That's why it had affected my emotions so deeply. But now, finally at the end of my rope, I cried out, "Jesus, I really need a next step here. I'm all out of options."

That's when a crazy thought came to my mind. I couldn't tell at the time if it was Jesus or my flesh, but I was so desperate for any sort of hope that I went with it.

I had a single one-dollar bill in my wallet. It was all the money I had. And I sensed the Holy Spirit say, "I want you to go buy a lottery ticket. Play these numbers, and I will give you everything you need."

I was giddy. I wrote down the five numbers that came to my spirit, drove to the gas station, and bought a lottery ticket.

One of my former pastors had once joked, "You're allowed to play the lottery, but only once. If God wants you to win it, that's all He'll need. So make sure you pray first and know it's the right week and the right numbers. If you don't win, then you didn't hear Him, and you don't ever need to play again." Well, I believed God had spoken, and I was expecting a huge win!

The next day, I listened for the lottery numbers to be called on the radio with my ticket in my hand.

The first number was correct.

The second number was correct.

I couldn't believe what I was seeing!

And when all the numbers had been called, I discovered that I had won!

No, I didn't match all five numbers. I matched three—just enough to win one dollar.

I started to cry happy tears. Jesus came through on His promise, and He used this silly method to convince me. He said that if I played those numbers, He would give me everything I need, and then all He did was give me back the one dollar I spent on that ridiculous lottery ticket.

I marched into the gas station with my one-dollar winning ticket and asked for my dollar. The clerk looked confused. "You sure you want just a dollar?" he asked, "Most people just use the dollar to buy their next ticket."

"Nope." I answered with a smile, "I want my dollar."

I kept that dollar for a long time as a reminder to me that Jesus promised to provide everything I need. We did make it out of that hole. Some perfectly-timed gifts from friends and family who didn't know our situation put us back into the positive numbers. We paid all our bills, and we even paid back the overdraft fees at the bank.

When you follow the Holy Spirit and keep your

eyes on Jesus, He will give you wisdom and insight for your finances. Sometimes He will instruct you to save. Sometimes He will instruct you to give. Sometimes He will instruct you what to spend or where to place your purchase or how to receive the best deal. Many times He won't instruct anything, trusting you to make the right decision (and if God trusts you to make the right decision, you're probably going to make the right decision).

But one thing is for certain. If you live your life fully for the sake of Him and His kingdom, He will provide everything you need. (See Matthew 6:19-34.)

Loving Others

> Limitless hope causes us to share everything we can with the Body of believers. Expected disappointment causes us to take care of ourselves first and share when it is convenient.

If we don't believe that our needs and desires will be met, then we will do what we can to hoard our possessions. But if we believe that God will meet our needs and give us the desires of our hearts, then we don't mind giving anything away. One perspective expects disappointment while the other is limitless hope.

During the beginning years of Christianity, the disciples understood the responsibility to care for others in the Body of Christ. They pooled together their resources. This wasn't socialism in the sense that a central power demanded such equality. Rather, it was goodwill toward their fellowman.

Acts 2:44-47 – All the believers were together and had everything in common. They sold property and possessions to give to anyone who had need. Every day they continued to meet together in the temple courts. They broke bread in their homes and ate together with glad and sincere hearts, praising God and enjoying the favor of all the people. And the Lord added to their number daily those who were being saved.

I have heard it said that "the trouble with socialism is socialism, and the trouble with capitalism is capitalists." Without turning this into a political rant, I have noticed in my home country of America that while we (for the most part) have the freedom to give our money to whomever we like for whatever reason we like, we still tend to be of the mindset, "Every man for himself." When a neighbor or friend expresses a need, our first thought tends to be, *Isn't there an organization or government program that can help this person?*

Could it be that God's preferred solution is to bless Christians with the finances needed to bless others who are in need? I believe so. Unfortunately, we tend to be so attached to the things of this world that God can't trust many of us with large incomes. If we're not willing to give when we have a little, then we can't be trusted to give when we have a lot.

My wife and I once led a house church of young adults between the ages of 16 and 35. When people were in need, those who were able would team together to meet that need. We helped people move into new homes. Our men teamed together and built one young woman a shed.

We took people in when they lost their homes, and we generally showed the love of Christ to each other in practical ways.

In my current small-group "church family," we've helped each other with hundreds of dollars of medical expenses, fixed each other's vehicles and homes for free, given unexpected gifts to each other, helped each other move, and more.

While it is indeed important to love those who are lost in the world, I love seeing Christians caring for each other. We have a responsibility to our brothers and sisters in the Body of Christ.

> **Galatians 6:10 –** Therefore, as we have opportunity, let us do good to all people, especially to those who belong to the family of believers.

Limitless hope does not focus on lack or surplus. Limitless hope focuses on Jesus Christ and the joy of serving Him. When we truly trust that our Father has our best interests in mind, we are liberated to focus on meeting the best interests of others.

This is love.

This is limitless hope.

Endnotes:

1. I need to be clear that giving beyond your means does not mean going into debt in order to give. Debt makes us slaves to our creditors. (See Proverbs 22:7.) Giving beyond your means is about making personal sacrifices for the sake of freeing up finances for others. On my second trip to Uganda, I discovered that on my first trip, Pastor Paul actually sold a lot of his possessions so that he could be hospitable and host me well. He lives in a little house in a village in the bush of Uganda, and yet he sold much of his own belongings out of love for me. That is sacrificial giving!

2. You read that right—God does want to please you. This does not, however, mean that God is our servant, bearing the responsibility of fulfilling our every whim. He only pleases us in accordance with His righteousness and on His terms. God loves to please His children, but that doesn't mean He caves into our whining. Notice in Romans 12:2 that God's will is "good, pleasing, and perfect." His will is pleasing! As David sang in Psalm 37:4, God truly does want to give you "the desires of your heart." In John 16:23, Jesus promised that the Father would give us whatever we ask in His name. Again, my responsibility is to please God, and His responsibility is to please me. I don't need to seek pleasure from anyone or anything else.

Chapter 12:

Limitless Hope and Raising the Dead

I n 2005, I read a new book that opened my eyes to
things God was doing all over the world. Until that time
I had no awareness of God's continued ministry of raising
the dead.

The book I read was titled *Megashift* by the now-
late James Rutz. While the main thrust of the book is to
promote and encourage a specific brand of decentralized,
grassroots networks of Christian fellowships—sometimes
called "house churches"—the entire first chapter is a
rousing battery of testimonies that stirred up my faith for
something more in my Christian walk.

Besides the many testimonies of miraculous
healings, explosive church growth, and supernatural signs,

Rutz shares several long and well-footnoted stories of resurrections. He reports on two teenage Mexican girls who died of black measles in 1998 and were raised to life a couple days later. He also shares the testimony of a victim of a deadly car accident, Daniel Ekechukwu, who had died and had even been injected with a chemical preservative to prepare his body for embalming. Daniel came back to life nearly two days after his death when his wife brought his corpse to a meeting where Evangelist Reinhard Bonnke was speaking.[1]

With one documented story after the next, Rutz opened my eyes to a ministry that I thought ended in the book of Acts. He writes:

> If you needed anything else to persuade you to rethink your life, this is it: God is once again in the business of raising people from the dead.
>
> I'm talking about many hundreds since the mid-'80s, perhaps over a thousand by now. There's a blizzard of reports. And I'm not referring to "near-death experiences"…I'm talking about people who were stone dead for up to three days.
>
> Five years ago, I was amazed to hear of resurrection reports from eight countries. Now it's exploded to 52…

Rutz then lists the fifty-two countries with endnotes pointing to the sources. He continues:

…Some of these people were dead
for less than an hour, some for three days.
The causes of death were all over the
map.

The process of resurrection ranged
from effortless to hours of extreme
prayer. There was no single "method"
that worked best. In fact the Holy Spirit
seems to be at pains to keep us from
imagining that some technique or
standard system will "work" at all. The
only thing that works is Jesus.[2]

Since being awakened by these testimonies in
2005, I have now discovered hundreds of testimonies from
throughout the world—including America. I even have
some friends who have raised the dead. God's power is
still at work today, and I find nothing stirs up limitless
hope within me like testimonies of His power over death.

In this chapter I want to do more than share
testimonies, though. I want to make this practical. I want
to stir up your faith to raise the dead and encourage you to
think with limitless hope. My honest belief and expectation
is that many human lives will be restored from death
because of what you and other hope-filled Christians are
about to read. Jesus is still in the business of raising the
dead.

In the interest of full disclosure, I have never
raised a person to life from the dead. I have made an
attempt at every funeral since 2005, and I've had more
dreams of it happening than I can recall. I want it, and I'm
shooting for it; but the only thing God ever helped me

resurrect was a kitten at my father-in-law's farm.

Limitless hope, though, is less about having constant results and more about a mindset that makes those results possible. If you never minister to the sick, you'll never see the sick healed. And if you never tell a dead person to rise in Jesus' name, then it definitely will never happen. But limitless hope opens us up to the possibilities, and it challenges us to go after the impossible. With God, nothing is impossible, and raising the dead is no exception.

Jesus: The Resurrection and the Life

> Limitless hope causes us to see that Jesus' identity as "the resurrection and the life" is relevant for today. Expected disappointment causes us to apply this reality only to Jesus' own resurrection and the future resurrection of the dead.

One of the classic statements Jesus made about Himself is, "I am the resurrection and the life. The one who believes in Me will live, even though they die..." (See John 11:25.) Strangely, I rarely hear this verse quoted within its context. It is true that in verse 26, Jesus takes this truth a step further by saying, "...whoever lives by believing in Me will never die." This does indeed have to do with our eternal salvation and points to the future resurrection of the dead. (See 1 Corinthians 15.) But in context, the beginning statement Jesus made about His own identity was prompted because of a man who had recently died and had already been entombed for four days.

Lazarus was the brother of Mary and Martha. When He fell ill, the sisters sent for Jesus; but Jesus didn't hurry as they had hoped. Before He could arrive to heal their dear brother, Lazarus died. The Jews carried out their customary three-day "wake" as they waited to see if he was merely in a coma. But when day four arrived, all traditional hope was lost. Martha, however, didn't have an ordinary, traditional hope.

As Jesus made His way into the village of Bethany, Martha ran out to meet Him.

> **John 11:21-25a** – "Lord," Martha said to Jesus, "if You had been here, my brother would not have died. But I know that even now God will give You whatever You ask."
>
> Jesus said to her, "Your brother will rise again."
>
> Martha answered, "I know he will rise again in the resurrection at the last day."
>
> Jesus said to her, "I am the resurrection and the life…

Jesus was clear that Martha didn't have to wait for the future "resurrection of the dead." Lazarus would be restored to her that very day because of the resurrection power of the Holy Spirit already resident within Jesus.

Shortly thereafter, upon reaching the tomb, Jesus declared the now-famous command, "Lazarus, come forth!" Lazarus, still bound like a mummy in grave clothes, hopped awkwardly out of the tomb. He was alive.

Jesus is the Resurrection and the Life. It is His identity. The same Holy Spirit who raised Lazarus from the dead also raised Jesus from the dead. And this is the same Holy Spirit who dwells within each of us as believers. (See Romans 8:11.)

As a Spirit-filled disciple of Jesus Christ, you have resurrection power within you. Jesus' identity has not changed since raising Lazarus.

It is time that we Christians stop expecting to remain disappointed when people die. Place your hope in the limitless Savior. He is the Resurrection and the Life— not simply when He stood by Lazarus' tomb but also as He is now seated at the right hand of the Father, living within you through the Holy Spirit.

Rethinking Funerals

Funerals are inevitable; they just don't have to be the last chapter of a person's life.

In Genesis 6:3, God limited the lifespan of mankind to 120 years. If you ask me, any person who dies short of 120 years is fair game for a resurrection. Admittedly, I don't believe everyone is supposed to reach this age. I just believe that it's biblically allowable— especially for those who have honored their parents and have been promised a long, enjoyable life. (See Ephesians 6:2-3.)

There is such a thing as people dying at an appropriate time. Several Scriptures speak of this. (See Genesis 47:29, 1 Kings 2:1, Ecclesiastes 3:2, and Romans 5:6.) But it is equally Scriptural that some people die before their time. (See Ecclesiastes 7:17.) And since I never know if a person should have lived more years, my only option left is to give it a try until someone finally ages out at 120.

Does that mean it will always happen? Probably

not, but this is age-limit is the only Biblical stipulation I can find. The only reason we believe otherwise is because of experience, but experience does not trump God's Word.

Does it work in practicality? Well, I did once hear a testimony of a 90-year-old man who came back to life after his Christian son prayed for him!

We have many reasons for struggling with the idea of God raising the dead. For one thing, it's typically not something we see everyday—at least not in America. Some ministries, like Freedom Ministries in Mexico and Iris Ministries in Mozambique, have witnessed more resurrections than they can accurately count. Between the two of these ministries, the number of resurrections may have already passed one thousand, and that's just within the last twenty-five years—most of them in the last decade. Apparently some Christians see funerals as opportunities rather than finales.

As far as we can gather from the record of Scripture, Jesus never attended any funeral where death was permanent (including His own). In one case, Jesus interrupted a funeral procession to correct something that was contrary to His Father's will.

> **Luke 7:12-15 –** As He approached the town gate, a dead person was being carried out— the only son of his mother, and she was a widow. And a large crowd from the town was with her. When the Lord saw her, His heart went out to her and He said, "Don't cry."
>
> Then He went up and touched the bier they were carrying him on, and the bearers stood still. He said, "Young man, I say to you, get up!" The dead man sat up and began to

talk, and Jesus gave him back to his mother.

People rarely die according to God's preferred timing. I say that for a few reasons: First, because He has allowed for 120 years, which people rarely reach. Second, because Jesus changed the plans of every funeral we ever read about Him attending. And third, because God's "preferred timing" is technically that no one die at all!

> **Limitless hope causes us to see death as an enemy of God. Expected disappointment causes us to say that death always happens according to God's timing.**

First Corinthians 15:26 is clear that death is an enemy of God. This makes us uncomfortable because most of us have lived our entire lives rationalizing death so that it could become more acceptable.

If it is true that death is an enemy of God, then we can no longer say phrases like, "Apparently it was just her time." I have seen people become downright angry with God for "taking" their loved one before their time. But did He? Remember, Scripture says that death is an enemy of God.

Death is not God's preferred design. God originally created human beings as eternal people, capable of living in relationship with Him forever. Only when Adam and Eve ate the fruit from the forbidden tree did death enter into history. (See Genesis 2:17.) God didn't create death. Death is simply the natural result of sin. (See Romans 6:23.)

With that said, death is a necessary component in

this fallen world. If not for death, then sin would run rampant for eternity. (See Genesis 3:22-23.) So in the context of a fallen world, death is a good thing; but this doesn't mean that it's what God would prefer. God's preference is a sin-free world where there is no death to steal away the people He so dearly loves. And that's why He sent Jesus—to destroy the power of sin and thereby remove the sting of death. (See 1 Corinthians 15:56.) One day we who believe in Him will live in that perfect world. (See Revelation 21:4.)

If people always die in God's timing, then why did Jesus raise the dead? Was He battling His Father? No. Jesus only ever worked in harmony with His Father. (See John 5:19.) Jesus came to destroy the devil's work, and it is the devil who comes to kill. (See 1 Peter 5:8, 1 John 3:8, and John 10:10.)

We struggle with this concept for a few reasons.

First, it's uncomfortable. It is uncomfortable to think that we might have known people who died before their time. It is even more uncomfortable to think that we had the Solution living inside of us the entire time we sat through their funeral.

Second, we have been conditioned to see death as a wonderful, blessed occasion for Christians. This is true because, as Paul said, when we are absent from the body, we are present with the Lord. (See 2 Corinthians 5:6-8 and Philippians 1:23-24.) Yet even then, God is not excited when believers die.

> **Psalm 116:15** – Precious [and of great consequence] in the sight of the Lord is the death of His godly ones [so He watches over them]. (AMP15)

Another word for "precious" here is "costly." As the Amplified Bible (2015) points out here, it is "of great consequence" to the Lord. Godly people are typically of much more use to the Lord alive. While He certainly rejoices their homecoming in heaven, He still grieves their departure from the earth right along with us.

But what about those who are not Christians? Have you ever considered the fact that Jesus never raised Christians from the dead when He walked this earth? Until He died, rose again, and poured out the Holy Spirit, there was no such thing as a Christian! Our God has compassion on those who are lost, and He wants everyone to have the opportunity to choose to follow Him.

This doesn't mean Christians can't be raised to life, because that happened in Scripture too. (See Acts 20:9-12.) My point is simply that of the tens of thousands of people who die every day, I have reason to believe the vast majority of them do so before their time. For one thing, most are statistically not Christians, and God does not want them to perish. As long as a person has a chance of repenting, I would say that their death is premature. Others who die are young Christians whose destinies were cut short. Only a small percentage are godly people who lived full lives and were ready to go home to be with the Lord. This would explain why some Christians, like those mentioned earlier, are seeing such regular results with resurrections.

I wonder, though, if death is even absolutely necessary for every Christian. Just because Elijah and Enoch are the only known humans to escape death does not mean that such a possibility is unavailable to others. It is one thing to recognize that we live in a fallen world where death is a natural occurrence, but this does not mean that we cannot hope for another possibility. I recognize that the odds are that I will physically die, but I sure would love to be whisked into heaven in a whirlwind like Elijah or simply be transported into heaven like Enoch! (See 2 Kings 2:11, Genesis 5:24, and Hebrews 11:5.) Wouldn't you?

If that last paragraph bothers you, it's probably because your hope has limits. The nature of limitless hope is that we don't base our expectation on earthly odds. We base our expectation on the biblically-rooted, limitless capabilities of the limitless God who loves us.

If I physically die, then I won't be upset. After all, I'll be with Jesus! But since escaping death is a Biblically supported possibility, I'm going to aim for such excellence, holiness, and intimacy with God that sin—the sting of death—can't take me down. Call me a heretic or call me crazy—I call it limitless hope—but my personal goal is to live on earth until I'm 120 and then either be translated into heaven or be martyred. Show me a Biblical reason to desire otherwise, and I'll change; but I have yet to find one.

This, however, is not my purpose in writing. The way we move from this life into heaven isn't technically up to us, but the decisions we make in this life are. I only mention this "alternative to death" in order to help you think differently about death. Paul called death an enemy of God, and the Church must embrace this truth if resurrections are going to become more commonplace among us. (See 1 Corinthians 15:26.) Limitless hope aims joyfully for the best possible outcome and then rejoices whether or not it happens.

A Better Problem in Ministering to Families

On June 21, 2010, I received a phone call from my retired parents. A man was added to the prayer list at their little Tennessee church who had been in the hospital after a serious accident. Not even 40-years-old and now brain-dead, the family was faced with the impossible decision to take him off life-support, which they did. The request came to pray for the family to be comforted and for the man to fully pass peacefully.

My parents and their church prayed for the family as requested; but my mom said she felt in her spirit that this man was supposed to live. She instead prayed that God would heal him and raise him up. The next day, the man was fully awake and walking around! The last we heard of this story, the man was fine and everyone was praying for the salvation of the family.

Which would you rather pray for: the comfort of family members whose loved one is still dead, or the salvation of family members whose loved one just came back to life in Jesus' name?

> Limitless hope causes us to seek the raising of the dead. Expected disappointment causes us to only pray for comfort for the family.

The aftermath of death comes with its list of problems. There are practical issues, like the cost of the funeral and burial. There are emotional issues as family members each grieve in their own unique ways. There are social issues as families try to carry on without a key member like a father or mother who is no longer part of the picture. If the person lived alone, there is then the responsibility of sorting through their belongings and possibly trying to sell their house.

Resurrections, on the other hand, come with their own list of problems. For example, who answers all the questions that family and friends have? How do we help the recently-raised individual understand what he or she just experienced? What happens legally when a death certificate has been issued and now the person is alive? How do we manage the influx of salvations that may result?

I would say the "problems" associated with resurrections are better than the "problems" associated with deaths. And I would also say that the more resurrections we encounter, the easier these questions will be to answer. Personally, I dream of a day when pastors spend more time learning to minister resurrection-life to the dead than they spend learning to conduct funerals.

These Are Not Uncharted Waters

I personally know a woman named Pam Walker who used to live in an apartment complex in Florida. For months, every time she entered that building, the Holy Spirit moved her to breathe deeply and declare, "I breathe the very life of Christ into this building." On March 16, 2000, at 6:30 in the evening, a man from across the hall came pounding on her door. When Pam opened the door, she found that the man wasn't alone. He was holding the lifeless body of his 7-month-old baby boy.

"I only left him in the bathtub for a minute!" he sobbed.

Pam had been a nurse. She knew what death

looked like. She knew what it felt like. When the father handed his baby boy to her, Pam knew that medical attention didn't have much help to offer. Nevertheless, she tossed the phone to the father and had him call 911. Pam checked all the vital signs and did everything she was trained to do, but the child had indeed died, and there didn't appear to be any earthly hope.

As paramedics raced to the apartment, Pam used the downtime to pray for the baby and command life into him in Jesus' name. Several minutes passed.

Suddenly, the baby boy's little chest began to rise.

By the time the paramedics arrived, he was perfectly healthy and alert.

Testimonies like Pam's don't need to be anomalies. Many will likely consider this to be the most controversial chapter in this book, but what I'm inviting you to is not a new teaching. For that matter, it is not a rare and unattainable experience. The same Holy Spirit who lives in Pam and in my mom lives in you. This is the same Holy Spirit who has been raising hundreds to life in Mexico, Mozambique, and around the world.

I'm not asking you to blaze a trail into uncharted territory. I'm encouraging you to step with me into the stream of what God has already been doing in hundreds (and perhaps thousands) of cases throughout the world—even in America.

We Have Been Commissioned to Raise the Dead

Raising the dead is one small piece of the authority that Jesus grants to His people. He actually commanded His twelve disciples to raise the dead in whatever villages they visited.

> **Matthew 10:7-8 –** As you go, proclaim this
> message: "The kingdom of heaven has come
> near." Heal the sick, raise the dead, cleanse
> those who have leprosy, drive out demons.
> Freely you have received; freely give.

Before you argue, "Yes, but that command was to
the twelve, not to me," I want you to consider what Jesus
said later in Matthew's Gospel:

> **Matthew 28:19-20 –** Therefore go and make
> disciples of all nations…teaching them to
> obey everything I have commanded you…

The twelve were commissioned to teach all future
followers of Jesus to obey every command that He ever
gave to them. Yes, that included things like, "Love your
enemies," and, "Pray for those who persecute you." But it
also included the command to raise the dead.

Notice that Jesus didn't say, "Pray that My Father
will raise the dead." He simply said, "Raise the dead." This
brings me back to the points I made in Chapter Ten when
we studied healing ministry. Do I cut wood in half or does
the saw cut wood in half? The answer is both—and neither
could do the work without the other. Yes, Jesus is the
resurrection and the life. We can only command life if we
speak on His behalf with His authority. Only the Holy
Spirit can raise the dead. But the responsibility of the
ministry has been placed in our hands as sons of God and
partners with Christ—extensions of His Body in the earth.

> **John 5:19-21 –** Jesus gave them this answer:
> "Very truly I tell you, the Son can do nothing
> by Himself; He can do only what He sees His

Father doing, because whatever the Father
does the Son also does. For the Father loves
the Son and shows Him all He does. Yes, and
He will show Him even greater works than
these, so that you will be amazed. **For just as
the Father raises the dead and gives them
life, even so the Son gives life to whom He
is pleased to give it.** (emphasis added)

"Freely you have received; freely give." Sometimes
we think the dead stay dead because God wants them
dead. But what if the dead stay dead because we aren't
pleased to give them life? What would happen if the entire
Church suddenly jumped on board with the ministry of
raising the dead? What if dead-raising became as common
as healing ministry? What if we were surprised when the
dead stay dead instead of being surprised when they wake
up?

I believe it's time for the Church to realize that
while Jesus is the Resurrection and the Life, we have been
commissioned to minister in His name and according to
His nature. We have been commanded, along with the
Twelve, to raise the dead. We have been instructed to
freely give what we have freely received. Even though we
can do nothing by ourselves, we are stewards of God's
grace; and we are invited to give life to whomever we are
pleased to give it, just like Jesus did.

The prophet Elisha once found his feet in the
trembling grip of a distressed mother whose son had died
in her arms. At that moment he did not bend down to
comfort her or pray for God's peace in her heart. He took
immediate action, fully expecting the boy to be raised back
to life. Sure enough the boy returned from the dead, but

not until Elisha went to the boy and made physical contact with his lifeless body, imparting life as he best knew how. (See 2 Kings 4:8-37.)

We read these historical accounts in the Bible and easily write them off as fairy-tales, exaggerations, or encounters relegated to a different era. But I hope you have discovered in this chapter that such experiences are still happening right now, today.

As for me, I'm convinced. I now know more than enough credible Christians who have raised the dead. I have even seen people who used to be corpses and are today healthy human beings. I don't question whether or not this is for today. So when I attend funerals, I always start by praying for resurrection. When I approach the casket I command the person to rise in Jesus' name.

I only pray for the family to be comforted if the dead person doesn't come back. For one thing, there are typically already enough people praying for comfort. For another thing, if the dead person is raised, the family won't need me to pray for comfort!

At the time of this writing, I have not yet seen God raise the dead with my own eyes, but by the time of this book's publication, I may have. How could this be possible? Because I'm regularly making opportunities for it to happen.

That's the main difference I've found between those Christians who have raised the dead and those who have not: The ones who have raised the dead are the ones who took action toward that end. Limitless hope doesn't just know what is possible; limitless hope acts on it.

Endnotes:

1. Daniel's resurrection was caught on video, and a documentary including the footage can be viewed at https://youtu.be/MZP5Gq7-WYM or purchased on Amazon.com in the DVD titled *Raised from the Dead*. This film includes interviews with Daniel, his wife, the doctor who declared him dead, the mortician, a state security officer, and two of the pastors who prayed for Daniel. Daniel now shares his testimony with his own death certificate in-hand!

2. Rutz, J. H. (2011). Chapter 1: The new kingdom explosion. In *Megashift: The best news since year one ...* (pp. 29-30). Washington, DC: WND Books.

Chapter 13:

Limitless Hope and Deliverance Ministry

I was in the little African village of Bubalya, Uganda. The church building—formed from mud, sticks, and grass—was about the size of my bedroom in America. Villagers flooded the tiny room and overflowed out the doors—some even hanging in the windows. Many miracles happened that day including a deaf man, a blind woman, and another woman with a paralyzed leg all being healed. By the time I left that village, every single sick, injured, diseased, or degenerating person was completely healed by the power of Jesus Christ.

One particular woman stood out to me, though. She came because of crippling pain in her legs that caused walking to be agonizing. I prayed for her and commanded the legs to be healed. Through my translator, I asked if anything had changed.

"This leg is now healed, but the other still hurts," came the translated reply.

I thanked the Lord for what He had done so far and commanded the other leg to be healed in Jesus' name.

This time, the translator said, "The pain has left this leg but has moved back to her other leg."

In my experience, any time pain starts to move around like this, I have found that a demon is at work. Demons are real spiritual beings that seek to steal from, kill, and destroy the people whom God so dearly loves. They not only attack the thoughts and emotions of humans but can also produce physical results, as evidenced in Jesus' ministry. (See Mark 9:17-18 and Luke 13:11.)

Rather than commanding healing again, I spoke to the spirit behind the problem. "Spirit of infirmity," I said quietly, "In Jesus' name, leave this woman now, and never return."

Remember, this woman did not speak English, so what happened next was not psychology or hypnosis. She began to shake and said to my translator, "I feel like I am beginning to panic."

"Tell her not to be afraid and that it will be over in a moment," I replied. I then turned back to the place of pain and said, "No, you are not allowed to make a show of this woman. Leave her alone."

Instantly, the shaking stopped, but the woman continued to breathe heavily.

"Come out now, in Jesus' name, and never return."

The woman let out a deep sigh and testified that

the fear, the panic, and all the pain had left instantly.

Speaking with Authority

As I ministered to that woman in the bush of Africa, the story could have gone differently. I could have been distracted by what the devil was doing. For that matter, I could have been completely unaware that a spirit was at work in the first place. In that case, when the woman began to shake and panic, I might have probably stopped seeking physical healing and started praying for the woman's peace and comfort. She probably would have calmed down, but her legs would still be in pain. The demon would still have a grip.

Unfortunately, this is what we often do. When people are experiencing emotional problems like panic, depression, rage, and so forth, we tend to assume that the problem is purely physical. In my experience, there are indeed cases where such an issue truly is purely physical— perhaps a gland that's not producing the correct balance of hormones. But demons can produce the exact same symptoms, so not everything is only physical.

For this reason I always start by ministering to the physical condition (commanding healing or prophesying authoritative words of peace and joy into the person's life), and most of the time this is sufficient to bring about the results. However, there are also cases where such ministry forces a demon to start fighting to maintain its grip, and this leads us into what many in the church now call "deliverance ministry."

I seem to run into demons far more often than I ever thought would be normal. Our modern culture shrouds them in medical diagnoses and suppresses their influence on the body with harsh chemicals, but science holds no authority to command the demon to leave. Jesus is the answer, and He always comes through.

I don't think I have ever "gone looking" for demons. This is often the unfortunate fallacy of many deliverance ministries in the world today—people so focused on demons that every problem must be caused by one. Such ministers go to great lengths trying to name demons, rank demons, and figure out their weak points. Unfortunately, this seems to place our focus on the demon's power rather than on God's power. We can become intimidated when we focus on the power of a demon, and this can cause us to shrink away from addressing them—especially if they are said to have significant influence over an entire region, which many have labeled "a territorial spirit."

> Limitless hope is not intimidated by demons of any sort. Expected disappointment ranks demons and considers some more powerful or formidable than others.

I like to say, "A rabbit is a rabbit. He is not considered more or less dangerous than other rabbits according to the number of carrots he stole from your garden." Likewise, a demon is a demon, and it is not considered more or less dangerous based on the number of people it influences. We deal with all rabbits the same, and we deal with all demons the same. Jesus' name has all authority, and demons only have the authority we give them.

To be honest, these studies of demons can make for fascinating reading. But my experience is that they they're completely unnecessary and they generally give far too much attention to the enemy.[1]

We don't need to look for demons. If we simply go about the work to which Jesus called us, they will show up. All we need to know is how to address the situation when it arises.

When my wife Robin and I had just begun courting, I had already been battling depression and emotional outbursts for several years. Those who know me today can't believe that as a fifteen-year-old, I would lay on the floor kicking and screaming—throwing a tantrum like an enraged toddler. I had some significant emotional dysfunction!

One weekend Robin and her family were leaving for a vacation. I was devastated. The "only person who made me happy" was going to be gone for two whole days! How was I going to survive?

Obviously I had more faith in Robin than I did in God, and that was idolatry. I sat in the car after our date— crying my eyes out—while Robin stared at me in stunned disbelief, not knowing what to do with her basket-case boyfriend.

Finally, Robin's discernment kicked in. "This isn't Art. Whatever spirit is behind this, you have to go right now!"

Instantly, it was as if the clouds parted in my mind and I was able to think for myself. Nearly seven years of clinical depression and emotional dysfunction was gone in an instant. Many had prayed for my peace. Many had prayed for me to have self-control. But what I really needed was for someone to command that demon to leave so that I could experience the peace and self-control that God had already made available to me. Since that time, I have lived consistently free from depression.

> **Limitless hope causes us to command evil spirits to leave in the name of Jesus. Expected disappointment causes us to pray for peace and comfort.**

The same principle we have already applied to the ministries of healing and raising the dead apply here. Yes, Jesus is the only One who actually has the authority to command a demon to leave; but He has invited you and me—despite our unworthiness—to sit with Him on His throne. (See Ephesians 2:6 and Revelation 3:21.) He has invited us to share the authority that He procured.

After Jesus rose from the dead He told His disciples, "All authority in heaven and on earth has been given to Me." (See Matthew 28:18.) If Jesus has "all authority," then this means the enemy has no authority. "All" means "all." But in the very next verse, He said, "Therefore, go…" In other words, by commissioning us with His authority, we have the responsibility to represent Him and to speak with His authority. This is why we can cast out demons rather than needing to pray for God to drive them out. Remember, we are presently seated with Jesus on His throne. (See Ephesians 2:6.)

Whenever Jesus instructed His disciples to cast out demons, that's how He worded it. He never said, "Pray for the demon to leave." To say that would be to imply that you have no authority, so you need to petition someone who does have authority.

I once found myself driving behind a drunk driver one night. I called the police and followed the driver until a squad car could meet up with us. As a citizen, I am required to follow all traffic laws; but the police department gave me permission to exceed the speed limit and to cautiously run red lights in order to follow this dangerous person and keep track of where he was. I had no authority to do these things on my own, but authority was delegated to me by the police to help them in their mission. I didn't have to ask permission at every red light or stop sign. Once I was given the authority, I maintained the authority until the mission was accomplished.

Until the devil's work is completely destroyed, our mission is incomplete, and we therefore maintain the authority needed for that mission. Once the devil is cast into the lake of fire at the end of time, we won't need that authority anymore. There won't be any demons left to cast out. Until then, the authority for the mission has been delegated; and for this reason, Jesus commands us to "cast out demons" in His name. (See Matthew 10:8 and Mark 16:17-18.)

After Jesus calmed a storm that nearly sank His boat, He and the disciples stepped onto land in the region of the Gerasenes.

> **Mark 5:2-5 –** When Jesus got out of the boat, a man with an impure spirit came from the tombs to meet Him. This man lived in the tombs, and no one could bind him anymore, not even with a chain. For he had often been chained hand and foot, but he tore the chains

apart and broke the irons on his feet. No one
was strong enough to subdue him. Night and
day among the tombs and in the hills he
would cry out and cut himself with stones.

In today's culture, we would put such a person in
an institution, sedate them with drugs, and hope for the
best. As Christians, we might even pray for healing or
peace. But none of these options are what Jesus
commissioned us to do with His authority. Jesus had a
different response. He commanded the demon to leave.

Authority that Works

Something interesting happened during Jesus'
encounter with that man. He commanded the demon to
leave, and it didn't!

Did you ever notice that? Look at what it says:

Mark 5:6-10 – When he saw Jesus from a
distance, he ran and fell on his knees in front
of Him. He shouted at the top of his voice,
"What do you want with me, Jesus, Son of the
Most High God? In God's name don't torture
me!" For Jesus had said to him, "Come out of
this man, you impure spirit!"

Then Jesus asked him, "What is your
name?"

"My name is Legion," he replied, "for we
are many." And he begged Jesus again and
again not to send them out of the area.

"For Jesus had said to him…" This means that
Jesus commanded the spirit to leave, and it didn't.

Place yourself in Jesus' shoes (or sandals if you

prefer historical accuracy). In that moment, it would be easy for you to think, *Wait a minute; that was supposed to work! Is there something wrong? Apparently I don't have the authority I thought I had!*

But Jesus didn't budge. Jesus knew the authority that He had from the Father. He knew that His mission included proclaiming freedom to prisoners and setting free the oppressed. (See Luke 4:18.) Jesus continued in ministry—not because He was stubborn but because He knew that He carried an authority that works, and He wasn't going to be swayed by contrary evidence. Jesus demonstrated what it is to "live by faith and not by sight."

When I find myself in a situation where deliverance ministry is called for, I always expect the demon to leave immediately. In most cases it does. Jesus rarely had conversations with demons. Casting out demons was typically a very fast and easy process.

> **Matthew 8:16** – When evening came, many who were demon-possessed were brought to Him, and He drove out the spirits with a word and healed all the sick.

Here we find Jesus ministering to "many," and the process of deliverance is nothing more than a single word. The Bible doesn't tell us what that single word was, but it's probably just as well—we would make a doctrine out of it because we like formulas. Instead, we have to rely on our own relationships with the Holy Spirit.

Many deliverance ministers use Jesus' one-time encounter with the demonized man in the tombs as their model for deliverance ministry. I, however, use the passage from Matthew's gospel, which seems to show a more common experience that worked with "many" (not a one-time encounter).

You don't need to know the demon's name, have a conversation with the demon, tell the demon where to go, or anything else like that. Simply practice faith in Jesus and trust that He will do the work as you merely speak in His name.

Immediate Deliverance

> Limitless hope causes us to expect the enemy to flee immediately. Expected disappointment causes us to expect circumstances to change "in God's timing."

Whenever we minister without results, it's easy to back down and cower. But remember when we talked about the epileptic boy who had a demon that the disciples couldn't cast out. Was that evidence that it wasn't God's timing to heal the boy and set him free? If it were evidence of that, then Jesus would have been rebelling against the Father to cast out that demon like He did. "Now is the day of salvation." (See 2 Corinthians 6:2.)

Jesus never gave an evil spirit time to pack its bags. If a demon stalled for time, this wasn't evidence that it wasn't God's timing. The legion of demons in the man Jesus encountered was stubborn. It says that Jesus "had been saying" for them to leave. But Jesus persevered, and the man was set free. Again: Now is the day of salvation!

When you see a person going through a rough situation, the right thing is to minister to them immediately. True biblical "comfort" in the pattern of

Jesus' ministry is found through actual freedom and wholeness. False comfort, however, takes the form of empty phrases that leave the person the same—statements like, "Things will change in God's timing."

I have learned something during my ministry: Things only change in God's timing when a Christian enforces God's timing. When Christians do nothing, God's timing is usually ignored because sin seems more interesting. When it comes to the things Jesus paid for in the atonement, God's timing is now; man's timing is later; and sin's timing is never.

I can't emphasize this enough: Now is the day of salvation! Do not waver when it comes to the authority you have received in Christ. If you find yourself in a situation where a person needs deliverance, simply command the demon to leave and expect it to leave immediately. If it argues or fights back, do not allow this to sway your expectation. Remain consistent, standing in faith.

> **James 4:7 –** Submit yourselves, then, to God. Resist the devil, and he will flee from you.

Clearly Defining the Enemy

Limitless hope sees the distinction between the work of Christ and the work of the devil. Expected disappointment causes us to blur the lines between good and evil.

First John 3:8 tells us that the reason Jesus came was to destroy the devil's work. In context this scripture is

279

talking about sin. But knowing the overarching theme of Scripture, we know that it includes the effects of sin: Sickness, disease, destruction, death, and so forth.

In a specific, direct sense, the devil's work is whatever the enemy is presently doing. In a broad, passive sense, the devil's work is everything that has been skewed by Satan's initial work in the Garden of Eden, leading to the fall of man. Jesus came to destroy all of that by transforming us into people of victory.

When did we become confused between what was the work of God and what was the work of the devil? In Chapter Two, I told you about the scars I used to have on my face. I spent two and a half years looking for ways that God could be glorified by me having those scars. Then I discovered that it wasn't God's will for me to have them at all. I can guarantee that God received (and still receives) glory from those scars because of the testimony of His ability to do the impossible. And I would argue that He receives more glory from that than if I still had them.

Jesus drew the line: "The thief comes only to steal and kill and destroy; I have come that they may have life, and have it to the full." (See John 10:10.) In summary, Satan is bad; Jesus is good. Stealing, killing, and destroying are the work of the enemy—at least until the end of time when God's righteousness will bring an end to everything that has not already surrendered to Jesus. Until that time, these things are only the work of the devil. Jesus came to give life.

When I minister healing or deliverance, I never question whether or not the problem is God's will. Jesus already revealed God's will. I simply ask the Holy Spirit how He wants me to address the problem for the sake of maximum effectiveness.

Every demon must submit to the name of Jesus. Our Lord is always victorious, and His Spirit dwells within us. We, therefore—as members of His Body—carry the ongoing responsibility of destroying the devil's work in today's world.

> **John 20:21 –** Again Jesus said, "Peace be with you! As the Father has sent Me, I am sending you."

Endnotes:

1. I'm currently working on a book about deliverance ministry that I believe will answer the most important questions about demons without distracting the reader from Jesus. It will likely be released in 2018 or 2019 and will be available at www.SupernaturalTruth.com.

Chapter 14:

Limitless Hope and Passionate Endurance

Perhaps by this point in the book you're beginning to think a little differently. That's good! When you really start giving yourself over to limitless hope, you begin to see possibilities where there used to be concern. You find yourself no longer worrying—not because you're a blind optimist but because you're aware of a limitless God who loves you. This mindset also stirs you to action as you trust that God really does want to team up with you to transform the world around you.

Limitless hope has a tendency to do that to people. We begin to think like Jesus. And as we think like Him, we begin to address situations in new ways. We embrace our authority as His representatives. We expect miraculous intervention in earthly affairs. We trust in His protection and provision wholeheartedly.

One of the most significant benefits I have discovered from limitless hope is the ability to passionately press forward through difficulties. In Christ we find the strength to endure. I'm not talking about merely "holding on" until Jesus takes us home. I'm talking about thriving in ministry as we persevere in the mission He has given.

In these final pages of the book, I want to introduce you to a few more concepts that will bring maturity and strength to everything you have learned so far. Limitless hope is not about a new theology. It is about a thriving relationship with a limitless God. And in the midst of this relationship, He grants us the joy of helping Him do what He wants to do.

You Are the Key to Changing Circumstances

I want to be clear about this. When I say that you are the key to changing circumstances, I'm not echoing the old cliché, "God helps those who help themselves." That's not biblical, and it often causes us to take matters into our own hands when God simply wants us to emotionally rest in Him. What I am saying is that within the context of your relationship with God, He wants your participation.

There is a difference between these two mindsets. The first seems to imply that we need to stay busy so God can help us. The second, however, implies that we need to be aware of what God is doing and join Him in it.

Sometimes we need a special revelation about what God is doing, but most of the time we simply need to look for opportunities to do the things He has already commanded us to do.

When it comes to relationships—whether family relationships, workplace relationships, or otherwise—the command from Scripture is to consistently represent Christ. Admittedly there are times when we represent Christ really well and yet our relationships still fall apart. Paul even gave such a scenario as one of the acceptable provisions for divorce. (See 1 Corinthians 7:12-15.) That's not what I'm talking about. On the contrary, I'm talking about the many relationships that desperately need Jesus to be tangibly present.

If you're feeling particularly ambitious, write down the names of the people in every strained relationship you currently have. Maybe it's a neighbor who has a dispute with you about your property line. Maybe it's a spouse who seems to be growing distant. Maybe it's one of your children or one of your parents—or a sibling. Maybe it's an obnoxious coworker or someone who wronged you at church. Take a look at that list and decide whose responsibility it is to represent Jesus in each relationship.

If you're honest, you'll realize that as the Christian it is always your responsibility to represent Jesus. If the other person is a Christian, it's their responsibility too; but that doesn't let you off the hook. You cannot force another person to be Christ-like. You can, however, choose to personally forgive, love, and actively demonstrate God's grace.

> Limitless hope sees that you are the key to relational restoration in your neighborhood, family, workplace, and church. Expected disappointment sees someone else as the key.

To wait for someone else to make the first move toward relational restoration is both petty and worthless. Yes, it does feel good to be pursued, but that's not Jesus' nature. When we were sinners, Jesus pursued us for the sake of restoring our relationship with Him. Now that we're saints, we represent Him. We have new natures. We are now pursuers. If you're waiting for someone else to fix a relational problem by pursuing you, then you're confused about your identity. Your identity is in Christ, and He is one who pursues for the sake of relationship.

Admittedly, He is also a gentleman and gives space when it is proper. Representing Jesus through pursuit does not mean we need to pester the person. On the contrary, it is entirely possible to pursue a person while giving them room to come around to the truth. What matters is the condition of your heart. Are you granting a person some space because you feel that this space will help them? Or are you giving them space as a means of escaping your own responsibility? Ask the Holy Spirit, and He will make the answer clear to you.

If you're bothered by the current condition of your marriage, family, neighborhood, church, etc., then you need to start praying for meaningful solutions. Don't wait around for someone else to "get their act together." Take responsibility for the problem and own it in prayer.

As you pray, you will receive strategies from the Lord. But as you implement the ideas He gives, do not become discouraged if things don't change immediately. Until you pray and act, the problems around you are your responsibility. But once you begin persisting in prayer and action, God takes the responsibility upon Himself. By praying and acting, you fulfill your role and open the door for God to fulfill His role. Your responsibility is Christ-like action; God's responsibility is success. If you act without success, do not be discouraged. Simply continue petitioning God for the next step and for the boldness and empowerment to carry out His instructions.

God wants consistent peace in every relationship you have, and He has chosen you as His representative. If a person is abusive and dangerous to you, then peace will likely involve keeping a distance from that person; but it will also require that you choose to forgive. Not every relationship needs to be reconciled, but every relationship does need the peaceful, loving influence of Jesus.

Only Some Suffering is to be Expected

The New Testament talks a lot about suffering. Strangely, many Christians have interpreted the meaning of these passages to say that we should expect to suffer with sickness, disease, poverty, and death. As mentioned in Chapter Seven, though, every New Testament passage that treats suffering positively has to do with persecution for the cause of Christ.

A quick look at the word "suffer" in a concordance will yield some interesting results. Throughout the Gospels of Matthew, Mark, Luke, and John, the word suffering (in the NIV) is basically used in reference to only two things: (1) the suffering Jesus would endure for our salvation and (2) the suffering involved with a sickness or disease that Jesus was about to heal. Never do we read in any of the Gospels about anyone suffering with a sickness or disease whom Jesus failed to heal. This is not the kind of suffering that we are to expect.

The first time we see the word "suffer" used in

reference to a Christian is in Acts 5:41. The apostles had been working many miraculous signs and were gaining quite a following, which made the High Priest and his associates jealous. He and the Sadducees threw the apostles in jail, but God miraculously set them free. They went right back to the streets to preach some more!

The High Priest and the Sadducees had them arrested again. After a trial the apostles were beaten with whips and released with a strict warning never to preach in Jesus' name again. Then we read that infamous word in this context: "The apostles left the Sanhedrin, rejoicing because they had been counted worthy of suffering disgrace for the Name."

Now that's godly suffering!

> Limitless hope causes us to rejoice in suffering for the sake of the Gospel and to not worry about other forms of suffering that could happen. Expected disappointment causes us to beg God for safety and protection.

You don't need to beg God for the things He is already pleased to give you. Jesus devoted only one phrase of His model prayer to protection: "...deliver us from the evil one." (See Matthew 6:13.)

Jesus was clear that we do not have to ramble on and on with prayer requests because our Father knows what we need before we ask Him. (See Matthew 6:8). To pray for safety is not necessarily wrong or sinful, but obsessing over it does seem to imply that we don't trust God to remember to follow through on the promises He has already made.

If I tell my wife that I'll pick her up from work, it doesn't make sense for her to repeatedly remind me to pick her up unless I have a track record of forgetting things like that. That just shows a lack of trust (translation: lack of faith).

Jesus doesn't forget His promises. Jesus vowed, "I am with you always, to the very end of the age." (See Matthew 28:20.) Jesus assured the disciples that because of the authority He has given us, "Nothing will harm you." (See Luke 10:19.)

Do I trust Him to remember these words? If I do, then I don't need to beg Him for something He has already promised.

In fact, one could even argue that the one line in Jesus' prayer about protection—"...deliver us from the evil one..."—is actually asking to be spared from a current trial, not a future one. I've ministered in a good number of dangerous and even life-threatening places; but to be perfectly honest with you, I don't really pray for protection. I simply trust Jesus to follow through on His promises. In Ephesians 6:16, Paul taught that our faith will successfully neutralize every single attack of the enemy. When I simply trust Jesus, He protects me.

Am I saying faith will protect you from all problems or that I never have problems in my own life? Not at all. Actually, faith makes you more likely to be persecuted. (See 2 Timothy 3:12.) Persecution is a promise for the faithful. (See Matthew 10:16-23 and John 15:20.) And even the ordinary problems that exist in this fallen world are to be expected. (See John 16:33.) Faith does not exempt us from problems altogether.

What I am saying, however, is that any inevitable suffering (like persecution and the basic, manageable troubles of this fallen world) will not be thwarted by prayer anyway (because Jesus promised it would happen); but any avoidable suffering (including avoidable persecution, attacks from evil spirits, and even a lot of natural calamities) will stay away when we simply trust Jesus. He will keep us safe.

Don't Fear Persecution or Death

When it comes to suffering persecution, the only biblical prayer seems to be for strength to endure. But when it comes to all other forms of suffering, I don't technically need to pray that God would protect me since Scripture already promises such protection to those who have faith in Jesus. There are plenty of more important things to pray about.

Consider the foreign mission trips that many churches take. Contrast our normal prayers for protection with the story of Paul and Agabus in Acts 21:10-14. Paul was planning a trip to Jerusalem, and the prophet Agabus grabbed Paul's belt and tied his own hands with it. He then prophesied, "The Holy Spirit says, 'In this way the Jewish leaders in Jerusalem will bind the owner of this belt and will hand him over to the Gentiles.'" Thus, Paul was warned of the danger ahead.

But Paul went to Jerusalem anyway! God gave Paul an opportunity to count the cost and know what he was walking into. Rather than praying for safety, I believe we should ask God what to expect when we go. Then, once He has revealed what will happen when we go, we have the opportunity to decide whether or not we are up for it. I would rather have God tell me that I'll be persecuted and then decide to go than pray for safety and find myself persecuted.

When I traveled to Uganda for the first time, I didn't need to pray for safety and protection. I knew the trip was dangerous, but I had confidence that God would protect me. I expected persecution, even though I didn't have a word from God about it. In fact, a little part of me expected that I might be killed. But because of the promises God has declared over my life—and the fact that I have many friends at home who believe in God's resurrection power—I had confidence that God would raise me back to life. (Is this any different from Abraham's faith, as discussed in Chapter One?) If I didn't have that confidence then there's no way I would have traveled alone to a country I didn't know to meet a man who e-mailed me a few times and could easily be a criminal. When we have confidence in Christ's love, we aren't concerned about persecution or death. Limitless hope is incompatible with a mindset that assumes God won't take care of us as we follow Him.

But again, persecution is sure to happen. In John 15:20, Jesus assured His disciples, "Remember what I told you: 'A servant is not greater than his master.' If they persecuted Me, they will persecute you also." If you're suffering persecution, you can rejoice in the fact that you were considered worthy to be associated with Jesus. (See Acts 5:41.) When it comes to persecution, Jesus said it would be normal, so don't be discouraged. Be excited that your walk with Jesus is so obvious to His enemies that they chose to attack Him by attacking you.

If you're not suffering persecution, then be

grateful because there are those in the family of God who currently are. Every day, an estimated average of around 482 Christians are martyred for loving Jesus and refusing to deny Him as their Lord.[1] That's around 20 every hour. In fact, during the time it has taken you to read this far into this chapter, it is statistically possible that 3 to 5 of your brothers and sisters in Christ were killed somewhere in the world for serving Jesus.

Persecution happens on some level in every nation of the world, but some locations experience more extreme attacks than others. In today's world, some Christians have their homes burned, their families murdered, and their belongings seized. Some are currently in prison and labor camps for spreading the Gospel. Some have suffered brutal beatings and all manner of disgraceful and evil acts from religious and political extremists.

Why don't they give up?

Because of limitless hope!

Paul wrote to Timothy from prison. In His second letter to the young pastor, Paul made the point I've been talking about here. He talked about the circumstances leading up to his current imprisonment but mentioned how in the midst of the persecution, God had miraculously protected Him.

> **2 Timothy 4:16-18 –** At my first defense, no one came to my support, but everyone deserted me. May it not be held against them. But the Lord stood at my side and gave me strength, so that through me the message might be fully proclaimed and all the Gentiles might hear it. And I was delivered from the lion's mouth. The Lord will rescue me from

every evil attack and will bring me safely to
His heavenly kingdom. To Him be glory for
ever and ever. Amen.

Paul had limitless hope. Paul rejoiced in suffering
for Jesus and completely trusted in God's protection at the
same time. He didn't focus on his natural circumstances
but rather kept his anchor of hope firmly fixed in the
throne room of God.

> **2 Corinthians 4:16-18** – Therefore we do not
> lose heart. Though outwardly we are wasting
> away, yet inwardly we are being renewed day
> by day. For our light and momentary troubles
> are achieving for us an eternal glory that far
> outweighs them all. So we fix our eyes not on
> what is seen, but on what is unseen, since
> what is seen is temporary, but what is unseen
> is eternal.[2]

Enduring Persecution

**Limitless hope grows from suffering. Expected
disappointment also grows from suffering.
Which one grows is up to you.**

Remember our study of Proverbs 13:12 in
Chapter Three: "Hope deferred makes the heart sick." As
we find ourselves in the face of suffering, we have the
decision either to allow our hearts to be made sick or to
nurture the hope we have developed thus far.

When you're over your head in the middle of a
lake, the difference between drowning or calmly floating to

shore begins in your mind. Will you panic and sink? Or will you take a deep breath and relax?

Sometimes the trials we face in the Christian life can seem like too much to handle. We can feel like we're drowning in the middle of a lake. If you fear the trial then you will indeed crumble beneath the weight of it. But if you maintain your limitless hope in the Lord then you will be able to endure it all.

The apostle Paul faced significant persecution— probably more than any of us are likely to experience. Take a moment to read some of the things he endured, and be encouraged by his unwavering faith:

> **2 Corinthians 11:24-28 –** Five times I received from the Jews the forty lashes minus one. Three times I was beaten with rods, once I was pelted with stones, three times I was shipwrecked, I spent a night and a day in the open sea, I have been constantly on the move. I have been in danger from rivers, in danger from bandits, in danger from my fellow Jews, in danger from Gentiles; in danger in the city, in danger in the country, in danger at sea; and in danger from false believers. I have labored and toiled and have often gone without sleep; I have known hunger and thirst and have often gone without food; I have been cold and naked. Besides everything else, I face daily the pressure of my concern for all the churches.

Despite Paul's constant suffering for the cause of Christ, he gladly pressed forward. In his letter to the Philippians—also written while in prison—Paul lets us in on his thought process. On one hand, He recognizes that his death would mean resting from the persecution and being with Jesus. On the other hand, His love for the church urges him to press on in this world.

> **Philippians 1:20-26** – I eagerly expect and hope that I will in no way be ashamed, but will have sufficient courage so that now as always Christ will be exalted in my body, whether by life or by death. For to me, to live is Christ and to die is gain. If I am to go on living in the body, this will mean fruitful labor for me. Yet what shall I choose? I do not know! I am torn between the two: I desire to depart and be with Christ, which is better by far; but it is more necessary for you that I remain in the body. Convinced of this, I know that I will remain, and I will continue with all of you for your progress and joy in the faith, so that through my being with you again your boasting in Christ Jesus will abound on account of me.

Paul exemplified perseverance. Perhaps that's because perseverance comes from trials.

> **Romans 5:2b-5** – …And we boast in the hope of the glory of God. Not only so, but we also glory in our sufferings, because we know that suffering produces perseverance; perseverance, character; and character, hope. And hope does not put us to shame, because God's love has been poured out into our hearts through the Holy Spirit, who has been given to us.

First, we see that trials produce perseverance.
Consider how physical exercise produces stronger
endurance, and the pains we endure in our muscles only
serve to make us stronger. As we endure trials in our
Christian walk, something psychological takes place: we
don't want the pain to go to waste! We choose to press
through for the sake of the reward promised. This alone is
enough to encourage us to persevere, but we also discover
the nearness of God in the midst of the trial. The result is
a strengthened relationship with Him. This takes us
beyond mere psychology and produces perseverance on a
spiritual level.

**Next, we read that perseverance produces
character.** The trials we endure help shape our
perspectives on life and the ways we love others. We are
reminded of how fragile this life is and therefore how
valuable our time is. We become even bolder in our
declaration of Christ. We become acutely aware of how
worthless the things of this world are. We begin to value
the kingdom of heaven above earthly wealth or comfort.
We focus on loving the lost while we still have the
opportunity. In these ways our perseverance in the face of
suffering produces strong, godly character.

**Finally, we learn that character produces
hope.** When we see how God has carried us and shaped
us through life so far, we begin to expect future good. We
look back on the testimonies of His faithfulness in the
past, and this renews our minds to expect testimonies in
the future. "Longing fulfilled is a tree of life." When we
see the natural progression from suffering to hope, it
strengthens our resolve when future trials come.

Rejoice in hope, and rejoice in the life experiences

that lead to increased hope—even when it's painful.

God's Unshakable Love

As we've already seen, not every struggle we face in life is necessarily persecution. Struggles and difficulties are normal in this fallen world—we just don't have to suffer in the midst of them. Notice what the Amplified paraphrase says of Jesus' words:

> **John 16:33b –** In the world you have tribulation and trials and distress and frustration; but be of good cheer [take courage; be confident, certain, undaunted]! For I have overcome the world. [I have deprived it of power to harm you and have conquered it for you.] (AMP)

Jesus has won the victory! It is perfectly normal to face tribulation, trials, distress, and frustration; but Jesus has deprived these things of power to harm you. He has already conquered them for you. Even though distress and frustration are still part of normal life in this world, we are not called to suffer from such things—these are different from persecution.

James instructed us to "consider it pure joy" whenever we "face trials of many kinds." (See James 1:2.) James didn't say that trials are joyful experiences. He simply said to "consider" it a joyful experience as you face them. This means that it is your decision. Furthermore, he didn't say to consider it joy when trials happen to you. Rather he said to consider it joy when you "face trials." In other words, face them head-on. Deal with them. Don't cower. Take action as a representative of Jesus, and trust the Father to work the situation out for your good.

> Limitless hope causes us to be convinced that God works everything together for the good of those who love Him. Expected disappointment causes us to question God's love for us in the midst of difficulties.

Sometimes we assume that God wants to cause problems in our lives. No.

> **Lamentations 3:31-33** – For no one is cast off by the Lord forever. Though He brings grief, He will show compassion, so great is His unfailing love. For **He does not willingly bring affliction or grief to anyone**. (emphasis added)

Not only does God dislike causing problems in our lives and only do it when absolutely necessary, but most problems in this world don't come from Him anyway.

Let's be clear: The devil causes problems; Jesus came that we may have life. And while God may discipline us when we need it, He is not the author of hurt. God is the One who turns hurtful situations around for our benefit. (See Genesis 50:20.) Trials and difficulties happen in this world, but if we love God, He uses those situations to our advantage. (See Romans 8:28.)

Every struggle I've ever endured has now become a testimony. What was once a weapon formed against me has now become a weapon in my own hand. The prophet

Isaiah declared, "No weapon formed against you shall prosper." (See Isaiah 54:17.) I would say that there is an exception in Christ: While the devil's weapons will not prosper against us, they will definitely prosper in our hands. What the devil uses to destroy, Jesus overcomes. And when Jesus overcomes, that evil circumstance becomes a glorious testimony. Testimony, as we know, is a weapon against the devil. (See Revelation 12:11.) No weapon formed against you shall prosper—until Jesus yanks that weapon from the devil and places it in your hands!

After struggling through grade school I was diagnosed with Attention Deficit Disorder (ADD) in the seventh grade. I couldn't focus on schoolwork or classroom lectures. I constantly forgot my homework. And I was often impulsive, which caused a lot of trouble for me. When I was finally diagnosed, I was placed on a medication called Ritalin, which stimulated my brain and removed those unwanted symptoms.

Unfortunately, I discovered that the medication had some unpleasant side-effects. Among other things, the worst seemed to be that I lost my creativity. The medication helped me focus, but I didn't feel like myself.

I continued on that medication for a year until one day I had an idea. I asked the Holy Spirit to heal me of all the adverse symptoms of ADD but allow me to keep the blessings that God designed in my personality. I stopped the medication and went from nearly failing school to nearly having perfect scores in every class.

Today I no longer struggle with distraction any more than the average person. I can maintain attention whenever it is needed. But I also have the good aspects of the so-called "disorder." I have regained my ability to think on my feet, be spontaneous, relate to strangers, and take risks—all of which have served me well in the mission field. The devil formed a diagnosis of "Attention Deficit Disorder" against me, but God worked it out for my good. Now I have valuable personality traits that serve me well in destroying the devil's work throughout the world.

We have a lot to learn from the suffering of Jesus, but one thing stands out to me in the context of this chapter: The crucifixion looked like a victory for the devil, but we now know better. God took the Roman world's most hideous suffering and transformed it into explosive, world-impacting power. You are a steward of that power. Every time you face a trial with a heart full of joyful hope and emerge victorious, the devil is reminded of the death and resurrection of Jesus.

Our Lord gladly suffered "for the joy set before Him." (See Hebrews 12:2.) Jesus is the Master of hope. He is our prime example. Know Him deeply, and you will find an endless supply of limitless hope.

> **Romans 12:12 –** Be joyful in hope, patient in affliction, faithful in prayer.

Endnotes:

1. Unruh, B. (2010, April 20). Martyred: 176,000 Christians in 1 Year. World Net Daily. Retrieved December 31, 2015, from http://www.wnd.com/2010/04/143493/
2. Remember that the context here is persecution, not sickness. When it comes to sickness and disease, these are things that Jesus paid for at the cross. If you're suffering from a natural, physical condition, don't use Scripture verses to falsely prop it up as something holy. Jesus did not go to the whipping post so that you could pretend that your disease has spiritual value; He did it for you to be healed. Don't suffer unnecessarily, and don't rob Jesus of His reward for the blood He shed. Seek healing and freedom. Until it happens, continue to love and serve God and rest assured of His love for you, but do not rationalize your condition. If Jesus paid for your healing and you are not yet healed, then this is an injustice. Pursue healing—not because you deserve it but because He deserves it. As mentioned in Chapter Ten, seeking healing is an act of worship.

Conclusion

Are you transformed? It's one thing to read a book that renews your mind, but it's another to allow it to actually change the way you think and behave. Romans 12:2 is spoken like a command: "...be transformed by the renewing of your mind..." The renewing is God's part, but you must choose to let it transform you.

The Greek word for "transformed" in this passage is the same word used in Matthew 17:2 when Jesus was "transfigured" and "His face shone like the sun, and His clothes became as white as the light." The transfiguration revealed the reality of Jesus' true identity. In the same way, if you allow the renewal of your mind to transform you, people will see the reality of your true identity in Christ.

The Greek word for "repent" literally means to change your mind. But the implication, in every Scripture where it is used, is that this change of mind will produce a change of action. It's not enough to merely think differently. You must allow that new way of thinking to permeate your actions.

My prayer for you is that this book has challenged you to believe God for the impossible. But most importantly, my desire is that this new way of thinking would move you into explosive, dramatic, faith-filled action.

Trust God in everything. Trust that Jesus' sacrifice was sufficient to transform you into exactly the person He intends for you to be. You are His representative on the earth, along with the rest of the Body of Christ. Remember who you are, express it with help from the Holy Spirit, and continually point people to Jesus. I can guarantee that your life will never be the same.

> **Expected disappointment is satisfied to have a theology that doesn't affect one's actions. Limitless hope, however, transforms you and moves you into a place of partnering with Jesus to transform the world.**

10 - Week

Small Group Curriculum

I f you'd like to conduct a ten-week small group study with this book, the following curriculum will help you facilitate discussion and engage in challenging activities. In this opening section you will receive some helpful information about effectively facilitating such a group, and this will be followed by ten weekly lessons with discussion questions and assignments.

First Steps:

It's really easy to lead a small group study on this book. You'll only need three things: (1) a consistent place and time to meet 90 minutes for 10 weeks, (2) a small group of 3-15 people who want to study the book along with you, and (3) a copy of this book for each participant. (Additional copies are available from bookstores, Amazon, or our web site, SupernaturalTruth.com.) No reading needs to take place until after the first meeting, so you can always distribute books to people on the first week.

Group Facilitator Guidelines:

❖ **Don't worry about needing to know everything—** You don't need to have all the answers, and you don't need to fix every problem. This way the people gathered won't become dependent on you. Instead they'll learn to be dependent on God, the Bible, and each other.

❖ **Remember you're not teaching a class—**The temptation for many of us—especially those who are really into the Word of God—is to dominate the discussion. The fact is, the more you allow others to talk, the more they'll become involved and open up…and the more they'll learn, too!

❖ **Be secure in your identity—**The more you make your goal "being liked," the worse you'll do. Be an ambassador of Christ. Don't be afraid to speak the Truth or challenge things that others bring up. God's Word will defend itself. Encourage others to achieve even greater things than you ever have!

❖ **Don't let religion take over—**By this I mean: Don't feel guilty if things went differently, you didn't have time to do something planned, or there wasn't enough time to complete the full curriculum for the week. The question is not whether or not the system was perfect or whether every element of the meeting took place. Rather it is this: Was God able to express His presence at our meeting?

❖ **Model Preparation—**Set the culture for your group

with your own actions. Read the chapters and curriculum a least a day before the meeting. Try to think about questions that might come up, and search the Scriptures ahead of time for possible solutions. Others will take the study seriously when they see you taking it seriously.

❖ **Keep the Attention on Jesus**—People in your group come from a wide variety of backgrounds and experiences. Because of this, they may also already have a lot of opinions (some of these connected to deep emotions). No matter what the discussion or disagreement, always point the conversation back to the example Jesus set. Did Jesus ever make the argument being made? Or did His life demonstrate the opposite? Did Jesus ever need to do or say what is being suggested? Or did His example point more to simple faith? We can often learn as much about life and ministry from the things Jesus never said or did as we can from the things He did say and do.

❖ **Be Excited about the Finished Work of Jesus**— Similar to the previous point, many arguments and debates can be resolved by remembering that the price for healing, forgiveness, deliverance, and overall wholeness has truly already been paid in full.

❖ **Encourage participants to share their thoughts and feelings**—This includes not shooting them down when they're wrong. When a person anticipates that you'll jump on them if they "mess up," they won't venture into discussion at all. If something comes up that you do feel is off-balance, ask the rest of the group, "What does everyone else think?" In almost every group the problem will fix itself. This demonstrates to everyone that you value their input, and it keeps you from being the "bad guy." If things do become out-of-hand, refer to the previous two points to bring biblical sensibility to the discussion.

❖ **Honor the authority of Scripture**—The apostle Paul said that all Scripture is useful for teaching, rebuking, correcting, and training in righteousness. Don't be afraid to ask, "Does anyone know what the Bible says about this?" Be careful about treating gray areas as doctrines or turning examples into prescriptions. For example, just because Jesus healed a blind man by rubbing spit-mud in his eyes doesn't mean that this is how it must be done every time. But whenever the Scripture is explicitly clear (from multiple references that agree), you can use Scripture authoritatively to settle disputes. In doing this, you'll also be teaching others to honor and value the Word of God as an authority.

❖ **Be grateful for every answer**—This will significantly increase the interaction that takes place in your group. Don't be cheesy, but do listen intently to everyone, maintain eye contact with the speaker, and throw in little encouragements whenever appropriate. Be careful not to "trump" a person's revelation by immediately piggy-backing off their comment with something you might consider deeper or more amazing. This can cause people to feel inferior and shut down. It's okay to hold in things that you know for the sake of honoring others in the discussion. Save your thoughts for later, and share them only if it becomes appropriate.

❖ **Keep the discussion moving**—Feel free to ask

questions about things that people say—even if you know what they mean. Keep the group dynamics going, and maintain the focus on the topic for that particular meeting.

❖ **Consider the makeup of your group**—Some may be quiet and reserved while others may be rather expressive! Don't be afraid to ask the talkative person to hold their answer as you direct the question specifically to the quieter people: "What do *you* think?" or, "I'm interested to hear what _____ has to say about this…"

❖ **Use silence to your advantage**—Give others (and maybe yourself) time to think and muster the courage to respond to questions. Don't be afraid of "awkward silence." It's not always your responsibility to make noise—often times silence occurs because God is moving on someone's heart! This will also encourage a culture in which the group expects that you're not going to let them off the hook until someone answers a question, which will lead to faster responses in the future.

❖ **Involve God in the discussion**—At various points, as the group interacts, something may be said or done that requires a response to God. Feel free to interrupt the normal flow of the meeting to briefly pray or worship God in response to something that came up in discussion. Allow God to participate in the conversation by bringing topics to a time of speaking with Him as a group.

❖ **Pray daily for the people in your group**—And if God shares something with you for one of those people, give them a call during the week to tell them!

Weekly Schedule: 90-minutes

Each week will follow a similar schedule. Feel free to adjust these approximate times as needed:

❖	Open in Prayer	2 min
❖	Welcome Everyone	3 min
❖	Opening Question	10 min
❖	Group Discussion Questions	60 min
❖	Application	10 min
❖	Give Assignments	3 min
❖	Close in Prayer	2 min

Each week's group discussion time will include 10 questions. Aim for spending an average of approximately 6 minutes on each. Ask probing questions and try to stir up deeper dialogue whenever necessary.

Some questions are likely to elicit a longer response or debate than others. Be sure to read the questions before the meeting, and anticipate allowing extra time wherever you think it might be needed.

On weeks when two chapters are being discussed, the questions are split between the two chapters. If you haven't finished the first questions by the time you reach 30 minutes into your discussion, you may want to skip ahead to the next topic.

There is no obligation to answer every question, so don't worry if you run out of time. There's also no obligation to fill the entire 60 minutes, so don't worry if you finish early. The goal here is encountering God and growing in Christ together.

Week 1: Orientation

Begin with prayer, and welcome everyone.   **(5 min)**

Opening Question: (10 min)

Allow each person in the group an opportunity to briefly answer the following question:

❖ What is your current definition or understanding of the word "hope"?

Group Discussion Questions: (60 min)

1. How many people here have witnessed a miracle? Share a few testimonies.

2. Read the entire "Preface" of this book out loud to the group. (Feel free to use one or more readers. This will likely take about 8-10 minutes.)

3. What stood out to you from the Preface? Were you challenged by anything? Surprised? Annoyed? Stirred?

4. How do you suspect that this study might affect you during these ten weeks?

5. What is it about "supernatural realism" that you feel is different from optimism or realism?

6. Have someone read Romans 12:2. As a group, list some things God can use to renew your mind?

7. Have someone in your group read the chapter titles in the Table of Contents out loud.

8. What seems like it will be the most exciting or interesting chapter to each of you?

9. What is something you're hoping to learn as we walk through this study together?

10. What is one area of your life where you recognize you need the most hope?

Application Activity: (10 min)

Take some time as a group to pray for each other, asking God to use this book and small group study to produce limitless hope in their life. (Perhaps have each person pray for the person to their right.) Especially ask the Lord to intervene in whatever area each person specified that they need the most hope (from question 10).

Assignments: (3 min)

Reading Assignment for Next Week —

❖ Introduction
❖ Chapter 1: The Anchor of Hope

Weekly Challenge —

❖ This week, identify and write down three situations that are troublesome in your life—whether ongoing or sudden, big or small. For each one, write down a sentence or phrase describing what pessimism expects, what optimism expects, what realism expects, and what "supernatural realism" expects. Bring it to next week's meeting.

Close in Prayer (2 min)

Week 2: Thinking about Hope

Begin with prayer, and welcome everyone.   **(5 min)**

Opening Question: **(10 min)**

Allow each person in the group an opportunity to briefly answer the following question:

❖ Choose one of the three situations you wrote down from last week's challenge. Read your description of the four forms of expectation applied to that scenario. Identify which of the four expectations would ordinarily be your default in this situation and briefly explain why "supernatural realism" is better.

Group Discussion Questions: **(60 min)**

1. How does Art's description of the men's meeting he attended affect how we might present prayer requests to our brothers and sisters in Christ?

2. Why do you think Art considers it important to ask Jesus to rebuke and correct any lack of faith in us?

3. How do the unbiblical limits we place on God affect our experiences with His power?

4. Why doesn't limitless hope make God do whatever we want? Follow-up: What *does* limitless hope do?

5. What is something you can do to help yourself think more about God's ability than about ordinary, natural outcomes?

6. Why is it important to hope in God as a Person and not merely to hope for good outcomes?

7. What is the difference between reasoning and rationalizing? (See page 25 if you don't remember.)

8. What specific ways do you see Abraham's relationship

with God being proven or expressed throughout the story of him going up the mountain to sacrifice Isaac?

9. What does it mean for hope to be an anchor for your soul? And how does that affect your daily life?

10. Was there anything about this week's reading or discussion that challenged you or stirred you?

Application Activity: (10 min)

Have each person share a prayer need with the group. After each one, have someone else share a hope-filled perspective of "supernatural realism" about what God could do in that situation. After that, ask if anyone can add to it or top it with something even better that God can do. When no one can think of anything better, pray specifically for the best outcome presented. Continue until everyone has received prayer. (For larger groups, you may want to divide into two or three smaller groups to save time.)

Assignments: (3 min)

Reading Assignment for Next Week —

❖ Chapter 2: Unshakable Boldness

Weekly Challenge —

❖ Look for someone this week who has a situation in their life that needs God's intervention. Tell that person what you believe God is capable of doing for them (remember to have hope!), and offer to pray for them right there and then.

Close in Prayer   (2 min)

Week 3: Letting Hope Take Root

Begin with prayer, and welcome everyone.   **(5 min)**

Opening Question: **(10 min)**
Allow each person in the group an opportunity to briefly answer the following question:

❖ What happened when you offered hope-filled prayer for someone last week? I'll share my story first, and then I want to hear yours.

Group Discussion Questions: **(60 min)**

1. On Page 36, we read, "A firmly anchored ship looks rather bold as it withstands the waves around it. That's because it has taken on the nature of the rock to which it is tethered. In the same way, limitless hope in a limitless God causes us to take on His nature— unimpressed with earthly circumstances and motivated by the kingdom of heaven." What aspects of God's nature can help us withstand earthly trials?

2. Read 2 Peter 1:3-4. In what ways does this verse encourage you? How does it affect the way you see yourself?

3. Knowing that hope will remain even in eternity, describe a little of what you suppose life in eternity could be like.

4. What are some specific, practical ways to "hold fast" to boldness and "rejoice in hope until the end"? (Hebrews 3:6.)

5. In this chapter, Art mentions speaking to the storm instead of loosening your anchor lines. What do you think he's talking about? (Pages 41-42.)

6.   How does hope affect your prayer life?
7.   Why does God want us to approach Him boldly?
8.   How does hope affect the ways we minister?
9.   Boldness by itself can be abrasive to people and may even do damage. What other qualities of God's nature do we need to express in order to put boldness into its proper context?
10. Was there anything about this week's reading or discussion that challenged you or stirred you?

Application Activity: (10 min)

Follow up with each other about the things you prayed for last week. Either share testimonies or an update.

Encourage each other with hope-filled expectation like last week, and then pray for anything that has not yet been resolved.

Assignments: (3 min)

Reading Assignment for Next Week —

❖   Chapter 3: Overcoming Deferred Hope

Weekly Challenge —

❖   In Acts 4:13, the boldness and courage of Peter and John indicated to the Sanhedrin that they had been with Jesus. Boldness comes from hope, and hope comes from time spent with the Lord. This week, journal three prayers. Write as much as you need for each, but try to write at least a couple paragraphs expressing your heart to God.

Close in Prayer   (2 min)

Week 4: Nurturing a Hope-filled Heart

Begin with prayer, and welcome everyone. **(5 min)**

Opening Question: **(10 min)**

Allow each person in the group an opportunity to briefly answer the following question:

❖ What was your experience with journaling prayers this past week? Was it difficult? Helpful? Meaningful?

Group Discussion Questions: **(60 min)**

1. What sorts of challenging or troublesome thoughts go through your mind when you pray for something and don't see results?

2. Why should we be encouraged even when prayers go unanswered?

3. What's the difference between the ordinary things of life that we ask God for and the things Jesus paid for with His blood?

4. Based on the previous answer, how should this difference affect the ways we pray and minister to people who need forgiveness, healing, or deliverance?

5. How would you counsel a person who thinks that God doesn't want to forgive them?

6. How would you counsel a person who thinks that God doesn't want to heal them?

7. On page 58, Art writes, "Never assume that waiting is necessary. Simply trust that if immediate results don't come when we expect them, God is growing the blessing behind the scenes." How does this affect us in the prayerful waiting process?

8. Why is it important to remind yourself about

testimonies of things God has done in the past?

9. Read Colossians 3:1-3. What are some practical ways to obey this scripture?

10. Was there anything about this week's reading or discussion that challenged you or stirred you?

Application Activity: (10 min)

Is there anyone here whose prayer need from the past few weeks is still unresolved? If so, take a moment to encourage those who are still waiting (even if they're already encouraged, it's good practice for ministry!). See if anyone in the group has a testimony about God's victory in a similar situation (from anytime in life), and share it. Declare again the hope-filled solution you're all expecting. Pray again as a group.

Assignments: (3 min)

Reading Assignment for Next Week —

❖ Chapter 4: Limitless Hope and Sin-Free Living

❖ Chapter 5: Limitless Hope and Hearing God's Voice

Weekly Challenge —

❖ Write a note (handwritten, print, or electronic) to someone who you know has been waiting for an answered prayer for a long time. Encourage them with what you learned in this week's chapter and discussion. Declare what God can do, and write a quick prayer for them at the end. Give them the note.

Close in Prayer (2 min)

Week 5: Relationship with God

Begin with prayer, and welcome everyone.   **(5 min)**

Opening Question: (10 min)

Allow each person in the group an opportunity to briefly answer the following question:

❖ Did anyone receive any feedback from the people you wrote the notes to? What are your reflections on the assignment?

Group Discussion Questions: (60 min)

1. In Chapter Four, we read about sin-free living. What were some of the most challenging or eye-opening components of this chapter?

2. What is the difference between deliberate disobedience and ordinary shortcomings? Why is it important to distinguish between these two types of sin?

3. Why is a list of rules insufficient to keep us free from sin?

4. What does it mean to "die with Christ?" Read Romans 6:11-14. What practical advice does this verse offer for how to die with Him?

5. What qualities of our "sonship" give us peace and assurance if we happen to sin?

6. In Chapter Five, we read about hearing God's voice. Did anything in this chapter surprise you or make you think about your relationship with Him in a new way?

7. Why is it important to remember that God often speaks subtly? How does this affect your relationship with Him?

8. Why do you think God wants you to hear His voice?
9. Why is it valuable to submit what we think God is saying to other believers for discernment?
10. Of the ways God speaks (discussed in this chapter), which seems to be the most common way He communicates with you?

Application Activity: (10 min)

Many Christians find themselves stuck at the cross. In other words, they come to Jesus for forgiveness, but they go right back out to the world and live the same way. That's not the "new life" to which you've been called. If you feel like that's you, and you want to be a new creation in Christ, we want to pray for you to have victory and a thriving relationship with God. Who needs to make that change? (If no response, ask if anyone feels like they've been living the resurrected life—born again as a new creation—but falling short of expressing their sonship.)

Assignments: (3 min)
Reading Assignment for Next Week —
❖ Chapter 6: Limitless hope and Prayer & Fasting
❖ Chapter 7: Limitless Hope and Studying Scripture

Weekly Challenge —
❖ Ask the Lord to give you an encouraging message about His love for someone you know. Watch and listen for His voice, and write down whatever comes to you. If you're not hearing something specific, simply write an encouragement from your heart.

Close in Prayer   (2 min)

Week 6: Communing with God

Begin with prayer, and welcome everyone. **(5 min)**

Opening Question: (10 min)

Allow each person in the group an opportunity to briefly answer the following question:

❖ How did your challenge go last week? Did you receive any feedback from the person to whom you gave the encouraging message?

Group Discussion Questions: (60 min)

1. In Chapter Six, we read about prayer and fasting. Was there anything in this chapter that changed your understanding of these two practices?
2. What is the purpose of prayer?
3. What is the purpose of fasting?
4. Why does God pour grace on humble people and oppose the proud?
5. What are some ways to identify what God's will is in a situation so that you know what to pray for?
6. In Chapter Seven, we read about studying and applying Scripture. Was there anything in this chapter that caused you to want to dig into the Bible more?
7. Why is transformation better than imitation?
8. In what ways does a hope-filled perspective on reading Scripture spare us from empty legalism?
9. How does limitless hope affect our interpretation of the Bible?
10. How does limitless hope affect our understanding of the high cost of following Jesus?

Application Activity: (10 min)

Read 2 Corinthians 5:14-21 together with a mindset of hope, expecting to encounter God and learn something fresh from the Holy Spirit. Discuss the implications this passage has for what it means to be a Christian. What practical actions can we take to apply this passage to our lives?

Assignments: (3 min)

Reading Assignment for Next Week —

❖ Chapter 8: Limitless Hope and Evangelism

Weekly Challenge —

❖ Try fasting for the sake of humbling yourself before God so that you're in the right position to minister to someone if a need arises. Ask the Holy Spirit how long to fast, and then give it a try. If you're new to it, maybe start with just a meal, and keep some fruit juice handy in case you have an unexpected problem with low blood sugar. If you have a medical condition, consult your doctor about the best way to fast without causing problems for yourself. (Note that in the Bible, fasting always has to do with food. It's great to abstain from other things, but that's "consecration," not fasting. You don't need something like television to survive, but you do need food, so these aren't the same. If you are not allowed to fast for medical reasons, try cutting out a part of your diet that is safe to remove. Only resort to some sort of consecration if there is legitimately no safe way for you to fast.)

Close in Prayer (2 min)

Week 7: Power for the Mission

Begin with prayer, and welcome everyone.   **(5 min)**

Opening Question: **(10 min)**

Allow each person in the group an opportunity to briefly answer the following question:

❖ How did the fasting go? Was it harder or easier than you expected? Did you notice an impact on your relationship with God? Did any ministry opportunities arise that may have benefitted from your fasting?

Group Discussion Questions: **(60 min)**

1. This week's chapter covered two topics: (1) the Holy Spirit's empowerment and (2) sharing the Good News about Jesus. But really, this was only one topic. Why is it important to see these two things as one topic?

2. Was there anything in this week's reading that challenged, stirred, upset, frustrated, emboldened, or otherwise affected you, either positively or negatively?

3. What are some things that can happen if we make disciples for Jesus apart from the Holy Spirit's power?

4. How does limitless hope affect the way people seek the empowerment of the Holy Spirit?

5. The word "evangelism" means "good news." Discuss what the Good News is that we are privileged to share. (Clue: Focus on the message, not the response. The word "repent" is not good news; repenting is what we do in response to good news. What is the message?)

6. What makes the "Good News" offensive?

7. How does limitless hope affect the frequency, target locations, and clarity of our evangelistic efforts?

8. Have each person name one person they know who does not yet know Jesus. Specifically, name the toughest case—the person least likely to repent. Next, describe (with limitless hope) what God will be able to do through that person once they surrender to Jesus.

9. What does it mean to make a disciple?

10. Describe the mission field God has given you.

Application Activity: (10 min)

If you have not yet had an experience with the baptism in the Holy Spirit, there's nothing wrong with you, and you're not an inferior Christian. However, that doesn't change the fact that God wants you to be clothed with His power! If you have not yet had this experience, those of us who have will do what was done in the book of Acts: We will lay our hands on you with expectation. There is no obligation to speak in tongues in front of us, but do at least try. Jesus will baptize you in the Holy Spirit, and you will receive power as the Holy Spirit overflows from within you.

Assignments: (3 min)

Reading Assignment for Next Week —

❖ Chapter 9: Limitless Hope and Spiritual Gifts

❖ Chapter 10: Limitless Hope and Physical Healing

Weekly Challenge —

❖ Lovingly tell someone the Good News about Jesus. It can be a friend or a stranger. Ideally, it should be a person who doesn't yet know Jesus; but feel free to practice with a Christian so you can get a feel for it.

Close in Prayer   (2 min)

Week 8: Walking in Power

Begin with prayer, and welcome everyone. **(5 min)**

Opening Question: (10 min)

Allow each person in the group an opportunity to briefly answer the following question:

❖ With whom did you share the Gospel this week? If it was a Christian, did they give you any constructive feedback? And if it wasn't a Christian, what was the person's response?

Group Discussion Questions: (60 min)

1. In Chapter Nine, we read about spiritual gifts. Did anything in this chapter stand out or encourage you?

2. What is the difference between eagerly desiring spiritual gifts and wishing you had a ministry like someone else's?

3. What is the scariest part about attempting a spiritual gift for the first time? What fears do you tend to face?

4. Why are spiritual gifts a valuable aspect of the Christian life?

5. What are some practical things we can do to desire, receive, and grow in spiritual gifts?

6. In Chapter Ten, we studied the ministry of physical healing. What did you find to be the most challenging or encouraging part of this chapter?

7. Why is humility necessary to succeed in healing ministry?

8. On page 215, Art wrote, "While I'm making some bold, impassioned statements here, I should interject that in the moment of ministry, I don't have these

arguments with people. There's a pastoral side to all this as well." Why are gentleness and tact important components in healing ministry?

9. What should we say or do if a person isn't healed when we minister to them? Why?

10. When it comes to healing ministry: (a) What is the sick person's responsibility? (Remember, they can be healed without faith, with or without medication, and with or without being a Christian.) (b)What is our responsibility as healing ministers? (c) What is Jesus' responsibility?

Application Activity: (10 min)

If anyone in your group needs physical healing, have one or more people ask if they can lay hands on that person and speak to them: "Be healed in Jesus' name." Remember, don't make it a long, drawn-out prayer. Just speak to it and test it as soon as you can. If no one in the group needs healing of anything, speak words of authority for people who aren't present. (See Matthew 8:5-13.)

Assignments: (3 min)
Reading Assignment for Next Week —

❖ Chapter 11: Limitless hope and Extravagant Giving
❖ Chapter 12: Limitless Hope and Raising the Dead

Weekly Challenge —

❖ Find someone this week who needs physical healing and ask if you can minister to them in Jesus' name. Have the person test their condition if they safely can.

Close in Prayer   (2 min)

Week 9: Trusting God's Ability

Begin with prayer, and welcome everyone.   **(5 min)**

Opening Question: **(10 min)**

Allow each person in the group an opportunity to briefly answer the following question:

❖ What happened when you offered to minister healing this week? Was it difficult? Did the person allow you to minister? Was the person verifiably healed?

Group Discussion Questions: **(60 min)**

1. In Chapter Eleven, we studied extravagant giving. What in this chapter stirred or challenged you?

2. What are some reasons why it's important to listen to the Holy Spirit when it comes to our finances?

3. Why is it important to financially support Christian organizations (especially the local church)?

4. Why is it also important to personally give money to people we see who are in need?

5. Why is it important not to go into debt for the sake of giving? (See Endnote 1 on p. 249 if you're stumped.)

6. In Chapter Twelve, we looked at the present-day ministry of raising the dead. What was the most surprising, amazing, or unexpected thing you learned?

7. How do we know when we should attempt raising a dead person and when we shouldn't?

8. Picture yourself at a funeral, and suppose you believe the person in the casket is supposed to be alive. As a group, write down a list of fears, social concerns, and other problems associated with attempting to raise the dead person in Jesus' name.

9. For each of the items on the list you just made, think of one practical solution or a reasonable, encouraging counter-argument until each item is crossed off the list.

10. How should God's ability to raise the dead affect the ways we live our everyday faith?

Application Activity: (10 min)

Break into groups of at least three people, and pray for each other's finances. First ask if anyone in the group has a specific financial need that needs prayer. Pray for God's provision, wisdom to budget and spend well, clarity about when and how to give, and insight into the proper, hope-filled handling of money.

Assignments: (3 min)

Reading Assignment for Next Week —

❖ Chapter 13: Limitless Hope and Deliverance
❖ Chapter 14: Limitless Hope and Passionate Endurance

Weekly Challenge —

Ask the Holy Spirit if there's a person or organization to whom He wants you to give financially this week. Ask Him how much He wants you to give, and then figure out if there are any personal sacrifices you'll have to make in order for it to be possible. Give as discretely as you can. Next week, we won't ask how much you gave or to whom you gave it, but we will ask for your reflections on the activity.

Close in Prayer (2 min)

Week 10: Fearless Living

Begin with prayer, and welcome everyone.   **(5 min)**

Opening Question: **(10 min)**

Allow each person in the group an opportunity to briefly answer the following question:

❖ How did last week's challenge make you feel (both during and afterward)? Was it difficult? Did you find that God provided for you in other ways?

Group Discussion Questions: **(60 min)**

1. In Chapter Thirteen, we read about deliverance from demons. Was there anything that stood out to you or that you found interesting in this week's chapter?
2. Why do Christians have no reason to fear evil spirits?
3. What are some unhealthy or psychologically damaging ways you've seen (or heard of) people attempt to minister deliverance?
4. What should you do if you tell a demon to leave and it doesn't?
5. What sort of things do we hope will happen after a person has been delivered from an evil spirit?
6. In Chapter Fourteen, we studied passionate endurance, no matter the cost. What was one of the most challenging or inspiring things you read?
7. What is the difference between godly suffering and unnecessary suffering?
8. Why is persecution a privilege?
9. Why don't Christians need to worry about persecution or constantly pray that it won't happen?
10. What are some things we can do now to prepare our

hearts and minds to endure persecution when it comes?

Application Activity: (10 min)

One of the things that sustains us in our faith and helps us to endure is encouragement. Take a moment as a group to focus on one person at a time and allow two or three other individuals to briefly encourage that person. Identify ways in which you have seen this person represent Jesus well. Encouragements should be directed at the person ("Something I see of Jesus in you is…" rather than, "Something I like about Bill is…"). Continue this activity with each of the other people in the group until everyone has had a turn being the recipient of encouragement.

Assignments: (3 min)

Reading Assignment —

❖ Right now, have someone read the "Conclusion" out loud to the group (pages 303-304).

Weekly Challenge —

❖ Take time as a group right now to pray together. Ask the Lord to help each of you to implement everything you've learned in the last 10 weeks.

Close in Prayer (2 min)

About the Author

Art Thomas is a missionary-evangelist who has preached the Gospel in diverse settings spanning from the inner city of Brooklyn, New York, to the bush of Africa. Now serving as the president and CEO of Wildfire Ministries International, Art has seen thousands saved and physically healed. He is the director and producer of the movies *Paid in Full* and *Voice of God* and has been actively involved in training tens of thousands of believers to minister in the power of the Holy Spirit since 2009. He lives with his wife Robin and their two boys, Josiah and Jeremiah, in Canton, Michigan.

Please consider sharing this book with a friend and writing a review on Amazon.com. Thanks a million!

Additional copies available at
www.SupernaturalTruth.com

53447167R00190

Made in the USA
San Bernardino, CA
17 September 2017